MW01292281

"When dealing with challenging texts please everyone all the time. But Merr to the text and there is much that ev of all, this is probably the most spiritual and Christ-centered reading of this part of Revelation I have seen."
—*Jon Paulien, PhD, Dean, School of Religion, Loma Linda University*

"No matter how Christians interpret and use the book of Revelation, all of us should take a Christ-centered approach, as James Merrills urges us to do."
—*Robert Van Voorst, PhD, Professor of New Testament Studies, Western Theological Seminary*

"This is a genuinely Christ-centered work with both devotional and scholastic value. It is written in the strongest possible Protestant tradition and demands considered thought on the part of the reader. I recommend it wholeheartedly with this warning . . . if your preconceived views are too highly cherished, Mr. Merrills' closely reasoned Scriptural evidence for Christ's primary position in the "Revelation" may challenge you beyond your limits."
—*Lt. Col. David DePinho, Chaplain (non-denominational), USAF*

"If you are interested in a scholarly approach to the four horsemen of the Apocalypse, then this book is for you. The author presents a Christ-centered understanding of these symbols in a manner that is both interesting and compelling . . . a fascinating read which I highly recommend."
—*Pastor Bruce E. Howell, Wesleyan Church*

"I find much to applaud. This major study clarifies the Christocentric message of the book, in these first seven chapters. A needed reply to futurist and preterist interpretations."
—*Dr. Richard Davidson, Professor of Old Testament Interpretation, Andrews University*

"Merrills' book sheds precious light on the Seals, and above all, centers them in the righteousness of Jesus Christ. Good job!"
—*Steve Wohlberg, Director, White Horse Media*

"Merrills' book is a scholarly masterpiece . . . as a Christ-centered book its message is made real to us."
—*Rev. Mathew Illikattil, Catholic Church*

"The Church has been given no greater gift than Jesus Christ. Whether or not one agrees completely with Merrills' Christocentric nature of the first horsemen in Revelation 6, there is no doubt that bringing Jesus back to the interpretative center of Revelation and a potential rider of the White Horse is a theological gift in and of itself to the Bride of Christ. We have nothing to fear when placing our trust in the Conquering Victor of Jesus. He is, has been, and will continue to be the center of the Church and the center of all Scripture—especially Revelation!"
—*Capt. Quentin M. Genke, Chaplain (Lutheran), USAF*

"The book of Revelation has birthed any number of interpretations. As early as the second century, it has been interpreted as apocalyptic or prophetic. Ripe with allegory and symbolism, it has defied easy answers. Merrills' Christ-centered interpretation moves the focus of the conversation away from the populist rapture and end times, and back to Jesus Christ where it belongs."
—*Rev. Rebecca Crise, Episcopal Church*

"I found Merrills' presentation of his word study surrounding the "four horsemen," and the resultantly more focused Christocentric view of these scriptures, intriguing. I find myself more compelled than ever to commit to studying this great book in its original language in context."
—*Scott A. Wiles, Trinity Bible (Baptist)*

"It is rare to find an author, when doing a commentary on the book of Revelation, keeping the focus on Christ, the Alpha and Omega. Yes, if Christ is the center of interpretation of the Four Horsemen of Revelation, the end result will lead us to a closer relationship with our Lord and Savior Jesus. This I believe the author has done."
—*Loren Nelson, former ministerial director, Michigan Conference of Seventh-day Adventists*

"Revelation is a complex scripture and Merrills' insight helps make the text understandable in a very practical way. He makes a compelling case for the Christ-centeredness of the Four Horsemen, and why these messages are important to us individually. While his studies are nondenominational in nature, they are Christ-centered and in keeping with main-line Protestant teachings. The author presents a solid scriptural foundation that provides an alternative to the apocalyptic fiction that is portrayed in the media today."
—*Pastor John Messner, United Methodist Church*

Victory in Christ

A CHRIST-CENTERED APPROACH TO THE

Four Horsemen of the Apocalypse

JAMES L. MERRILLS

Copyright © 2014 James L. Merrills

Cover: Guy Puffer and Diane Myers
Layout: Diane Myers
Edited by Tim Lale

Printed in the United States of America
All rights reserved
You can obtain additional copies of this book by contacting:
www.4horsemenofrevelation.com

Unless otherwise marked, Scripture quotations are taken from the HOLY BIBLE, NEW INTERNATIONAL VERSION®. Copyright © 1973, 1978, 1984 Biblica. Used by permission of Zondervan. All rights reserved.

Bible quotations marked YLT are from the 1898 Young's Literal Translation by Robert Young.

Scripture quotations marked AMP are taken from the Amplified® Bible, copyright © 1954, 1958, 1962, 1964, 1965, 1987 by The Lockman Foundation. Used by permission. (www.Lockman.org)

Scripture quotations marked NKJV are taken from the New King James Version. Copyright © 1982 by Thomas Nelson, Inc. Used by permission. All rights reserved.

ISBN-13: 978-1495342103

DEDICATION

JON PAULIEN, PhD
Who continually pointed me to the Answer:
Jesus Christ, Our Victor

And all who supported me in this journey.

ACKNOWLEDGMENTS

I want to express my appreciation to those close friends in Christ whose unending support helped me see this work through to the end:

> David DePinho, Terry Nelson, Benjamin Orian, Jonathan Peinado, and Chuck Randall. And my wife, Vicky, who patiently endured everything that this work required of me, and more.

Finally, my appreciation to all who have contributed over the years, through discussions, proofreadings, and otherwise encouraging this publication.

CONTENTS

Introduction

I have always been captivated with the book of Revelation. Perhaps it's the bizarre symbols and puzzle-like character that first captured my interest. I preached my first sermon on Revelation in high school. But the experience of a lifetime came during college, when my pastor invited me to conduct a class on the book. It was also then that my naïve understanding of Revelation was badly shaken.

Schooled in the early Protestant or Reform view of prophecy, I had accepted the position that the visions in the first half of Revelation (7 churches, 7 seals, 7 trumpets, and cosmic war) were panoramic views of church history—from the Cross to the Second Coming. Naturally, each of the four horsemen (6:1–8) represented a period of church history, with the advancement of the gospel, subsequent persecution, and the church's departure from the teachings of Scripture.

You can imagine my confusion, then, when a visitor in my class asked, "If the first horseman is the antichrist, are you suggesting that Satan was guiding the early church?" I was dumbfounded. I had never given any thought to who the riders may be, focusing instead on the horse's colors, the rider's instruments, and a historical application. As I recall, my response went something like this: "That's an excellent question. Obviously, the answer is, No! But I'll come back to that point later." Although "later" never came, the question never faded from my mind, and over the ensuing years, I kept searching God's Word for the answer.

Revelation's opening story

My perseverance and study were rewarded when the Holy Spirit led me to discover that chapters 1–7 are the "opening story" of Revelation, a condensed version of the book. This story is about the *victories of Jesus and His church*. It begins with the revelation of Jesus Christ, who is our heavenly High Priest (Rev. 1). Through seven brief letters, Jesus admonishes all in His church to overcome temptation to sin (Rev. 2–3), just as He did (3:21). The focus then shifts to the throne room in heaven, where we see the Father sitting on the throne, and a seven-sealed scroll—the "scroll of destiny." A Lamb—once slain, but now victorious—enters the scene and takes the scroll (Rev. 4–5). As the Lamb begins to remove the seals, four cosmic horsemen ride forth on colored horses. Their activity has great impact on the earth. In the wake of their activity, the world is found to be divided into two camps—the righteous and the wicked (Rev. 6). As the story closes, our attention is drawn back to heaven, where a great multitude of victors—the Israel of God—is found standing before God's throne (Rev. 7).

The over-arching theme in the story (and the entire book) is *victory*. The Greek word *nike*, which can be translated as "overcome," "prevail," "conquer," "triumph" or "victory"[1] (compare 3:21; 5:5; 6:2; 12:11; 17:14; 21:7) is the controlling thematic word of the book of Revelation.

Not the antichrist

The "four horsemen of the Apocalypse" (6:1–8), as they are commonly called, are situated in the middle of the opening story. They play a key role in identifying and separating the mere professors in the church from those who are true spiritual victors. Today, most Christians hold one of the following views of the four horsemen.

- **First-century fulfillment.** Also called the preterist view; the horsemen represent events that occurred in the ancient times of

---

1. God's "throne"—the victor's greatest reward (3:21)—is also a central theme in the opening story (3:21; 4:2; 5:7; 6:6; 7:9).

*Author beside a relief
of Nike in Ephesus
(Turkey).*

Revelation's author (i.e., war, famine).

- **Antichrist—literal view.** Also referred to as the futurist view; the four horsemen represent the antichrist, who comes on the world scene after the church is raptured. A small group of 144,000 converted Jews will lead those on the earth who were "left behind" into an acceptance of the gospel.

- **Antichrist—symbolic view.** Though the first horseman may represent the antichrist, or something sinful, or possibly Jesus Christ, the other three are most likely evil. The church is not raptured before the final tribulation but is represented by the 144,000, which are "spiritual Israel."

- **Christ-centered (author's view).** Revelation 1–7 is a story about Christ and His people. The four horsemen represent the various ministries of Jesus Christ: Conqueror, High Priest, and Judge. There is no secret pre-Tribulation rapture. The 144,000 represent all of God's faithful people—"spiritual Israel." (By default, this position is the backbone of the church-centered view, as held by the Protestant Reformers.)

This book is a Christ-centered challenge to the prevailing, but erroneous, view that the four horsemen represent the antichrist. Furthermore, it candidly confronts some of the popular teachings that misuse Revelation for their support, e.g., the pre-millennial rapture (4:1–2) and a prophetic mandate for the political state of Israel (7:4). My friends in the preterist camp will be challenged to go beyond the first-century application and consider what the four horsemen's messages mean to Christ's church today. Futurists will be forced to face the shallow evidence in Revelation for the rapture. Finally, I encourage those of the Reform view to give consideration to what the Revelator actually wrote and how the passage relates to Jesus Christ.

It's my sincere prayer that every reader will come to know our Lord Jesus Christ more fully through this study. He alone can give us the power to overcome and become the victors that He wants us to be, "even as He overcame" (3:21).

Chapter 1

The Revelation of Jesus Christ: Revelation 1

"The Revelation of Jesus Christ,
which God gave him to show his servants
what must soon take place. . . .
Blessed is the one who reads the words of this prophecy,
and blessed are those who hear it and take to heart
what is written in it, because the time is near."

The story begins

Revelation 1–7 is a short story about victory. A condensed version of the whole book of Revelation,[1] it reveals Christ's victory over death, highlighting His resurrection, ascension, and present ministry in heaven. It also highlights the victory of His church. In chapters 2 and 3, Jesus identifies many of the weaknesses in the church and then shows the believers how they can overcome temptation and sin through His power. At the conclusion of the story, the faithful are with the Lamb, dwelling together forever (7:15–17).

---

1. The book of Revelation is a story. Jesus admonishes the churches to "overcome" (Rev. 1–3), and then He removes seven seals from what is commonly called the "scroll of destiny" (Rev. 4–7). After the four horsemen complete their mission, seven trumpet warnings are sounded throughout the world (Rev. 8–11). In response, the dragon, or Satan, organizes all of his forces against God's people (Rev. 12–14), until God responds by pouring out seven plagues on the earth and destroying the city of Babylon (Rev. 15–18). Upon Christ's return, a millennium of peace and judgment passes before evil is completely annihilated (Rev. 19–20). Finally, the New Jerusalem settles upon the new earth, where the saints dwell forever with the Lamb (Rev. 21–22).

The question has been asked, exactly how do the believers in the churches overcome in preparation to meet the Lord? The answer is found in the ministry of the four horsemen (6:1–8). In order to fully appreciate the victory theme of the story, and the four horsemen's messages, we must start at the beginning of the story.

God communicates with His people

Just as God the Father sent His Son into the world (John 3:16, 17), He has given believers an additional revelation of Jesus Christ, another sign of His care, in the book of Revelation. The word *revelation* comes from the Greek word *apokalupsis*, or apocalypse, which means to unveil or uncover (*apo-*, "from" and *kalupto*, "to cover"). The last book of the Bible is a further revealing of Jesus and His ministry in heaven. And yet, despite the book's opening promise of a blessing for the one who hears with understanding (1:3), the book remains sealed for many Christians, "seldom read and often relegated to a curiosity."[2] At worst, "for many Revelation remains a closed book,"[3] which is an affront to the title word "revelation."

Jesus Christ is the subject of Revelation. His title-name is mentioned seven times.[4] As the "most important key" to understanding the entire book, He is described as a Lamb, High Priest, Warrior, Conqueror, and King.[5]

As if God had pulled back the curtains, He wants His people to know what is happening behind the scenes in the great cosmic battle between Christ and Satan. Through the Revelation, we can see how much heaven and earth are intimately connected.

According to the apostle John's perspective, some two thousand years ago, the prophesied events *must soon take place.* How important it is, then,

---

2. Elisabeth Schüssler Fiorenza, *The Book of Revelation: Justice and Judgment,* 2nd ed. (Minneapolis: Fortress, 1998), 1.
3. Leon Morris, *The Book of Revelation: An Introduction and Commentary* (Grand Rapids, MI: Eerdmans, 1987), 17.
4. The name Jesus is found fourteen times.
5. Merrill C. Tenney, *Interpreting Revelation* (Grand Rapids, MI: Eerdmans, 1957), 29.

that every believer be fully prepared now for earth's closing scenes and Jesus' return.

Communicating to Christians through a divine chain of command, God signified (*semaino*, "made known") the revelation. Note the first four letters—"*sign*-ified."[6] From the start, we're told that God is speaking through symbols and signs, or "picture language."[7] As Mounce points out, "This should warn the reader not to expect a literal presentation of future history, but a symbolic portrayal."[8] In many respects, Revelation is like the book of Daniel. They are what is commonly referred to as apocalyptic literature.

Why would God choose this method? Perhaps because John was under the watch of Roman guards. Writing in this manner may have been less risky—the portions that are political would seem meaningless and non-threatening to the Empire. Under those circumstances, God could convey more through word pictures. A picture is worth a thousand words, the saying goes. That is certainly the case with Revelation.

Because of Revelation's symbolic nature, many too quickly assume that the book is impossible to understand. But that is not the case. First, the Revelator explains what many of the symbols mean. Second, the symbolism makes Revelation one of the most beautiful literary works ever written.

---

6. "If you look up the Greek word for 'signified' in other parts of the New Testament . . . [there is] a very particular connotation. It means something like 'a cryptic saying or action that points to a future event.' . . . The author of Revelation here defines the whole book in one word." Jon Paulien, *The Deep Things of God: An Insider's Guide to the Book of Revelation* (Hagerstown, MD: Review and Herald, 2004), 104. ". . . *semaino* . . . more typically has the connotation 'make known by means of signs' (e.g., Dan 2:45 LXX)." Joseph L. Trafton, *Reading Revelation: A Literary and Theological Commentary*, rev. ed. (Macon, GA: Smyth and Helwys, 2005), 15. "The Book of Revelation is a study of signs. . . . Through signs, we come to an understanding." Jack Van Impe, *Revelation Revealed* (Troy, MI: Jack Van Impe Ministries, 1982), 55.

7. George R. Beasley-Murray, *Revelation*, The New Century Bible Commentary (Grand Rapids, MI: Eerdmans, 1981), 51.

8. Robert H. Mounce, *The Book of Revelation*, The New International Commentary on the New Testament (Grand Rapids, MI: Eerdmans, 1977), 42.

William Hendriksen calls it "a work of art, marvelous art, divine art."[9] Ladd points out that it is written "in the style of modern surrealistic art with great fluidity and imagination."[10] Third, most of Revelation's symbols and themes—perhaps as many as two thousand allusions[11]—are borrowed from the Old Testament. Scholars have noted the following: "The Revelation has many Jewish ideas, characters, and expressions."[12]

> The book [of Revelation] is absolutely steeped in the memories, the incidents, the thoughts, and the language of the church's past. To such an extent is this the case that it may be doubted whether it contains a single figure not drawn from the Old Testament.[13]

And again, "It is a book of symbols deeply rooted in Old Testament history. We mistake their meanings when we fail to hear the background music of the Old Testament."[14] Tenney says,

> Jewish literature, Jewish imagery, and Jewish theology appear in the book of Revelation. . . . Without a knowledge of the Old Testament one cannot interpret Revelation successfully. The book is a mosaic of allusions, quotations, and images taken from the Jewish Scriptures, and it interprets these in terms of the person of Christ.[15]

9. William Hendriksen, *More Than Conquerors: An Interpretation of the Book of Revelation* (Grand Rapids, MI: Baker, 1940, 1967), 59.
10. George Eldon Ladd, *A Commentary on the Revelation of John* (Grand Rapids, MI: Eerdmans, 1972), 111.
11. Jacques B. Doukhan, *Secrets of Revelation* (Hagerstown, MD: Review and Herald, 2002), 10.
12. Edward Bickersteth, *A Practical Guide to the Prophecies* (Philadelphia: Orrin Rogers, 1841), 75.
13. William Milligan, *The Revelation of St. John* (London: Macmillan, 1886), 72.
14. Hank Hanegraaff, *The Apocalypse Code* (Nashville: Thomas Nelson, 2007), 117.
15. Tenney, *Interpreting Revelation*, 25.

The Old Testament is the "key to the code of Revelation"[16] (see John 5:39).

The Revelator refers to himself as God's servant (Greek, *doulos*), which is literally "slave." The apostle Paul explains: "He who was a free man when he was called is Christ's slave. You were bought at a price" (1 Cor. 7:22, 23). Believers enter into a unique relationship or agreement with Christ called the "new covenant" (Heb. 12:24; cf. 13:20; 8:10). Because it cost Jesus His life, the choir in heaven sings, "You [the Lamb] were slain, and with Your blood You purchased men for God" (Rev. 5:9). With this background in mind, we can better appreciate Osborne's reflection on what it means to be a servant of Christ: "[The phrase] is used metaphorically by Paul and here by John to stress the absolute dependence and service of believers toward God, who owns them as their master."[17]

John testifies to everything he saw, and it is based on the word of God and the testimony of Jesus Christ. As one of the twelve disciples, John had been very close to Jesus during His time on earth. Now he was a "father figure" in the Christian community, and the members of the churches trusted his word. The "word" and the "testimony" are probably references to the Old Testament (the Scriptures of John's time) and the ministry of Jesus Christ (cf. 1:9; 6:9). In Revelation, "all the other books of the Bible end and meet."[18]

The first of seven beatitudes ("blessed") in Revelation[19] says, "Blessed is the one who reads the words of this prophecy, and blessed are those who hear it and take to heart what is written in it." It speaks to the "the fullness of blessing to be bestowed on the reader or hearer who faithfully obeys."[20]

---

16. Paulien, *Deep Things*, 101.
17. Grant R. Osborne, *Revelation*, Baker Exegetical Commentary on the New Testament (BEC) (Grand Rapids, MI: Baker Academic, 2002), 290.
18. Robert Jamieson, A. R. Fausset, and David Brown, *A Commentary, Critical, Experimental, and Practical, on the Old and New Testaments*, rev. ed. (Grand Rapids, MI: Eerdmans, 1961), 1526. "The book of Revelation is like the finale of the biblical symphony, drawing all of the Bible's themes together in a thrilling conclusion." Jon Paulien, *The Gospel From Patmos* (Hagerstown, MD: Review and Herald, 2007), 15.
19. See Rev. 1:3; 14:13; 16:15; 19:9; 20:6; 22:7; 22:14.
20. Richard Bauckham, *The Theology of the Book of Revelation* (Cambridge, UK: Cambridge

The entire Revelation is set in an aura of worship (cf. 4:10; 14:7; 15:4; 22:9).[21] Osborne writes: "Revelation instructs us in worship. It shows us where, why, and how to praise God. Worship takes our minds off our problems and focuses them on God. . . . Worship lifts our perspective from the earthly to the heavenly."[22]

Notice that the reader ("the one who") is singular and the listeners ("those") are plural. The entire revelation was addressed to the church (1:4) and would have been read out loud to the congregation.[23] It's believed that Revelation was intended as an "oral enactment" or "dramatic performance,"[24] modeled on the ancient Greek play,[25] divided into seven acts.[26]

What nearness means

If Revelation was written two thousand years ago, why would John say "the time is near"?[27] From a human perspective, two thousand years seems like

---

University Press, 1993), 26.

21. Fiorenza, *Book of Revelation*, 35.

22. Grant R. Osborne, *Revelation*, Life Application Bible Commentary (LABC) (Wheaton, IL: Tyndale House, 2009), 15.

23. Mounce, *Book of Revelation*, 77.

24. Bauckham, *Theology of the Book of Revelation*, 10.

25. John Bowman, "The Book of Revelation," in *The Interpreter's Dictionary of the Bible*, edited by George Arthur Buttrick, vol. 1; cf. John Sweet, *Revelation* (London: SCM Press, 1979), 45.

26. "Series of sevens." Frank E. Gaebelein, ed., *Hebrews Through Revelation*, The Expositor's Bible Commentary, vol. 12 (Grand Rapids, MI: Zondervan, 1981), 411. "Seven major parts with a prologue and an epilogue." Paulien, *Deep Things*, 122. J. Massyngberde Ford states, "However, there is an even stronger possibility [of] . . . six series of six, that is, a symbol of incompleteness congruous with the 666, the number of the beast expressing a lack of fulfillment." *Revelation*, The Anchor Bible, vol. 38 (New York: Doubleday, 1975), 48. Based on Revelation's chiastic structure, Strand contends, "Aside from the prologue and epilogue, there are *eight* major prophetic sequences—four that precede and four that follow a line drawn between chapters 14 and 15." Kenneth Strand, "The Eight Basic Visions," in Frank B. Holbrook, ed., *Symposium on Revelation – Book 1* (Silver Spring, MD: Biblical Research Institute, 1992), 35.

27. Beasley-Murray believes that John thought the church of his day was the last church. *Revelation*, 140. While that was undoubtedly true of all the disciples following Jesus' ascension, the Revelator may well have understood through the visions that the Messiah's return would be in the future. Compare Daniel 9:25–27, where Daniel saw that the Messiah's coming was nearly five hundred years in the future.

eternity. But in the light of eternity, the devil understands that "his time is short" (Rev. 12:12), and he's well aware of God's prophetic time clock. From Heaven's viewpoint, the faithful must at all times be ready for the Lord's return. Peter wrote, "He is patient with you, not wanting anyone to perish, but everyone to come to *repentance . . .* [so] *what kind of people ought you to be?*" (2 Pet. 3:9–11). Peter and John are both concerned about spiritual readiness rather than the hour of Jesus' return or how long the wait might be (Rev. 3:3; 16:15).

Seven churches (1:4)

Written by the apostle John,[28] the letter[29] was addressed to seven churches located in the province of Asia (modern-day Turkey). The cities were Ephesus, Smyrna, Pergamum, Thyatira, Sardis, Philadelphia, and Laodicea.

Seven is an important and predominant number in Revelation, used more than fifty times. Throughout the Bible, it is a symbol of completeness or perfection, "beginning with the days of creation in Genesis."[30] "The fact that the number seven is biblically imbued with a sense of completeness or wholeness should immediately alert us to the reality that Revelation is relevant to the whole church throughout the whole of history,"[31] as confirmed by Revelation 22:16.[32] Revelation speaks especially to Christians today. Roy Allan Anderson writes, "While this Revelation was particularly helpful for the persecuted saints in John's day, and has spoken to every age since,

---

28. "There is ample evidence that it was written by John the apostle." Hanegraaff, *The Apocalypse Code*, 139. "The prophet simply calls himself 'John,' as though there were no other Christian leader in that area with whom he could be confused." Donald Guthrie et al, eds., *The New Bible Commentary: Revised* (Grand Rapids, MI: Eerdmans, 1970), 1279; J. Massyngberde Ford argues that the author was John the Baptist. *Revelation*, 50.
29. "Indeed the whole Book from i. 4 to its close is in fact an Epistle." R. H. Charles, *A Critical and Exegetical Commentary on the Revelation of St. John* (Edinburgh: T & T Clark, 1920), 1:8.
30. Tenney, *Interpreting Revelation*, 37.
31. Hanegraaff, *Apocalypse Code*, 110.
32. Sweet, *Revelation*, 77.

yet it has a special message for those living just before our Lord's return."[33]

There is also a "time-honored belief" that the seven churches represent successive periods of church history, stretching from the Cross to the time of the end.[34] For example, the characteristics of the church in Ephesus (2:1–6), the first of the seven, match the characteristics of the apostolic period (AD 30–100). Smyrna, the second church (2:8–10), is well matched to the years that followed, when the church came under great persecution for her faith (AD 100–313). Laodicea, the seventh and last church (3:14–21), with a sense of needing nothing and a false sense of assurance, well represents our own day.

What Christ did for people

John's greeting, "Grace and peace to you," blends the languages of the old and new covenants (Hebrew, "peace," Greek, "grace"; see Mt. 26:28; Heb. 8:8–10; 9:15). As the student of Revelation will discover, "while he [John] writes in Greek, he thinks in Hebrew."[35]

The number three represents unity. "From him who is, and who was, and who is to come, and from the seven spirits before his throne, and from Jesus Christ" (1:4–5). John wants us to know that the Trinity, all three members of the Godhead, is involved in this revelation.

John highlights the Father's eternal nature—He always was and always will be. He then describes the seven-fold perfection of the Holy Spirit.[36] Following Jesus' ascension, the Holy Spirit was poured out on the earth in His fullness on the day of Pentecost (Acts 1:8; 2:18).

John now describes Jesus in three different ways. First, after descending from the Father's throne, the Son of God is a faithful witness of the Father's loving character. The word *witness* is translated from the Greek

---

33. Roy Allan Anderson, *Unfolding the Revelation* (Mountain View, CA: Pacific Press, 1953), 5–6.
34. Tim LaHaye, *Revelation Unveiled* (Grand Rapids, MI: Zondervan, 1999), 36.
35. Charles, *Critical and Exegetical Commentary*, 1:cxliii.
36. In Zechariah's vision, the seven lamps represent God's Spirit; see Zech. 4:1–10.

word *martus*, from which we get *martyr*. Christ, the true witness of God's character, is the ultimate martyr. Second, He is the firstborn from the dead (Acts 26:23). Because of His resurrection, we all have hope in the final resurrection (John 11:25). And third, He is described as the ruler of the kings. After He ascended, Christ "sat down at the right hand of the throne of the Majesty in heaven" (Heb. 8:1). Someday soon He will return to earth as "King of kings" (Rev. 19:16).

In another set of threes that deal with salvation, John goes on to describe Christ's intimate relationship with His people. First, He loves them, even as the Father loves them (John 3:16). Second, by His sacrifice, Jesus has atoned for sins with His blood and has thereby freed His people (Greek *luo*, "to loosen"; "washed," KJV) or released them from the bondage of their sins (Titus 3:5; 1 John 1:7). Third, He has made them to be both a kingdom and priests to serve God.

John has already used terms and concepts that point the reader back to the Old Testament. Indeed, Revelation's entire structure is fashioned around the ancient temple[37] and set in the context of worship (cf. Rev. 4:10; 14:7). But now he applies the spiritual privileges of Israel to the larger Christian community—the church.[38] Similar wording is found in Revelation 5:9, 10, which "recalls God's original charge to Israel at Mount Sinai in Exodus 19."[39] Just as God commissioned Israel at the Passover, so the church finds its commission under the True Lamb (5:6–10).[40] Peter

---

37. "At the beginning of each of the seen cycles the vision returns to the temple with a liturgical note that alludes to the calendar of Israel's high holy days (as prescribed by Leviticus 23). . . . The author invites us to read the Apocalypse in the light of the Jewish festivals." Doukhan, *Secrets of Revelation*, 14. For a similar pattern in the Gospel of John, see George R. Beasley-Murray, *John*, 2nd ed., Word Biblical Commentary 36 (Nashville: Thomas Nelson, 1999), lix.

38. "Places, persons, and objects which occur in the historical books reappear in the Apocalypse as symbols of facts in the life of the Church or of the new world to which the Church points and which lies behind the visible order." Swete, *Apocalypse*, cxxxii.

39. Paulien, *Gospel From Patmos*, 163.

40. Ladd, *Commentary on the Revelation*, 27; "Much in Rev 1 recalls the giving of the covenant at Sinai. Jesus 'freed us from our sins' . . . ; 'by his blood' suggests the blood of the Passover lamb. . . . He 'made us a kingdom, priests to his God.' . . . Jesus appeared to John

addressed this when he likened the early Christians (Gentile and Jewish believers) to the nation of Israel:

> But you are a chosen people, a royal priesthood, a holy na-
> tion, a people belonging to God, that you may declare the
> praises of him who called you out of darkness into his won-
> derful light. Once you were not a people, but now you are
> the people of God (1 Pet. 2:9–10; compare Rom. 2:28–29;
> 9:6–8; Gal. 3:29; Phil. 3:3).

Peter was acknowledging that Israel's vocation (Ex. 19:6) was extended to the church.[41] Swete writes: "As Israel when set free from Egypt acquired a national life under its Divine King, so the church, redeemed by the Blood of Christ, constituted a holy nation, a new theocracy. . . . The Church, like Israel, is a great sacerdotal society."[42] Building on this, the Revelator is saying that "the 'priesthood' belongs to the church as a whole."[43] True Christian faith is heir to Israel's heritage, as demonstrated in Hebrews 11. In Christ, the Israel of God is expanded to include all peoples of the earth[44]: "The promises made to literal, physical Israelites were fulfilled by a literal, physical Israelite, Jesus the Messiah. He is *the* Seed of Abraham."[45] "Reve-

---

with 'a loud voice . . . ' reminiscent of the trumpet blast at Sinai. . . . His 'eyes were like a flame of fire' . . . recall the fire on the mount (Exod. 19:16, 19). John's prostrate response recalls Israel's fear before the overpowering theophany." Beatrice Neall, "Sealed Saints and the Tribulation," in Frank B. Holbrook, ed., *Symposium on Revelation – Book 1*, 247.

41. Guthrie et al, eds., *New Bible Commentary*, 1288.

42. Swete, *The Apocalypse*, 8.

43. Sweet, *Revelation*, 66.

44. This is not to say that the church has "replaced" Israel. As Goldsworthy states, "For the new covenant is not a new thing replacing the old, but rather the old renewed and applied in such a way that it will be perfectly kept." *Gospel and Kingdom* (Minneapolis: Winston Press, 1981), 85. Even John Hagee, a staunch dispensationalist, who holds that the church and Israel are two separate entities in Bible prophecy, acknowledges: "There is also a spiritual Israel . . . (the church)." *In Defense of Israel* (Lake Mary, FL: FrontLine, 2007), 146. We will revisit the topic of Israel in Revelation 7, where John mentions "the tribes of Israel" (verse 4).

45. Hanegraaf quoting Keith A. Mathison in *The Apocalypse Code*, 50. Compare Kenneth Davies's response in "A Response to the False Witness of Keith Mathison," http://www.pret-

lation uses the events, geography, and terminology of the Old Testament, and then brilliantly applies them universally to Jesus Christ, the Israel of God."[46] Trafton writes:

> John has applied to *Christians* language that, in the Old Testament, depicts *Israel*. Indeed, John gives the reader no reason to distinguish Israel from the Church. . . . [He speaks of] Christians in terms that had previously been reserved for Israel. . . . *The failure to understand what John is doing in the doxology [1:4-6] leads many interpreters into much confusion regarding what they mistakenly view to be the separate roles of Israel and the Church in the visions that unfold.*[47]

Beginning here, "descriptions of the old Israel are piled up and applied to the church."[48] The faithful in the seven churches, Jew and Gentiles alike, represent the new or "true Israel."[49] According to the text, believers have been elevated to the status of kings and priests in Jesus Christ.[50] The believer, like ancient Israel's priest, may bring his petitions directly to the throne (ark of the covenant) of God through Jesus Christ (Heb. 4:16).

"To him be glory and power for ever and ever! Amen." Like John, the

---

erist.org/articles/mathisons_false_witness.asp. "All God's promises and prophecies to the Jews, all their priesthoods, sacrifices, Temple, and sacraments, preached Christ." Roy C. Naden quoting Christopher Wordsworth in *The Lamb Among the Beasts: A Christological Commentary on the Revelation of John That Unlocks the Meaning of Its Many Numbers* (Hagerstown, MD: Review and Herald, 1996), 12.

46. Steve Wohlberg, *End Time Delusions* (Shippensburg, PA: Destiny Image, 2004), 184.

47. Trafton, *Reading Revelation*, 21. "Darby contended . . . [that there remains to the end] two distinct people with two distinct plans and two distinct destinies. Only one of those peoples—the Jews—would suffer tribulation . . . due to the murder of their Messiah." Hanegraaff, *Apocalypse Code*, 41.

48. Morris, *Book of Revelation*, 114; see Caird, *Revelation of St. John*, 17; Harrington, *Revelation*, 46. "For the author of Rev. Israel is identical with the church, since he no longer knows of the distinction between the Jewish-Christian and Pagan-Christian communities." Fiorenza, *Book of Revelation*, 65.

49. Hanegraaff, *Apocalypse Code*, 116.

50. Paulien, *Gospel From Patmos*, 20.

true believer desires to praise the Savior for who He is and what He has done. With longing anticipation, he looks forward to the day when he can shout, "Behold our King! He's coming with the clouds of heaven!" But on that day, not everyone will be praising His name—not those who pierced Him, not the peoples of the earth who have resisted His Spirit and fought against His people. They will mourn because of Him (Rev. 6:12–17; Zech. 12:10). So shall it be! Amen. "The Greek for 'even so' [KJV] is *amen*, and *amen* is the Hebrew for even so. John is literally shouting the praise or praises of God in two languages as he says, 'Amen and Amen, He is coming!' "[51]

This section of the vision concludes with God giving a three-fold self-description, which applies equally to Jesus Christ, because it is "God who has revealed himself in Christ."[52] Notice how God's words (1:8; 21:6) are identical to Jesus' words (1:17; 22:13). His eternal nature, without beginning or end, is reflected in the words "I am the Alpha and the Omega," the first and last letters of the Greek alphabet. The second description—"who is, who was, and who is to come"—is similar to the first, and may be Christ's challenge to the god Zeus, who bore the same title.[53] Third, He is "the Almighty" or All-Ruling One, an Old Testament expression for God (Exod. 6:3; Ps. 91:1; Joel 1:15). Addressing this passage, Theodore H. Epp, founding director and speaker of the *Back to the Bible* broadcasts, highlights the inseparable relationship between the Father and Son:

> Christ is both the Originator and the Consummator of all that exists [see Isa. 44:6]. . . . Since He is the One who always was and who now is and always will be, He is the Jehovah of the Old Testament and the Christ of the New. He is the Almighty One.[54]

---

51. Van Impe, *Revelation Revealed*, 16.
52. Harrington, *Revelation*, 47.
53. Barclay, *The Revelation of John*, The New Daily Study Bible (Louisville, KY: Westminster John Knox, 1976), 1:35.
54. Theodore H. Epp, *Practical Studies in Revelation* (Lincoln, NE: The Good News Broadcast-

As altogether glorious as these verses are, they are but a few among the many descriptions of Christ. Revelation contains a "virtual gallery of pictures" of Him.[55]

Daniel—companion of Revelation (1:9)

The book of Daniel has been called the companion of Revelation because the two have many things in common. The authors, John and Daniel, were both taken prisoner, suffering for their faith (Dan. 1:1–2). Much of the imagery in Revelation is taken from Daniel.[56] Even the writing style—"I, John"—is similar (cf. Dan. 7:15; 8:15; 12:5).[57]

Feeling a bond with other Christians who had suffered "tribulation" (KJV) for their faith, John called himself their brother and companion (cf. Rev. 2:9, 10). In this world, the faithful should anticipate persecution for obedience to God (Matt. 10:22; John 16:33). It was precisely because of the word of God and the testimony of Jesus that John was exiled to the island of Patmos. According to tradition, he was exiled only after the Roman authorities attempted to take his life by boiling him alive in a cauldron. We're reminded of Daniel's three Hebrew companions who were cast into a furnace—and lived!—because of their faithfulness to God (Dan. 3:16–25).

On the Lord's Day (1:10)

It should come as no surprise that John would find himself in the Spirit—as in a trance[58] or ecstasy[59]—on the Lord's Day. After all, this is the "revelation of Jesus Christ," who declared that He is the "Lord" of the Sabbath (Mk. 2:27, 28; cf. Ex. 20:10; Deut. 5:14). And, as mentioned above, Revelation is formed by sanctuary language.

---

ing Association, 1969), 1:42.

55. Lichtenwalter, *Revelation's Great Love Story*, 21.

56. For example, the beasts (Dan. 7:1–8; Rev. 13:1–2), specific time periods (Dan. 7:25; Rev. 12:14).

57. "Daniel is always in John's mind." Barclay, *Revelation of John*, 1:57.

58. Mounce, *Book of Revelation*, 55.

59. Barclay, *Revelation of John*, 1:50.

There's been plenty of debate, however, over which day John was referring to. Was it the seventh day, the Sabbath of Creation? Or Sunday, the first day of the week, on which some Christians may by then have begun to commemorate Jesus' resurrection? Or the eschatological "Day of the Lord" (cf. Joel 2:1, 11; 13:14; Rev. 6:17; 11:18), since Revelation portrays scenes from the time of the end?[60]

For most Christians, Sunday seems like the logical answer. But a closer examination shows that the case for Sunday is lacking. To begin with, New Testament scholars confess that

> *there was nothing in Jesus' teaching (as recorded in Luke) to encourage transfer of Sabbath theology to another day.* . . . Eight times we hear in Acts of what happened on the *seventh* day Sabbath, but only *once* of the day that supposedly eclipsed it in importance . . . *but in all this there is not the barest hint of the inauguration or observance of Sunday!* . . . We must conclude that it is barely imaginable that first-day Sabbath [Sunday] observance commenced before the Jerusalem council. Nor can we stop there; we must go on to maintain that first-day Sabbath observance cannot easily be understood as a phenomenon of the apostolic age or of apostolic authority at all. . . . The story of the origin of the Lord's Day remains in many respects obscure.[61]

The problem with this position is that "there is no firm evidence that this means Sunday till much later."[62] Since "the connection between Sun-

---

60. "He was taken across the centuries to the time the Bible calls the Day of the Lord. That Day is the day of the consummation of all things." Epp, *Practical Studies*, 1:47. Mounce points out, however, that "if the reference were to the eschatological day of the Lord, we would have expected the more usual [Greek wording]," as found in 1 Thess. 5:2 and 2 Pet. 3:10 (56).
61. D. A. Carson, *From Sabbath To Lord's Day*, 134–136, 240. "Its identification is difficult." Gaebelein, ed., *Hebrews Through Revelation*, 424.
62. Sweet, *Revelation*, 67. The Lord's Day is "a phrase which became technical in the 2nd

day and the resurrection of Jesus was not made explicit until the second century," and this is "the only such reference in the New Testament and the earliest in Christian literature,"[63] one can only assume that this is the "beginning" or the "emerging language"[64] for the phrase, "Lord's Day." In light of the historical facts, LaHaye seems to be correct: "[Rev. 1:10] probably does not refer to being in the Spirit on the first day of the week."[65]

The biblical evidence points to the seventh day, the Sabbath of Creation, but not necessarily for the reason that Sabbatarians may think. First, Revelation is immersed in the Old Testament, of which the creation Sabbath was a "sign" (Ezek. 20:12). Second, the apostle John "is Jewish, nourished by the Hebrew Scriptures and steeped in the tradition of his ancestors."[66] As such, he would have faithfully observed the Ten Commandments, which included the Sabbath, the memorial of Creation (Exod. 20:8–11; John 1:1–2). The Creator and His Law are highlighted in Revelation (4:11; 11:19; 12:17; 14:7; 21:1). Third, the apostles, we're told, were still preaching in the synagogues on the Sabbath, decades after Christ's ascension (Acts 13:42–44). Fourth, the Sabbath introduced the yearly cycle of festivals (Lev. 23:3).

Fifth and perhaps most important, the number seven, the most prominent numeral in Revelation, is tied to the Sabbath of Creation.[67] Commenting on the relationship between the book of Revelation, the Old Testament, and the number seven, Wilcock observes that "the music of eternity is reverberating with the same seven-beat rhythm. . . . Creation,

---

century for Sunday." Guthrie et al, eds., *New Bible Commentary*, 1282.

63. Trafton, *Reading Revelation*, 27.

64. Ladd, *Commentary on the Revelation*, 31.

65. LaHaye, *Revelation Unveiled*, 34.

66. Doukhan, *Secrets of Revelation*, 21.

67. According to the *Dictionary of Biblical Imagery*, the number "seven is the most important. . . . Underlying all such use of the number seven lies the seven-day week, which, according to Genesis 1:1–2:3 and Exodus 20:11, belongs to the God-given structure of creation." Leland Ryken, James C. Wilhoit, Tremper Longman III, eds., *Dictionary of Bible Imagery* (Downers Grove, IL: InterVarsity, 1998), 774.

religion, society, all seem to go in sevens."[68] Ford notes the inseparable tie between the number and its Old Testament background: "Seven. This is a sacred number. For the Jews it was sacred because of the Sabbath (the seventh day), the seven days of creation, the seventh year which was the year of release, and in the temple the seven altars, seven lamps, and the sprinkling of sacrificial blood seven times."[69]

Agreeing that no one can say with certainty that John meant Sunday, Harrington goes to the heart of the Lord's Day inclusion: "In the liturgical bent of Revelation it is probable that 'the Lord's day' is the day of *worship*."[70] In other words, the reference to the Lord's Day is most probably a call to worship (as the Sabbath was), rather than a treatise on the day of the week. The Reverend Billy Graham may have captured the spirit of the text best when he wrote, "Perhaps, in their 'benevolence,' John's Roman captors allowed this Jewish seer his *ancient Old Testament practice* of keeping one day out of seven holy. Perhaps, that day, they had already herded the other grumbling *non-Jewish* prisoners to their [labors] . . . [leaving John to] wander up and down the beach at Patmos that Sabbath."[71] Like other words and phrases in Revelation, the Lord's Day may have been an allusion to the "day of the Lord" in both the Old and New Testament.[72]

"What you see, write in a book and send it to the seven churches which are in Asia" (Rev. 1:10). The book of Revelation was actually "one circular letter,"[73] reaching all the churches. Fiorenza makes the following observations: "The concentric ABCDC'B'A' pattern [the chiastic structure] of Rev. shows that the whole book is patterned after the epistolary framework."[74]

---

68. Wilcock, *Message of Revelation*, 62.

69. Massyngberde Ford, *Revelation*, 84.

70. Harrington, *Revelation*, 50, italics added.

71. Billy Graham, *Approaching Hoofbeats* (Waco, TX: Word, 1983), 31, 33, italics added.

72. "Yohanan received his vision about the day of the Lord (day of the final judgment and the Parousia) during the Sabbath day (the other day of the Lord)." Doukhan, *Secrets of Revelation*, 21, 22.

73. Bauckham, *Theology*, 2.

74. Fiorenza, *Book of Revelation*, 175.

"It is therefore not accidental that Rev. as a whole has the form of the early Christian apostolic letter."[75] Fiorenza goes on to point out that Revelation's unity has been achieved by far more than just its structure:

> The author achieves a unified dramatic composition primarily by using a common stock of symbols and images . . . [and] by employing image clusters and symbol associations that reinforce each other. . . .
>
> Another primary means . . . consists in the author's use of numbers and numerical patterns. . . . [76]

Revelation is a work of art indeed.

Our heavenly high priest (1:12)

While in this visionary state, John heard a loud voice like a trumpet from behind him. Turning to look, he saw, walking among seven golden lamp stands, one "like the son of man," who was dressed in a robe, with a golden sash[77] around his chest.

Several times in Revelation, John will hear something, but when he turns to look he sees something completely different. And yet what he sees and hears are one and the same (e.g., lion/lamb, 5:5–6; water/beast, 17:1, 3). Caird writes: "What John hears is couched in the traditional messianic imagery of the Old Testament; what he sees constitutes the most impressive rebirth of images he anywhere achieves."[78] Sweet refers to the two aspects as the "theological comment" and the "outward reality."[79]

---

75. Ibid., 170. "The book of Revelation . . . takes the form of a letter." Mounce, *Book of Revelation*, 44.

76. Elisabeth Schüssler Fiorenza, *Revelation: Vision of a Just World* (Minneapolis: Augsburg Fortress, 1991), 33, italics added.

77. Keener notes that the only other occurrence of the girdle is found in 15:6, which also contains priestly imagery in the temple. *Revelation*, 95.

78. Caird, *Revelation of Saint John*, 73.

79. Sweet, *Revelation*, 149, 150.

In the context of the vision, the trumpet's sound would no doubt remind John of the giving of the law at Mount Sinai.[80] This scene, then, is foundational for the sanctuary/throne room scene in the next vision (chapters 4 and 5).

The description *Son of Man* "is full of Old Testament phrases [cf. Dan. 7:13, 14]. . . . His aim is to set the echoes of memory and association ringing."[81] Jesus often applied this title to Himself (John 3:14; 6:53; 8:28; 12:23; Mk. 13:26). With Jesus dressed here in garments that are intended to remind us of the high priest performing his ministry of intercession in the ancient tabernacle,[82] John sees the glorified Savior, our heavenly High Priest (Heb. 2:17), walking among the seven lamp stands. Barclay concludes:

> All this means that the description of the robe and the girdle
> of the glorified Christ is almost exactly that of the clothes of
> the priests and of the high priest. Here, then, is the symbol
> of the high priestly character of the work of the risen Lord.[83]

Gaebelein points out that the sashed robe probably signifies "Christ as the great High Priest to the churches in fulfillment of the OT Aaronic priesthood,"[84] and who is now "to enter into judgment."[85]

We're reminded of the Old Testament covenant, where God promised to walk among His people (Lev. 26:12). As the priests entered the taber-

---

80. Barclay, *Revelation of John*, 1:50.
81. Caird, *Revelation of Saint John*, 25. Barclay, *Revelation of John*, 1:52. Gaebelein, ed., *Hebrews Through Revelation*, 426.
82. Mounce (*Book of Revelation*, 58) notes that, in the LXX, six of the seven usages of the garb are used in connection with the attire of the high priest, which strongly "suggests that this part of the description is intended to set forth the high-priestly function of Christ." See Sweet, *Revelation*, 68; Wilcock, *Message of Revelation*, 41; Osborne, *Revelation* (LABC), 11; Tenney, *Interpreting Revelation*, 54.
83. Barclay, *Revelation of John*, 1:53.
84. Gaebelein, ed., *Hebrews Through Revelation*, 427.
85. John Phillips, *Exploring Revelation: An Expository Commentary* (Grand Rapids, MI: Kregel, 2001), 26.

nacle, a seven-branched menorah stood on their left hand (or south) side, in the Holy Place (Ex. 25:31, 32). This scene is reminiscent of the priest who attended to the candelabra daily; the only source of light, it burned continually. Later, John is told that the seven lamps—a standard symbol of Judaism—represent the churches (1:20), stressing the Jewishness of the Christian faith.[86] "That central message is this: Christ is working out the creation of the one people of God [Jew and Gentile], a priestly nation of all peoples of the world."[87]

Because Revelation is heavily dependent upon the Old Testament, let's reflect for a moment on the sanctuary's background. After freeing the Israelites from bondage in Egypt and guiding them into the Sinai peninsula, God instructed them to construct a portable, tent-like sanctuary, where He could dwell with them (Ex. 25:8, 9). According to the Bible, the structure was "a copy of the true one" in heaven (Heb. 9:24), which is the "more perfect tabernacle" (Heb. 9:24, 11; Ex. 25:40). The sanctuary's furnishings and services illustrated God's plan for the salvation of man. Foreshadowing the Messiah's ministry (Ex. 35–40),[88] every sacrifice pointed forward to Christ, types pointing to the true Antitype (Ex. 12:3, 5; Isa. 53:7, 12; John 1:29). According to the New Testament, Jesus, the Son of God, became like us ("flesh") and "did tabernacle [Greek, *skene*; "tent"] among us" (John 1:14, YLT). Seen through the lens of the sanctuary, Christ is both the true Lamb and High Priest: "For Christ did not enter a man-made sanctuary that was only a copy of the true one; he entered heaven itself, now to appear for us in God's presence. . . . But now he has appeared once for all at the end of the ages to do away with sin by the sacrifice of himself" (Heb. 9:24, 26). "Therefore, since we have a great high priest who has gone through the heavens, Jesus the Son of God, let us hold firmly to the faith we profess" (Heb. 4:14). "Therefore he is able to save

---

86. Paulien, *Gospel From Patmos*, 27.
87. Harrington, *Revelation*, 51.
88. M. R. DeHaan, *The Tabernacle* (Grand Rapids, MI: Zondervan, 1955); Ada R. Habershon, *Outline Studies of the Tabernacle* (Grand Rapids, MI: Kregel, 1974); see especially p. 59.

completely those who come to God through him, because he always lives to intercede for them" (Heb. 7:25).

The book of Revelation can be separated into seven sections, each beginning with a scene from the sanctuary (1:12–20; 4:1–5:14; 8:2–6; 11:19; 15:5–8; 19:1–10; 21:1–8). These introductory scenes lead the reader through the sanctuary's services. Beginning with the sacrifice in the court-yard (5:6), we move into the Holy Place of the tent-tabernacle, past the seven-branched candelabra (1:12) to the altar of incense (8:3–5). Next, we enter the Most Holy Place, where the ark of the covenant was kept, which housed God's moral law, the Ten Commandments (11:19). God's Shekinah presence resided over the mercy seat (compare Exod. 25:22; Lev. 16:2). As Paulien concludes, Revelation, through the sanctuary compound, reveals the necessary "path people take back to God."[89]

Blessed assurance, Jesus is mine (1:14)

John described Christ's glory as follows:

> His head and hair were white like wool, as white as snow, and his eyes were like blazing fire. His feet were like bronze glowing in a furnace, and his voice was like the sound of rushing waters. In his right hand he held seven stars, and out of his mouth came a sharp double-edged sword. His face was like the sun shining in all its brilliance.

Some scenes in Revelation simply demand our contemplation, and this is one of them. Before we jump in and dissect the imagery, allow this entire picture of Christ to make an impact on the mind. Scenes like this, filled with symbols and bizarre imagery, set apocalyptic literature apart from every other form of biblical genre.

---

89. Paulien, *Deep Things*, 126.

Once again, the imagery is borrowed from Daniel. Christ bears the characteristics of the "Ancient of Days" (Dan. 7:9–13). As Jesus told His disciples, "If you have seen me, you have seen the Father" (John 14:9). But the comparisons between the Father and Son are not confined to the opening vision alone: "The application to Christ of the attributes of God is a constant phenomenon in this book."[90] Swete writes:

> The doctrine of God maintained in the Apocalypse cannot be rightly understood apart from its Christology. Our author's revelation of the Father is supplemented by his revelation of the Son. . . . Our writer's Christology leads him frequently to assign to the glorified Christ attributes and titles which belong to the Father.[91]

A two-edged "sword" protrudes from Jesus' mouth. The sword is often used as a symbol of the Bible: "For the word of God is living and active. Sharper than any double-edged sword, it penetrates even to dividing soul and spirit, joints and marrow; it judges the thoughts and attitudes of the heart" (Heb. 4:12). Paul instructs the believer to arm himself with the "sword of the Spirit, which is the word of God" (Eph. 6:17). Possessing a sword-like tongue, Christ is appropriately called "the Word" of God (John 1:1; 5:38; cf. Rev. 19:13, 15), and His power is the "sword of his mouth" (1:16; 2;12, 16; 19:15, 21),[92] which can be seen in how He overcame Satan's temptations (Mt. 4:4, 7, 10). Indeed, as Creator and Redeemer, the very sound of His voice can bring forth life (John 1:3; 11:43). And in the present scene, flanked by corresponding pairs of images—white head/shining face, eyes/mouth, feet/hand—for the purpose of heightening what is

---

90. Guthrie et al, eds., *New Bible Commentary*, 1282.
91. Swete, *Apocalypse*, clx, 16.
92. Wes Howard-Brook and Anthony Gwyther, *Unveiling Empire: Reading Revelation Then and Now* (Maryknoll, NY: Orbis, 1999), 140.

revealed at the center,[93] is Jesus' "voice" (Greek, *phone*) that thunders like the "sound" (Greek, *phone*) of rushing waters.

Beasley-Murray observes that Christ's white hair, piercing gaze, and sword-like word are all indicative of divine judgment.[94] As evidenced in the Gospels, Christ's words "cut both ways by either killing or bringing to life, . . . [offering] salvation for the believer but destruction for the unbelievers."[95] As the coming visions will demonstrate, Jesus offers words of life and death to His churches (cf. 2:23). He is salvation to the believer but a presence of horror to those who despise His grace (6:16, 17).

Conqueror over death (1:17–18)

Overwhelmed by the glory of Christ's presence, John fell to the ground as though dead (cf. Dan. 10:5–10). Who wouldn't? But the beauty in this scene is found in the utter contrast between John's human weakness and Christ's divine power. John tells us that Jesus bent down and gently placed His right hand on him and spoke these words: "Do not be afraid. I am the First and the Last. I am the Living One; I was dead, and behold I am alive for ever and ever! And I hold the keys of death and Hades." How could you be afraid of anything after hearing the sovereign King utter those words?

After narrowly escaping death and being exiled to a lonely isle, John hears Christ, the Conqueror over death, assure him that he is not alone. Jesus is closer to John than he could have imagined—Jesus is the true Ladder connecting heaven and earth. John may have recalled Jesus' words: "In the world you will have tribulation, but take courage; I have conquered [*nike*] the world!" (John 16:33). Jesus overcame temptation through prayer and the study of the Holy Scriptures. Jesus triumphed over Satan through His selfless gift on the Cross. And He has conquered eternal death through His

---

93. Eugene Peterson, *Reversed Thunder: The Revelation of John and the Praying Imagination* (San Francisco: HarperOne, 1991), 37.
94. Beasley-Murray, *Revelation*, 67; Mounce, *Book of Revelation*, 79.
95. Lichtenwalter, *Revelation's Great Love Story*, 76.

resurrection. Jesus Christ, our heavenly High Priest, is our Victor.

The words "the first and . . . the last" are found in Isaiah 44:6, which identifies Christ as the Lord of the Old Testament (Isa. 48:12). But the first-century Christians probably read more into this self-description. Because the early Christians were under constant societal pressure to worship the pagan gods (Rev. 2:14–20), Christ was probably taking a direct shot at Hecate, a popular Asian goddess who went by the title "first and the last."[96]

In warrior-like fashion, Christ takes down Hecate with the "sword" of His mouth, one piece at a time. She bears a triple-sided form, with three faces; the Trinity is composed of the Father, Son and Holy Spirit (1:4-5). She claims the land, sea, and sky as her realm; the Christ-like figure in Revelation 10:5 assumes authority over the entire earth and the heavens. Hecate refers to herself as the "beginning and the end"; Christ claims this title as His own (21:6).[97] She holds out a flaming torch; He holds a host of blazing stars, created by His words alone (1:20). She carries a sword; He will "strike down the nations" of the earth with His sword (19:15). She possesses keys, presumably to the underworld; by His death and resurrection, He has conquered "Hades" (the grave)[98] and holds "the keys" (1:18). Hecate is no match for the "King of kings, and Lord of lords" (19:16).

The church's mission (1:19–20)

As the introductory vision comes to a close, Jesus bids John once again to "write, therefore, what you have seen, what is now and what will take place later" (1:19, NIV, cf. verse 11). Some—especially futurists—have used this text to divide Revelation into a rigid threefold literary structure: (1) "have seen," chapter 1; (2) "what is now," chapters 2 and 3; and (3) "what will

---

96. Paulien, *Gospel from Patmos*, 34.
97. The titles for Jesus and the Father (1:8, 17) are found in the parallel passages at the close of Revelation (21:6; 22:13).
98. "Contrary to modern usage, Hades is not a synonym for Hell. . . . It is the Greek equivalent of the Hebrew 'Sheol,' the place of the dead (i.e., the grave)." Trafton, *Reading Revelation*, 30.

take place later," chapters 4–19. Such a strict division has been rightly called "a grotesque over-simplification"[99]; "the division is rough and superficial."[100] Consider, for example, that the throne-room drama of chapters 4 and 5 and the birth of the man-child in chapter 12 now belong in the past at the time John is writing. Also, the septets (seven seals, seven trumpets, and cosmic conflict scene of chapters 12–14) covering the first half of the book repeatedly conclude with Christ's second coming. Osborne concludes that this "option is weak because the seven letters are not just dealing with the present situation, for eschatological warnings and promises are featured throughout. Moreover, the visions of chapters 4-19 also have past, present, and future aspects intertwined throughout."[101] Indeed, there is "perpetual movement between past, present, and future in the visions," and to miss the obvious has been "a cause of frequent misunderstandings."[102]

Upon closer examination of the text we see only a "twofold" division, not threefold.[103] Mounce writes, "Translate, 'Write, therefore, the things you are about to see, that is, both what now is and what lies yet in the future.' *This relationship between present and future underlies the entire Apocalypse.*"[104] Thus, the vision that unfolds through the book will include present and future events intertwined.[105]

Holding seven stars securely in His hand, Jesus explains that they are the "angels of the seven churches." The word *angels* is probably a reference to the church leaders (the word *angelos* literally means "messenger"; cf. Dan. 12:3; Phil. 2:15), since John is told to address the letters to "the

---

99. Caird, *The Revelation of Saint John*, 26.

100. Swete, *Apocalypse of St. John*, 21.

101. *Revelation* (BEC), 97.

102. Beasley-Murray, *Revelation*, 68.

103. "However, a better translation of 'what is now' [NIV] is 'what they are,' that is, the explanation Jesus provides for the imagery." For the symbolic meaning of the stars and the lampstands is immediately given for John to write down." Mark W. Wilson, *Revelation*, Zondervan Illustrated Bible Backgrounds Commentary (Grand Rapids, MI: Zondervan, 2007), 17.

104. Mounce, *Book of Revelation*, 81, 82, italics added.

105. Osborne, *Revelation* (LABC), 14.

angel" of each church in the seven letters (Rev. 2–3). Just as stars guide sailors through the darkest hours, Christ has provided ministers to guide His church (1 Cor. 12:28). But how important is the role of the minister? Tenney believes that this scene suggests "rigid inspection" of God's leaders and people in the light of the "day of judgment on the world, for judgment must 'begin at the house of God' (1 Pet. 4:17). Christ cannot judge the world until He has purged His church and made it ready for taking it to Himself."[106]

Standing among the seven golden lamp stands (1:12), Jesus explains that they represent the seven churches. Just as the priest maintained the burning lamps inside the temple, Jesus is assuring His church that He is vigilantly caring for her (Mt. 28:20). But like ancient Israel, the church should be a true witness of the God of heaven, radiating the light of His truth and love—"lights in the world, through whom the Light of the world shines."[107] Paul wrote, "Don't you know that you yourselves are God's temple and that God's Spirit lives in you?" (1 Cor. 3:16).[108] Of course, the seven lamp stands, resembling the temple's seven-branched lamp stand, emphasize "the Jewishness of our faith."[109] Harrington notes that the central message here is this: "Christ is working out the creation of the one people of God, a priestly nation of all peoples of the world."[110]

Summary

John, as an exile on the island of Patmos, has just had an encounter—through a vision-like trance—with the resurrected and glorified Christ,

---

106. Tenney, *Interpreting Revelation*, 55.

107. Beasley-Murray, *Revelation*, 70.

108. The Christian is likened to the entire sanctuary: as priests, we serve God continually (Rev. 1:6); we're "living sacrifices" (Rom. 12:1); like the candlestick, we are His "light" (Matt. 5:14); approaching the table of consecrated bread, we partake of the "the bread of life" (John 6:35); our prayers go up from the altar of incense, mingled with the sweet savor of Christ's sacrifice; like the ark of the covenant, in the Most Holy Place, His moral law is inscribed on our hearts (Heb. 8:10).

109. Keener, *Revelation*, 92.

110. Harrington, *Revelation*, 51.

victor over Satan and death. In this vision, Christ was dressed as a high priest, walking among seven sanctuary lamp stands, symbols for seven of His churches. The vision, which carries into chapters 2 and 3, portrays the close relationship between Jesus in heaven and His people on earth. Though separated from us by inestimable space, Jesus seems to be as close to us now, through His Spirit (1:10), as in the days when He walked on earth with the twelve disciples—and perhaps closer.

Chapter 2

The Seven Churches: Revelation 2–3

"Write on a scroll what you see and send it to the seven churches:
to Ephesus, Smyrna, Pergamum, Thyatira, Sardis,
Philadelphia and Laodicea."

As John's vision continues, Jesus gives him seven short messages for the seven churches. Many refer to these as "seven letters," although the entire revelation is a letter,[1] not just chapters 1–3. Adapted to meet each congregation's unique societal situation and spiritual condition, these are intimate messages from the God of heaven who knows His people's needs. Some churches will receive words of praise and encouragement, while others will hear censure and warning, much as a loving parent might need to give to a child (3:19; Matt. 23:37; Gal. 3:26; 1 John 2:28). But regardless of their background or condition, God desires that all would "overcome"[2] (Greek, *nike*) and share His throne throughout eternity (3:21).

Seven messages of victory

Before we examine the seven messages individually, let's take a look at what they all have in common.

---

1. "Linguistic analyses have established that the seven letters form an integral part of the book." Fiorenza, *Book of Revelation*, 20. Since the promises to the victors in the churches are taken up again in chapters 21–22, the seven churches "frame and encircle" the entire Revelation. Ibid., 52. "It is therefore inappropriate to separate the letter septet from the following visions of the book." Ibid., 173.
2. Rev. 2:7, 11, 17, 26; 3:5, 12, 21.

To begin with, scholars believe that all seven cities were located along the same main road, possibly a Roman postal route. The book of Revelation probably traveled from one community to another in the order that John lists them (1:11).

All seven messages follow a definite literary pattern, consisting of seven parts.[3] First, each begins with a brief description of Jesus Christ, which is borrowed primarily from Revelation 1. Commendation or censure follow, along with a call to repent (2:5, 16, 21; 3:3, 19). Each message contains an end-time promise or "eschatological gift"[4] for those who overcome and are victorious. Finally, each concludes with a universal appeal: "He who has an ear, let him hear what the Spirit says to the churches." Tenney breaks it down as follows: Commission, Character, Commendation, Condemnation, Correction, Call, and Challenge.[5] William M. Ramsay notes: "The promise made to the victors at the end of every letter [Rev. 2–3] is to be understood as addressed to the Christians of the city, *but still more to the true Christians of the entire Church.*"[6]

As a whole, the letters reveal a pattern of spiritual decline. In the first few churches, only a minority have strayed from their first love of the gospel; but in the last few churches, there's only a faithful remnant. In a world full of temptations, it's a normal tendency for any church to fall away from the Truth.[7] But note that as the churches wander further from Jesus, His presence grows more intimate,[8] there's an "increasing imminence of the Lord's coming,"[9] and the number of promises increases.[10] A divine principle is at work here. Just as grace does "much more abound" over sin (Rom. 5:20), so too does Christ's love "much more abound" over our

---

3. Gaebelein, ed., *Hebrews Through Revelation*, 431.
4. Osborne, *Revelation* (BEC), 165.
5. Tenney, *Interpreting Revelation*, 51.
6. Ramsay, *Letters*, 206, italics added. Barclay, *Revelation of John*, 1:34.
7. Paulien, *Gospel From Patmos*, 64.
8. Doukhan, *Secrets of Revelation*, 28.
9. Tenney, *Interpreting Revelation*, 68.
10. The number of promises increases by one with each successive church.

weaknesses. Our Great Physician is the remedy for all of our spiritual ills.

Bible students have observed (as did historian Phillip Schaff) a correlation between the character of the seven churches and what appears to be "seven basic periods or stages" of church history,[11] reflected by "seven different sets of conditions."[12] The spiritual characteristics of the seven churches parallel the church's actual history, from the first century down to the end. Perhaps the best way to look at the seven churches is to say, "If the shoe fits, wear it," and the history appears to fit well. Most, if not all, believe that the seventh church, Laodicea—spiritually indifferent and self-sufficient—represents today's Christian church.

As already pointed out, every professed member in the church was called and expected to overcome (Rev. 2:7, 11, 17, 26; 3:5, 12, 21).[13] Victory was not a foreign concept to the early Christians. It was "an athletic and military metaphor."[14] The winners of games and the conquerors of warfare were highly exalted under Nike, the Greek goddess of victory. Victory (*nike*) is also a prominent theme in the seven messages and is woven throughout the Revelation (e.g., 6:2; 11:17; 13:7; 17:14).[15] At the close of each message, Christ admonishes every believer to "*nike*" ("overcome," KJV; "conquer," RSV) even as He did (3:21). The form of this verb in the letters is "a present active participle, [which] implies continuous overcoming/victory . . . as a pattern of life" (see 3:21).[16] And how did Jesus overcome? Jesus overcame Satan by living in faithful obedience to His Father's will. The same is true for our overcoming.

Nike can denote battle or warfare, another prominent theme in

---

11. LaHaye, *Revelation Unveiled*, 35–36. Interestingly, while LaHaye maintains a separation between the initial churches (Ephesus, AD 30–100; Smyrna, AD 100–312; Pergamum, AD 312–606; Thyatira, AD 606 through the Dark Ages), he proposes that the last three all extend simultaneously to the time of the rapture/Tribulation.

12. Van Impe, *Revelation Revealed*, 11.

13. Osborne, Revelation (LABC), 18. Ladd, *Commentary on the Revelation*, 69.

14. Osborne, *Revelation* (BEC), 122.

15. The word *victory* is used in the title of many books on Revelation (e.g., Warren Wiersbe, *Be Victorious* (Wheaton, IL: Victor Books, 1985); Hendriksen, *More Than Conquerors*).

16. Lichtenwalter, *Revelation's Great Love Story*, 96.

Revelation and throughout the Bible. Because "the Christian life is an unrelenting warfare against the powers of evil,"[17] Paul exhorts the Christian to prepare himself for battle against Satan and "put on the full armor of God" (Eph. 6:11). Our sword is the "word of God" (Eph. 6:17) in our daily conflicts against Satan's temptations. First John 2:14 notes the decisive relationship between God's Word and our victories over temptation: "The word of God lives in you, and [because of this] you have overcome [Greek, *nike*] the evil one." John's crowning statement is this: "For everyone *born of God* overcomes [*nike*] the world. This is the victory [*nike*] that has overcome [*nike*] the world—even our *faith*" (1 John 5:4, emphasis added). Beasley-Murray notes: "But the idea of a victor or conqueror entails the concept of the Christian as a warrior for Christ . . . The essential characteristic of the conqueror, therefore, is that he participates in Christ's conquest [Rev. 3:21; 5:5] by *faith*."[18] And thus, "overcoming demands the reader's active participation in the divine war against evil."[19]

The messages to the churches are "vitally important for a proper understanding of Revelation"[20] and are a guide for victorious living in Christ Jesus.

Seven Intimate Messages

Ephesus (2:1–7)

Steeped in paganism, Ephesus had a plurality of gods. Here sat the temple of Diana, one of the Seven Wonders of the World. Against this background, Ephesus became a center for Christian evangelism. Paul, Timothy, Aquila and Priscilla, and John the Revelator all visited this city.

Borrowing imagery from the opening vision, Christ is depicted as walk-

---

17. Ladd, *Commentary on the Revelation*, 40.
18. Beasley-Murray, *Revelation*, 71, 79, italics added.
19. Lichtenwalter, *Revelation's Great Love Story*, 97.
20. Harrington, *Revelation*, 76.

ing among them. Earlier, we saw Him holding stars in His hand (1:16). Here He holds [Greek, *krateo*] the Ephesians with a mighty grip. The same word is used to describe the manner in which Christ seizes the dragon and binds it (20:2). This is reassuring to the church community—no power on earth can wrestle them from His hand. He redeemed the church with His blood (Rev. 5:9), and it's His forever!

Jesus says, "I know your deeds, your hard work and your perseverance. You have persevered and have endured for my name." The words *I know* imply an intimate knowledge—a close relationship. His words would be a compliment for any church. Despite the consistent pressure from the pagan society around them, the members of this church have succeeded in remaining untarnished by outside influences.

But the real challenge comes from *within*.

Some of the church members—called apostles here—spoke as if they had an "in" with Christ, some special insight into Truth. Whatever their motive (a desire for authority perhaps), they could not support their views by the Scriptures (cf. John 5:39; 2 Tim. 2:15). The church tested or examined their ideas and found them to be false, out of sync with God's truths. Accordingly, the church did not tolerate these erroneous influences.

There are more problems. The church had taken the necessary steps to stand up to a more formal group that had been gaining ground among some of the members. Aware of this, and pleased with the church's decisive actions in the name of truth, Jesus said, "You have this in your favor: You hate the practices of the Nicolaitans, which I also hate." The word *Nicolaitan* (a combination of the Greek words *nike* and *laity*) literally means "to conquer the people." In short, a small but calculating group of theological dissenters had come in with the goal to triumph over the members of the church. There appears to be a play on words here, since Christ closes the message with an appeal for the church to *nike* (verse 7; "overcome," KJV).

Bible scholars have suggested that these practices were members' participation in the community's pagan activities. Pagan worship was an integral part of society; even the trade guilds—the occupational unions—gave honor to certain gods. The festivities for the gods included food that had been offered to idols and sensual activities (cf. 2:14, 20; Dan. 1:8). The Nicolaitans may have reasoned that the church was too strict, isolating herself from the very society that she hoped to win over. "How can we expect to attract new converts," they may have argued, "if we are closed minded and refuse to mingle with our neighbors? We're acting like a bunch of legalists! Didn't Paul say that we're *free* in Christ? You need to loosen up a bit, or this church will eventually fade away!" This rationale could have easily "overcome" some of the members.

The apostle Paul may have been seeing some of these seeds of discontent when he warned the Ephesians about trouble ahead: "I know that after I leave, savage wolves will come in among you and will not spare the flock. Even from your own number men will arise and distort the truth in order to draw away disciples after them. So be on your guard!" (Acts 20:29–31; 2 Cor. 11:13). And Peter warned: "There will be false teachers among you. They will secretly introduce destructive heresies" (2 Pet. 2:1). It's no wonder that John had instructed them to "test the spirits [members] to see whether they are from God, because many false prophets have gone out into the world" (1 John 4:1; 1 Thess. 5:19).

Ephesus had a problem that was much bigger than the presence of a few stray visionaries or a band of controllers. Although the members had persevered and endured hardship for the sake of the gospel, the church at large had experienced a serious loss—"You have forsaken your first love." It was as if they had intentionally "abandoned" (RSV)—the Greek literally means, "to send away"—the most essential part of who they were. Clinging too tightly to their doctrinal purity, they had pushed aside the essential aspect of the gospel—God's love. While the surrounding churches were looking at Ephesus and making glowing remarks like, "Look at what the Ephesians are doing. They're on fire for the Lord!" God's love had faded away. But as Beasley-Murray points out, "If the price paid by the Ephesians for the preservation of true Christianity was the loss of love, the price was too high, for Christianity without love is a perverted faith."[21]

Something had to be done, and right away. Christ admonishes the members: "Remember the height from which you have fallen! Repent and do the things you did at first." At some point in time, the church had been on a genuine spiritual "high." The gospel of Jesus Christ was relatively new and something to be excited about. But in the process of confronting situations in the church and occupying their interest with "church work," the members' focus shifted and their priorities changed, and they soon lost sight of their "first love"—a relationship with Jesus.

The Ephesians needed to change direction. The word *repent* (*metanoeo*) means "to turn around." True repentance is a change in thought and attitude that results in a change of behavior. Evangelist Mark Finley, commenting on Ephesus' situation, writes, "In order to feel what we once felt we need to do what we once did."[22] This means that we must be willing to reestablish that connection with God. Some Christians, strangely, think there is nothing more to do after they have accepted Jesus Christ as their Lord and Savior. But that is not what God says, as Trafton explains:

> One of the themes that pervades the book is that Christians are not merely passive recipients . . . Christians are still called, for example, to repent and conquer, as the letters to the seven churches make clear . . . [even to] bear witness (6:9; 12:11), prophesy (11:3), follow the Lamb (14:4), keep the commandments of God and the faith of Jesus (14:12), and do righteous deeds (19:8).[23]

How spiritually dangerous is the track they're on? So much so that

21. Beasley-Murray, *Revelation*, 75.
22. Mark Finley, *Letters From a Lonely Isle*, 15.
23. Trafton, *Reading Revelation*, 86.

Christ warns them that He may be forced to remove their lamp stand from its place. This warning is also aimed at His broader church. The warning "appears to signify the total destruction of the church."[24] Is there any hope? Yes, because Jesus' statement—"unless you repent" (NKJV)—"signifies that the judgment is not irrevocable."[25]

As the first message comes to a close, Jesus says, "He who has an ear, let him hear what the Spirit says to the churches." The Spirit speaks on behalf of Jesus (John 16:13). By its very nature, this is an individual and universal appeal—"whoever has an ear." Beyond the seven churches, it is addressing every member of the church, in every generation (cf. 1 Cor. 2:13–14). The message "is eternal."[26] Like every other New Testament letter for the church, Revelation is addressed to all who will listen. When you sense the Spirit pricking your mind, you can know that Jesus wants to come into your heart (Rev. 3:20).

Christ closes His message to the Ephesians with this promise: "To him who overcomes [nike], I will give the right to eat from the tree of life, which is in the paradise of God." All who refuse to partake of the feast of this world will eat freely from the Tree of Life. A symbol of eternal life, the Tree of Life had been located in the Garden of Eden at the beginning. Just as the serpent had deceived Eve into believing that God was holding back something wonderful from her, so the Nicolaitans had sought to win over others in the congregation with their erroneous teachings on Christian "freedom." But as the story of Eden reminds us, compromise can lead to destruction.

Ephesus reminds us of the early church (AD 31–100). Because of the early Christians' initial or "first" love for Jesus, the gospel spread rapidly throughout the then-known world (Rom. 10:18). But the fervency wouldn't last forever. As we will see, the church would go on to suffer from spiritual compromise and growing apostasy over the coming centuries.

---

24. Morris, *Book of Revelation*, 61.
25. Ibid.
26. Barclay, *Revelation of John*, 1:162.

Smyrna (2:8–11)

The Christians in Smyrna paid a heavy price for their faith, suffering severe afflictions and poverty. Some were ostracized in the community because they didn't participate in emperor worship. Some conscientiously chose to turn away work, because the trade guilds (potters, tentmakers, and other occupations) celebrated the pagan deities. It comes as no surprise that Christ does not have a single word of criticism for this church. They're hurting, and He knows it. Instead, He speaks to them with words of comfort: "I know what you are facing."

The believers in this community were coming face to face with death—martyrdom—for their faith in Jesus Christ. Knowing this, Jesus reminds them that He died as a martyr but came to life again! And if He could lay down His life and rise again (John 10:17, 18), He could raise them up into eternal life. The point is that tribulation, even martyrdom, is temporal (Matt. 10:28). But the one who has been born again from above has already received eternal life and part of God's eternal kingdom—this is what it truly means to be rich.

The pagans were not the only source of trouble. Many unbelieving Jews were a source of slander. Jesus addresses this when He states: "There are some who say they are Jews [that is, God's elect] and are not, but are [in reality] a synagogue of Satan."[27] The synagogue must have been active in its hatred of Christians.[28] The attitude and actions of many Jews toward Christians showed that an ungodly spirit was in their hearts (Luke 9:55). They rejected the Messiah and turned on Jewish believers. They didn't realize that they "were in fact blaspheming God as they persecuted his church under the guise of doing him service (Jn. 16:2)."[29]

We must bear in mind that Christianity was actually a sect of Judaism. Jesus' disciples and most of His followers, as well as the apostle Paul, were

---

27. "Christians saw themselves as God's Israel." Sweet, *Revelation*, 68.
28. Tenney, *Interpreting Revelation*, 59.
29. Wilcock, *Message of Revelation*, 45. "By rejecting their Messiah and attacking his followers they have forfeited the right to be called Jews." Caird, *Revelation of Saint John*, 35.

all Jews (Acts 2). Following the outpouring of the Spirit on Pentecost, thousands of Jews came to accept Jesus as the Messiah when they heard the gospel (Acts 6:7). By and large, Jews and Christians did live side by side over the first few centuries.[30] But many Jews, not accepting the gospel of Jesus, tried to disassociate themselves from the Christians for a number of reasons. For example, just before the Roman invasion in AD 70, the Christian believers heeded Christ's prophetic counsel and fled the city (Matt. 24:15–20).[31] This was an act of treason to an unbelieving Jew. Also, many Jews saw the new Jewish converts as heretics who had denied the faith of their fathers. Now, cognizant of the fact that the Christian would not participate in the community's pagan feasts or emperor worship (the Jews were exempted under Roman law), some of the Jews seized upon this opportunity and accused their Christian neighbors of being unpatriotic to society. Charges like these caused great hardship on the church.[32]

It should be noted that Bible scholars have been somewhat divided over who these Jews actually were. Some hold that these Jews

> are without question Jews by race and religion [literal Jews]. . . . But in reality, inwardly, they are not [true] Jews, because they have rejected Jesus as their Messiah. . . . John makes a real distinction between literal Israel—the Jews—and spiritual Israel—the church.[33]

But others see the term *Jew* as a symbolic reference for those Christians[34]

---

30. "History shows that Jews and Christians remained together, even after the revolts, at least until the fourth century. . . . Besides, that Jewish Christians were free to attend synagogue, as attested in the book of Acts, is clear evidence that Christians never suffered excommunication in the full sense." Jacques Doukhan, *Israel and the Church: Two Voices of the Same God* (Peabody, MA: Hendrickson, 2002), 36.

31. Kenneth L. Gentry, Sam Hamstra, Robert L. Thomas, and C. Marvin Pate, *Four Views on the Book of Revelation* (Grand Rapids, MI: Zondervan, 1998), 139, footnote.

32. Compare the events in Dan. 6:1–13; Acts 17:6–7; Rev. 13.

33. Ladd, *Commentary on the Revelation*, 43, 44.

34. "[The Church's] enemies; [any] who pretend to be the people of God, as the Jews boasted

who were "false professors,"[35] having already wandered from the truths of the gospel (cf. 1 Tim. 4:1). As the seven messages in Revelation 2–3 reveal, some members in the first century had already begun to reject certain aspects of the gospel, returning to their pre-Christian practices. The "slander," then, was coming from professed believers who were intent on rebelling against some of the church's teachings and deceiving other members into error (and as we just saw, this was the case in Ephesus). In another place, Jesus refers to these professed Christians as being like "Balaam" (2:14) or "Jezebel" (2:20).

While both views have their merits, it's more important to remember: "The point of view taken in the Apocalypse is that the Christians were the true Jews,"[36] the spiritual Israel of God[37] (cf. Rom. 2:28–29; 9:6–8; Gal. 3:29; Phil. 3:3). In light of the Cross, the "true Jews are the people of the Messiah."[38] Thus, "true Israel [is] represented by the faithful in [the] seven churches."[39]

Knowing that the tribulation will soon intensify, Christ forewarns the young church that it will soon be put to a great test and suffer persecution for ten days. Some think that this reference to time might simply mean a short, limited period—as if Christ is assuring the members that it will not last forever, and they will survive. Others have suggested that it should be interpreted as a prophetic time period, representing ten specific years:

---

themselves to be . . . assemblies that promote and propagate errors, in opposition to the purity and spirituality of gospel worship." Henry, *Commentary on the Holy Bible*, 3:452. "Today we would accuse our fellow believers of not living up to their 'Christianity,' and call their gathering place a 'church of Satan.' " Doukhan, *Secrets of Revelation*, 32.

35. "They did not really believe" but only "claim to be Christians." Jack Van Impe, *Revelation Revealed*, 27.

36. William M. Ramsay, *Letters to the Seven Churches* (Grand Rapids, MI: Baker, 1985), 142.

37. Even though Pastor John Hagee is an adamant defender of Judaism and a contemporary voice against replacement theology, he acknowledges that "*there is also a spiritual Israel*, with a spiritual people and a spiritual New Jerusalem. *Spiritual Israel (the church)* may have the blessings of physical Israel." *In Defense of Israel* (Lake Mary, FL: FrontLine, 2007), 146, italics added.

38. Ladd, *Commentary on the Revelation*, 43.

39. Hanegraaff, *Apocalypse Code*, 116.

AD 303–313.[40] During that period, Christianity was banned throughout the Roman Empire by Emperor Diocletian. But there's a third view that has not received due consideration. Throughout the Bible, the number *ten* is a symbol of testing: for example, Pharaoh was given ten opportunities in the form of plagues; Daniel and his friends were tested for "ten days" (Dan. 1:12–20);[41] standing on the edge of the Promised Land, ten faithless Hebrew spies convinced the children of Israel that they were powerless to conquer it; every Israelite searched his soul for ten days prior to the Day of Atonement, a day of judgment (Lev. 26:23–29); ten virgins waited for the bridegroom, but only five had enough oil when he arrived (Matt. 25:1–13). We could add that God's Law, the Ten Commandments, is the standard for all humanity, and one tenth of our increase (tithe) belongs to the Lord.

Christ ends His second message with two promises. First, those who remain faithful at all costs will receive the crown (*stephanos*) of life. Distinct from a king's royal *diadema* (cf. Rev. 19:12), the *stephanos* was a wreath bestowed upon the victor in the Greek games. Here, the crown is a symbol for eternal life (cf. 4:4; also 2 Tim. 4:8; James 1:12; 1 Pet. 5:4). Second, those who remain faithful to Jesus will not be hurt by the second death (referring to eternal death, or the "lake of fire" [Rev. 20:14]). As these rewards demonstrate, "the principle of the Christian life is not escape [from either persecution or death] but conquest."[42]

As we look back over the details of Christ's message, it's easy to see why Bible students have seen a relationship between the church of Smyrna and the second phase of church history. True to the prophecy, persecution followed in the wake of the gospel's advances (AD 100–313). But this didn't hinder Christ's work on earth.

---

40. In Bible prophecy, a day represents a year. See Ezek. 4:6; Num. 14:34.
41. It's highly probable that Daniel 1 is the background of Smyrna's ten days. The Septuagint, the Greek translation of the Old Testament, uses the same word—*peirazo*—to denote the test of the four faithful Hebrews (Dan. 1:8).
42. Barclay, *Revelation of John*, 1:101.

Pergamum (2:12–17)

Pergamum ("Pergamos," KJV) was one of the greatest cities in the province of Asia. But with the city's multitude of pagan temples dotting the landscape and its being a seat of emperor worship and host of a large altar dedicated to Zeus,[43] we can see why Christ referred to Pergamum as the place where Satan has his throne. Zeus worship was an affront to Christ for several reasons: the pagan god was titled the "king of the gods" (cf. Rev. 19:16); he was associated with the eagle, the king of birds (cf. 12:4); he was thought to oversee the heavens (cf. 10:1–4; 12:1–5); and he was esteemed as the god of victory (cf. 3:21; 5:5; 17:14).

Despite all the pressures to conform to society, the majority of Christian believers in Pergamum had held fast to their faith, and Christ commended them for it: "You remain true to my name. You did not renounce your faith in me, even in the days of Antipas, my faithful witness, who was put to death in your city."

Though we know nothing more about Antipas, the word *witness* comes from the Greek word *martus*, from which we get the word *martyr*.[44] Jesus, of course, is the "faithful *martus*" (1:5). Years ago, Zenith Corporation ran an advertisement that said, "The quality goes in before the name goes on." Likewise, when we take the name of Jesus, we ought to be a witness for Him with His same qualities.

Unlike Ephesus, the church in Pergamum was tolerant of those who

---

43. The Pergamum altar, built and dedicated to the Greek god Zeus in the second century BC, can be seen today in the Pergamon Museum in Berlin. Ramsay explains: "The Zeus who was worshipped at Laodicea was the Hellenised form of the old native god. . . . When the new seat of Hellenic civilisation and speech was founded in the valley, the people continued to worship the god whose power was known to be supreme in the district, but they imparted to him something of their own character and identified him with their own god Zeus. Thus in Sardis and elsewhere the native god became Zeus Lydios, 'the Zeus who the Lydians worship'; and the same impersonation in outward appearance was worshipped at Laodicea, though with a different name in place of Lydios." *Letters to the Seven Churches*, 418.

44. Though a number of Christians were martyred for their faith before John wrote Revelation, the Roman power itself had not formally engaged in the persecution of Christians up to this time.

advanced erroneous doctrines like the teaching of the Nicolaitans. Unable to find a balance between love and truth, or love and discipline, the church allowed the disease of compromise to spread. Soon another group formed, whom Christ describes as holding to the teaching of Balaam. As you'll recall, Balaam was the prophet who helped Balak, a pagan king, to entice the Israelites to sin by eating food sacrificed to idols and by committing sexual immorality (Num. 22–24). And now the first-century Christian in Pergamum is enticed by the same two practices.

Balaam is a Hebrew name meaning "to devour [or destroy] the people." Essentially, it's the Old Testament equivalent of the Greek name *Nicolaitan* (meaning "to conquer the people"). The original audience would have caught the play on words.[45] The context here reminds us of Paul's words: "These things happened to them [literal Israel] as examples and were written down as warnings for us [spiritual Israel]" (1 Cor. 10:11). Having apparently flaunted their participation in the community's pagan activities, the members of the Pergamum church must have understood exactly what Christ was saying.

As compromise spread like a deadly cancer in the assembly, the Chief Surgeon decided it was time to intervene with His sharp, double-edged, surgical sword. If the "body" is to survive, the cancer must be removed! With a voice of urgency, Christ cries out, "Repent therefore! Otherwise, I will soon come to you and will fight against them [who have apostatized] with the sword of my mouth!" This may be a startling picture for those who have known Jesus only as the Lamb and not the Warrior/Judge of truth (cf. 6:16).[46] This same weapon (Greek, *rhomphia*), which is used here against the unbeliever, is the same one that Christ uses against His enemies (Rev. 19:15, 21). His word, which proceeds from His mouth, can destroy the evil in the world and the wickedness in the church.

---

45. Barclay, *Revelation of John*, 1:74.
46. Ibid., 103. To those who "fail to repent, Christ will come as judge." Harrington, *Revelation*, 62.

Why is it necessary for Christ to present such a serious picture? Because the church was permitting compromise "where there could be no compromise."[47] Though we may not want to admit it, compromise is often nothing less than "yielding to sin," regardless of how innocuous it may seem, and it is "enough to set a process of ultimate annihilation into motion."[48] As Tenney concludes: "The judgment of the world at large will be visited upon the churches if they do not sever themselves from its evils by repentance."[49]

The faithful in Pergamum are promised three rewards. (Notice how the number of promises is increasing with each church.) First, those who overcome the temptation to participate in the pagan feasts and remain faithful to their Lord will receive the *hidden manna* of heaven. After Israel built the sanctuary in the wilderness, Moses was instructed to place a sample of the heavenly manna inside the Ark of the Testimony, beside the Ten Commandments (Exod. 16:32–36; Heb. 9:1–4; Rev. 11:19). Jesus made the connection between the manna and Himself when He said,

> "I tell you the truth, it is not Moses who has given you the bread from heaven, but it is my Father who gives you the true bread from heaven. For the bread of God is he who comes down from heaven and gives life to the world. . . . I am the bread of life. Your forefathers ate the manna in the desert, yet they died. But here is the bread that comes down from heaven, which a man may eat and not die. I am the living bread that came down from heaven. If anyone eats of this bread, he will live forever. This bread is my flesh, which I will give for the life of the world" (John 6:32–33, 48–51).

Second, the overcomer will receive a white stone. That may not sound

---

47. Osborne, *Revelation* (LABC), 30.
48. Paulien, *Gospel From Patmos*, 62.
49. Tenney, *Interpreting Revelation*, 61.

very impressive today, but a white stone served a variety of important purposes in John's day. In a courtroom, black and white stones were used to signify one's guilt or innocence. (The believer in Christ is declared not guilty of all Satan's accusations [12:10]). Used also in John's day as a ticket to enter a banquet, this white stone may very well represent "the Conqueror's ticket of admission to the heavenly banquet, a very permanent ticket to the eternal feast."[50]

Third, there is also a promise that the white stone will have a new name written on it, known only to him. The Lord changed Jacob's name to Israel after he wrestled with his greatest weaknesses and triumphed (Gen. 32:24–30). This new name reflected his new character, earned this side of heaven. So too, every victor will have a new name, an eternal witness of his or her triumphs in Christ here on earth (2 Cor. 5:17; Phil. 3:14).

The name Pergamum means "marriage" and is a fitting symbol for the third phase of church history (AD 313–538). During this period the church, though engaged to Christ, "became more Roman [Catholic] and less Christian in its practices."[51] After his so-called conversion, the Emperor Constantine sought to Christianize the Roman Empire. Raised as an adherent of Mithraism (worship of the sun god), Constantine sanctioned the blending of paganism with Christianity. Like the Nicolaitans in the church who "promoted laxity toward the pagan practices,"[52] these practices entered through the front door of the church during this period and were "baptized" as Christian sacraments. Reportedly, Constantine even baptized his army by marching the ranks through a river. "Sunday, the Roman day of the sun, came to [officially] replace Saturday as the God-given Sabbath day,"[53] and the first sun-day law was enacted, only permitting the most necessary work

---

50. Caird, *Revelation of Saint John*, 42.
51. LaHaye, *Unveiling Revelation*, 59.
52. Ladd, *Commentary on the Revelation*, 48.
53. Doukhan, *Secrets of Revelation*, 35.

on "the Lord's Day," such as milking cows. Many Christians welcomed the change in the church because it served to stem the tide of persecution. But compromise—spiritual adultery—as the faithful would soon discover, would give the church more to fear from within than without.

Thyatira (2:18–29)

With a brilliance that cannot be conveyed through words, Christ approaches the church in Thyatira with eyes like blazing fire and feet like burnished bronze. It may have been His intention to outshine the sun god Apollo Tyrimnaeus, the patron deity of the city.[54] But to the eyes of the unfaithful, Christ's appearance is a reminder that He searches hearts and minds—there's no need to pretend with Him, because He *knows* us.

Jesus begins, "I know your deeds, your love and faith, your service and perseverance, and that you are now doing more than you did at first." That sounds good, doesn't it? So far they're keeping pace with the Ephesian assembly. And yet, despite all of their efforts and accomplishments in church ministry, there was something wrong—*very* wrong—within the church's walls.

Unlike the previous churches, where only a minority of the members had strayed, this church was divided over the teachings of a self-made leader, whom Christ calls "Jezebel." We must return to the Old Testament to understand the allusion.

Jezebel was the wicked wife of Ahab, the king of Israel (1 Kings 16:31). A daughter of the king of Tyre, she had a pagan background. Ruthless in her tactics and wicked to the core, she pressured her husband to promote worship of Baal, the ancient Phoenician and Canaanite sun-god.[55] In one of the most infamous stories in the Old Testament, Elijah, a prophet of

---

54. Trafton, *Reading Revelation*, 41.
55. "The tutelary [guardian] god of [Thyatira], Tyrimnos, had been identified with the Greek sun-god, Apollo, and appears on the city's coins grasping the hand of the Roman emperor." Caird, *Revelation of Saint John*, 43.

Yahweh, took on all of Jezebel's prophets in a hilltop battle over worship. After a three-and-a-half-year drought on the land, the battle on Mount Carmel came down to this: "Who is the true god—is it the Lord Yahweh or is it Baal?" (see 1 Kings 18:16–45). The matter was settled when fire reached down from the heavens and consumed Elijah's water-soaked altar. (Revelation 11:3–6 and 13:13 allude to this great event.)

Unlike the small clique of libertarians in the church in Pergamum, "Jezebel," a self-proclaimed prophetess, brazenly led some of the members into overt pagan practices—namely, sexual immorality and the eating of food sacrificed to idols (apparently, "Jezebel," Balaam, and the Nicolaitans were creating similar problems in the churches; 2:14). The church's leadership, for whatever reasons, chose to tolerate her immoral teachings. But Christ's response is altogether different:

> "I have given her time to repent of her immorality, but she is unwilling. So I will cast her on a bed of suffering, and I will make those who commit adultery with her suffer intensely, unless they repent of her ways. I will strike her children dead" (2:21–23).

Jesus had warned His disciples, "Many will turn away from the faith and will betray and hate each other, and many false prophets will appear and deceive many people" (Matt. 24:10–11). Such was the case in Thyatira, where many of the members had accepted the teachings of "Jezebel." If this were left unchecked, the entire congregation would fall into spiritual ruin, to be subjects of the "second death" (Rev. 2:11).

Though they were small in number and probably felt as though they were standing alone for truth, the rest[56]—the faithful remainder—refused to hold to her teaching, which Christ refers to as "Satan's so-called deep

---

56. Or "remnant" (*loipoy*). Cf. Rev. 12:17.

secrets" (2:24). Osborne suspects that these were "secret insights that were guaranteed to promote deeper spiritual life."[57] Morris may be closer, stating, "They held that to triumph over Satan it is necessary to know Satan's works."[58] The point is, some mysteries in this world a Christian should not explore. One doesn't need to experience the depths of sin to appreciate the heights of grace (Rom. 6:1)!

Acutely aware of the pressure on the true believers, Christ nevertheless urges the remnant in this church to overcome (*nike*). And how do they do that? Christ explains: "Hold on to what you have until I come . . . and [do] my will to the end." As Osborne points out, the author has created a chiasm here—"an ABA pattern"—sandwiching the word *nike* between His expectations: "The only way to be a conqueror is to persevere in Jesus' *words* (v. 25) and *works* (v. 26) until the eschaton. . . . It is only Christ's deeds that can be the basis for Christian victory. . . . Jesus' *words* (2:25) must be lived out in *deeds* (2:26)."[59]

Those who are faithful and endure to the end of this world are promised authority over the nations in the future. Adam was given dominion over the earth (Gen. 1:26), but he forfeited his privilege through his disobedience. But Christ, the second Adam (1 Cor. 15:22), won it back, and He promises to share it with all who are victorious (Rev. 3:21; 20:4). The promise includes an iron scepter (Num. 24:17; Ps. 2:9), which finds its ultimate fulfillment in Christ, who "will rule them with an iron scepter" (Rev. 19:15). The victor's greatest reward is Jesus Himself, the Morning Star: "I am . . . the bright Morning Star" (Rev. 22:16).

Thyatira's condition can be likened to the condition of the church during the Dark Ages (approximately AD 500–1500). The union of church and state created a long, dark history of spiritual apostasy. Having the support of the state, the church persecuted those who dissented from her ex-

---

57. Osborne, *Revelation* (LABC), 34.
58. Morris, *Book of Revelation*, 73.
59. Osborne, *Revelation* (BEC), 165.

tra-biblical teachings and manmade traditions, many of which were nothing more than baptized paganism. As the church turned to the Inquisition and other measures to achieve her goals, the remnant in Europe was forced to withdraw from society socially, politically, and economically, and find refuge in the solitude of the mountains.

Those who have a spiritual "ear" will hear Christ's call to remain faithful until the end.[60]

Sardis (3:1–6)

Sardis is dead? But how? With all of her deeds—program ministries, community outreach, and more—she had a reputation among the churches of being alive! Christ can see right through all of her activities, however; He knows her true condition. And He knows that she will not survive much longer if she doesn't take immediate steps to address the situation. Shaking her cold, lifeless body, Christ cries out, "Wake up! You are about to die!"

Barely opening her eyes, she whispers, "But I don't want to die."

To which Christ responds, "Then strengthen what remains!"

That seems like an odd response—a dying soul being told to strengthen itself. But then, it must have seemed odd to the dying Israelites when they heard Moses say, "Look to the figure of the snake and live," after being bitten by a snake!

The Chief Physician knows exactly what this dying church needs to survive, and He offers them the one and only antidote. "Remember what you received and heard at the beginning, and obey it!" He admonishes them. Like Ephesus, Sardis had lost that "first love" experience. Cold, calculated church programs had overcome the warmth of the gospel. If Sardis is to survive, she must recall her former days with her Savior and reflect on

---

60. Like the seven seals, with four horsemen (6:1–8), and the seven trumpets, with four creation scenes, and the three woes that follow (8:7–13), there is a 3 | 4 division in the seven letters: "In the foregoing epistles [the first three messages], this demand ["He who has an ear"] comes before the concluding promise; but in this [message to Thyatira] and all that follow, it comes after [the promises]." Henry, *Commentary on the Holy Bible*, 3:454.

what brought her to love the gospel at the beginning. Then, pushing all of her self-made plans and goals aside, she must repent and surrender her will to God once again. Returning to His Word, she'll find what she had first received and can obey it again. Obedience is an identifying mark of the true believer (Rev. 12:17; 14:12)—"Those who listen to it being read and do what it says will also be blessed" (Rev. 1:3, TLB).

Jesus knows that a true, daily surrender of the will doesn't come easily to us. He adds this warning: "If you don't wake up, my coming will be like a thief—you will not know at what time it will happen." Christ uses the word *gregoreu*, meaning "to awake and remain alert," twice for emphasis! He discussed this very need with His disciples:

> "Therefore keep watch [Greek, *gregoreu*] because you do not know on what day your Lord will come. But understand this: If the owner of the house had known at what time of night the thief was coming, he would have kept watch and would not have let his house be broken into. So you also must be ready, because the Son of Man will come at an hour when you do not expect him" (Matt. 24:42–44).

Jesus included this warning in the parable of the ten virgins. [61] All ten maidens fell asleep as they waited for the bridegroom's arrival. When he did arrive, only five of them had enough oil (Holy Spirit) in their lamps to join him (Matt. 25:1–13); the others were left in the dark. "For you know very well that the day of the Lord will come like a thief in the night. While people are saying, 'Peace and safety,' destruction will come on them suddenly, as labor pains on a pregnant woman, and they will not escape. But you, brothers, are not in darkness so that this day should surprise you like a thief" (1 Thess. 5:2–10).

---

61. Following His appeal in Matthew 24 for believers to remain awake, Jesus shares a series of parables in Matthew 25 that illustrate how the Christian ought to live.

Matthew Henry notes that "whenever we are off our watch, we lose ground."[62] How true! Our sinful nature is as real as gravity, always pulling us down. We can't earn salvation by working at it, but God has given us a role to play in our salvation. To begin with, we must make a sincere decision. We must choose to surrender our will—everything we are—to Jesus. Like a child running up the descending escalator, our character begins to grow more like Jesus' as we spend time with Him daily (2 Pet. 1:5–8). Sure, we might misjudge a step along the way and fall back momentarily. But Christ's Spirit is there to comfort and strengthen us as we continue our ascent. As the words of the childhood song go, "We are climbing Jacob's ladder."

True to Sardis's name, which means "that which remains," only a few had not soiled their clothes or compromised "with the world's filth" (TLB). These Christ compassionately refers to as "worthy," a word normally reserved for the Father and Himself (5:9, 12; 4:11).

The victors are promised many rewards. First, Jesus says, "I will acknowledge his name before my Father and His angels" (Luke 12:8). Next, "I will never erase his name from the book of life." In light of the Greek language, Paulien notes: "Remaining in the book of life is the result of an ongoing process of 'overcoming' ([here, *nike* is] a Greek participle in the present tense). . . . As long as they remain in relationship with Him, their position with God is secure."[63] Jesus' statement, of course, goes against the popular belief of "once saved always saved." As Osborne points out: "The promise is empty if the 'blotting out' could never occur. . . . The only way to be sure of one's salvation is to persevere."[64] To the one who does overcome, Jesus promises: "He will walk with me, dressed in white" (see Rev. 7:9, 13).

Sardis's spiritual condition is reflected in the Reformation period (early

---

62. Henry, *Commentary on the Holy Bible*, 3:455.
63. Paulien, *Gospel From Patmos*, 79, 81.
64. Osborne, *Revelation* (BEC), 183. Also, "Those 'erased' are members of the Sardian church who failed to remain true to Christ. Moreover, there are other passages in Revelation on the possibility of losing one's place in the kingdom (cf. 2:5; 21:7-8; 22:17-18) as well as corroborating material in the rest of the NT (e.g., John 15:1-6; Heb. 6:4-6; 10:26-31; 2 Pet. 2:20-22)." Ibid.

1500s to mid-1700s), which included defining moments like Martin Luther nailing his Ninety-Five Theses to the church door in Wittenberg, Germany. With the invention of the printing press, Bibles that were heretofore limited to monasteries and pulpits found their way into the hands of the common people. Though small at first, a bright light was shed across the European continent as the Reformers—such as John Wycliffe and William Tyndale in England; John Huss and Jerome in Bohemia; Martin Luther in Germany; Ulrich Zwingli in Switzerland; and John Knox in Scotland—began to challenge the unbiblical teachings and long-standing traditions of the church. But the glowing warmth of this movement did not last, as the cold rigidness of doctrinal debates took preeminence. As the Reformers faded from the scene, their successors became more and more involved in doctrinal debates and controversies. As a result, many members of the church became satisfied with the teachings of certain men and stopped there (i.e., Lutherans, Calvinists, Wesleyans). Unfortunately, as LaHaye points out, the Reformation leaders "did not proceed to complete the works of reforming the church, but stopped far short of scriptural standards."[65]

Philadelphia (3:7–13)

The name Philadelphia means "brotherly love." It would be a wonderful name for this church if it were not for the fact that only a small number of members demonstrated godly love. Speaking to this faithful remnant, Christ says, "I know that you have little strength, yet you have kept my word and have not denied my name. . . . You have kept my command to endure patiently" (3:8, 10, cf. 1:9).

This faithful little group had "patiently obeyed [Jesus' words] despite the persecution" (TLB) from the unbelieving Jews around them—that is, those who are of the synagogue of Satan, who claim to be Jews. Warren Wiersbe writes, "These people may have been Jews in the flesh, but they

---

65. LaHaye, *Revelation Unveiled*, 74.

were not 'true Israel' in the New Testament sense (Rom. 2:17–29)." Like the believers in Smyrna, the Christians were probably excluded from worshipping in the local synagogue and falsely accused.[66]

Jesus is described as holy and true: "['The true one', RSV] recalls the covenant made with Israel in Old Testament times which God has now faithfully fulfilled with his church in Jesus Christ."[67] In contrast to their weakness, Christ is pictured here in His regal strength. The heir in the line of Judah (5:5), He holds the key of David, a symbol of His authority over the house of God (cf. Isa. 22:20–22, where the authority to open and shut the doors of the kingdom was placed in the hands of Eliakim).[68] He's the true King of true Israel (cf. 19:16)! Not only does He possess the key to the "city of David, the heavenly Jerusalem,"[69] but Christ Himself is the open door by which every believer is able to enter God's kingdom. All who believe on Him have the assurance of salvation by His Spirit; what He opens no one can shut, and what He shuts no one can open.

Knowing full well what these believers have endured for their faith, Christ promises them that their enemies will one day hear Him say of them, "I have loved you!" Those are words of encouragement, giving them renewed strength. "[So] hold on to what you have," He continues, "so that no one will take your crown [*stephanos*]," the "crown of life" (2:10).[70] Over and over, Jesus tells His disciples that "they have a responsibility to persevere [here, it is to 'hold fast']. . . . The emphasis is on the continual effort (present tense) needed to maintain their walk with Christ."[71] This is a sobering reminder that others, even in the church (e.g., the Nicolaitans, Balaam, and "Jezebel"), can have a negative influence on our eternal decisions. As

66. Wiersbe, *Be Victorious*, 42.
67. Ladd, *Commentary on the Revelation*, 58.
68. Harrington, *Revelation*, 70.
69. Morris, *Book of Revelation*, 78.
70. Some believe that the crown represents the believer's salvation (Paulien, *Gospel From Patmos*, 86), but others say that it is "not salvation, but rewards" (Van Impe, *Revelation Revealed*, 40).
71. Osborne, *Revelation* (BEC), 194, 195.

Paul said, "The race isn't over until it's over" (see 1 Cor. 9:24; 2 Tim. 4:7).

Switching to an eschatological tone, Christ promises to keep the church from the hour of trial that is going to come upon the whole world to test those who live on the earth. The language seems to refer to earth's final hour. The Greek phrase, *tereo ek*, "kept from," is used in only one other place (John 17:15) and means "to preserve from the attack of evil rather than to remove from it by physical separation."[72] "Hence, any notion that the same expression in [Rev.] 3:10 depicts a physical removal (e.g., a pre-tribulational 'rapture' of the church) is surely misguided."[73] This phrase indicates "special protection in the trial, rather than exemption from it."[74]

The Bible is filled with stories about the faithful who endured tribulation (see Hebrews 11:32–38).[75] Though some, like Daniel and his friends, were miraculously spared, many of God's people in the Bible offered up their lives for His sake. The same is true for the Christian age. Many now believe that Christ will rapture His church to heavenly safety before the final Tribulation. But if the Old Testament account of the plagues on Egypt is any clue (Exod. 7–12), the true believers will be protected by the Lamb's blood during the seven last plagues (Rev. 16), just as ancient Israel was.

In keeping with her name, Christ promises His brothers and sisters that they will soon enjoy close, intimate fellowship with Him: "[The victor] will be a pillar in the temple of my God. Never again will he leave it." The pillar and temple are metaphors. There will be no need for any semblance of a temple in the New Earth, because sin will have been eradicated. And with the capital of the universe—New Jerusalem— seated upon the earth, God will not need a special place to dwell with His people. "The Lord God Almighty and the Lamb [are] the temple" (21:22),

---

72. Tenney, *Interpreting Revelation*, 65.
73. Trafton, *Reading Revelation*, 50.
74. Harrington, *Revelation*, 71.
75. "All the righteous blood that has been shed on earth, [beginning] from the blood of righteous Abel" (Matt. 23:35; cf. John 17:15).

and They will openly dwell with the redeemed. The very fact that we are called God's "temple" demonstrates the close relationship that already exists between us because of Jesus Christ (1 Cor. 6:19). The last promise is personalized: "I will write on him the name of my God and the name of the city of my God, the new Jerusalem . . . and I will also write on him my new name" (Num. 6:27; Rev. 14:1; 22:4). Verse 12b contains another small chiasm, or A-B-A pattern: the New Jerusalem is situated between God's name and Christ's name.[76] At last, the victor will be at one with God because of the great atonement of Jesus Christ.

The church of Philadelphia reminds Bible students of the revivals in the 1700s and 1800s, which included the Great Awakening. During this period, Christians from a variety of denominations engaged in serious Bible study. "A historian of the time, John B. McMaster, reports that nearly 1 million people out of the 17 million in the United States participated in this movement. . . . Interestingly, the same fever also gripped [the] Jews and [the] Muslims."[77] Topics like Bible prophecy, the heavenly sanctuary, and Christ's second coming dominated small-group Bible studies and church revivals. A heightened zeal to fulfill the great commission gave way to a vast expansion of missionary work overseas. A door of opportunity had indeed opened before the church (cf. Acts 14:27; 1 Cor. 16:9; 2 Cor. 2:12; Col. 4:3), and the gospel spread rapidly around the globe.

Laodicea (3:14–22)

The seventh and last message was to the Laodiceans, whose name means "a judged people." Laodicea was a thriving and prosperous city. Renowned for its hot springs, eye salves, and products like black wool, Laodicea appealed to the senses of the wealthy. While all of this may be great for a city, it can be detrimental to one's spirituality.

Like the city that surrounded her, the Laodicean church boasted, "I am

---

76. Osborne, *Revelation* (BEC), 199.
77. Doukhan, *Secrets of Revelation*, 43.

rich; I have acquired wealth and do not need a thing." The Lord looks right through this church's beautiful structure, elaborate furnishings, and other treasures and searches her heart. Her lifestyle is similar to "the inhabitants of the earth" (6:10), and He finds that her primary interests are on "material and earth-centered pursuits."[78] For "these all but apostate Christians,"[79] the senses have been dulled—numbed even—by the world's attractions and riches. This assembly of "self-centered, self-occupied, self-satisfied, self-sufficient, and over-confident"[80] souls has become spiritually lethargic.

Considering how independently wealthy and successful the church is, what praise could Jesus possibly offer this community that she had not heard before? The answer is *none*. And therein lies the problem: Jesus doesn't have a single good thing to say about her current spiritual condition.

But that doesn't mean Christ has nothing to say. And He's ready to get right down to it!

Jesus begins by comparing those who profess to know Him to the tepid waters that poured into the city from the hot springs on the nearby hill. "You are lukewarm—neither hot nor cold," He declares. Of course, lukewarm water is "useless to him."[81] Laodicea is the height of compromise—what a patchwork religion composed of a little of self and a little of Christ looks like. That's a very disturbing thought when you consider that the purpose of the church is to fulfill God's will and mission on earth. Imagine the silence that must have fallen over this assembly as the minister read this out loud. Knowing full well that their name means "to be judged," the members must have felt painfully uneasy as the words began to sink in.

And the Great Physician isn't finished.

"I know your deeds," He continues. You can't hide from someone who knows you. "You are spiritually wretched, pitiful, poor, blind and naked!"

78. Osborne, *Revelation* (BEC), 216.
79. Gentry et al, *Four Views*, 1287.
80. Epp, *Practical Studies*, 190.
81. Gaebelein, ed., *Hebrews Through Revelation*, 458.

Could the picture of this church be more pathetic? "I am about to spit you out of my mouth!"

So why does Christ use such harsh language? Because, more than just being His witness on earth, the church is Christ's *bride* (19:7)! He loves her. He gave everything for her, even assuming her humanity forever! But Laodicea is so utterly self-deceived that she does not realize how bad her condition is or that her marriage is on the rocks! She's been relying on her possessions and self-designed accomplishments as the tools to evaluate her relationship with Christ. Satisfied with herself, she has become spiritually "indifferent, nominal, [and] complacent."[82] In the end, all of her "deeds of love" have added up to nothing, because the Spirit was not in them. It should come as no surprise that Christ would take key words from this last message to the church—garments, shame, nakedness—and insert them into the middle of earth's final battle, Armageddon. This should serve to remind us that the spiritual principles involved in the final war between Christ and Satan are just as vital for Christians today.

So, what action should Christ take with such a church? This time, it's "tough love." Speaking like a father who has his child's best interests in mind, He says, "Those whom I love I rebuke and discipline" (Heb. 12:6). On the one hand, these are words of warning; things must change. "The very harshness of his censure" that follows "is the proof of a love that is satisfied only with the best."[83] On the other hand, Christ's words serve to assure these believers that He has not removed their candlestick from its place (Rev. 2:5). The cure has arrived in time—but now they need to apply it.

"I counsel you to buy from me gold refined in the fire, so you can become rich."

Over the course of her relatively short history, the Laodicean community had slowly exchanged a spiritually rich relationship with Christ for "corruptible" worldly materials (1 Cor. 9:25). The gospel had become dull

---

82. Ladd, *Commentary on the Revelation*, 64, 65.
83. Caird, *Revelation of Saint John*, 57.

in comparison to the worldly goods and entertainment around her. Thus, the question has been raised, can one be both a faithful Christian and prosperous?[84] Is there anything wrong with having my needs met, being financially secure, and enjoying what I have? No, there isn't. "Except," as Mark Finley points out, "when you're actually poor, blind, and naked *and don't even know it!*"[85]

In order to revive this church, Jesus must first purge her with the purifying fire of the Spirit, just as gold is purified by fire. In order to do this, however, the soul will have to endure deep and painful self-examination and respond with abiding faith in His discipline.

Next, Christ bids her let go of her "filthy rags" (Isa. 64:6), which cannot hide her shameful nakedness, and accept the white clothes that only He can offer—a robe purchased through His saving act on Calvary. "They must receive from Christ the white raiment he purchased and provided for them; his own imputed righteousness for *justification* [the new birth] and the garments of holiness and *sanctification* [growing up in Him daily]."[86] (Compare Isa. 61:10.) She has long been clinging to her self-made and self-righteous garments. But Christ cannot accept a patchwork faith, composed of heavenly and earthly materials.

Finally, in spite of the fact that Laodicea is renowned for her medicinal eye salves, Jesus offers this church "salve to put on your eyes, so you can see." In order for her to see her need for a Savior, she must be able to see herself as she truly is, and Jesus as He truly is. Without the discernment of the Holy Spirit, we're all spiritually blind.

That's a lot of medicine to swallow. But the heavenly Physician isn't quite finished.

To close His message, Jesus creates a solemn word-picture, a visual aid.

84. Adela Yarbro Collins, *Crisis and Catharsis: The Power of the Apocalypse* (Philadelphia: Westminster Press, 1984), 133.
85. Finley, *Letters From a Lonely Isle*, 72.
86. Henry, *Commentary on the Holy Bible*, 3:457, italics added.

He is standing outside the door of His own church—"an incongruous concept."[87] He knocks . . . and knocks. Then, with a passionate plea, He cries, "Here I am! I stand at the door and knock!" The church must be willing to open the door and invite the Great Physician to enter, in order to receive the life-changing prescriptions that she so desperately needs. Her need to respond reveals her "human responsibility"[88] to Jesus' invitation.

Christ goes on to explain, "I want to eat with him, and he with me." Mealtime has lost much of its value and significance in Western society. But in Bible times a meal was an opportunity for fellowship.[89] A bumper sticker reads, "The family that eats together stays together." Christ wants an intimate fellowship with all of His children.

Christ has repeatedly admonished the churches to repent (2:5, 16, 21, 22; 3:3), which literally means to "turn around," to begin doing things differently. Not unlike today, many members in the churches needed to do a 180-degree change in life! But now He adds, "Be zealous!" The Greek word *zelos* means "to heat." Laodicea's passion for the gospel of Jesus Christ had cooled. The flame needed to be rekindled.

Many families have played a game with their children called "Hot or Cold." To begin with, the parent thinks of an object in the room. Next, the children move about, trying to guess which object the parent is thinking of. As a child gets closer to the object, the parent says, "You're getting hotter!" This, of course, makes the game exciting. And so it is with Jesus—He desires a church that is excited about His presence. The good news in the message to Laodicea is that it is still possible to recapture the warmth of that "first love" experience. Knowing this, one should never give up on a spiritual brother or sister, or even a church, that appears to have become indifferent to God's truths.

---

87. Tenney, *Interpreting Revelation*, 67.
88. Barclay, *Revelation of John*, 1:161.
89. "There is inescapable reference back to the Last Supper . . . and forward to 'the marriage *supper* of the Lamb.'" Sweet, *Revelation*, 109.

Christ has promised almost everything imaginable to the victors in the first six churches. What could He possibly offer to Laodicea, who believes that she has everything she needs? Actually, the answer is contained in the question: He'll offer her *everything*! "He who overcomes and is victorious, I will grant him to sit beside Me on My throne, even as I was victorious, and have sat down beside My Father on His throne." Considered by some to be the "main symbol"[90] in Revelation, the heavenly throne was seen at the beginning of the vision (1:4) and is mentioned in almost every chapter of the book. The mention of the Father and Son together on the throne reveals again the "progressive assimilation of God and the Lamb."[91] Here too (verse 21) is "the essence of Revelation 4-7 in advance," that is, a picture of the Father's throne (Rev. 4), Jesus joining His father (Rev. 5), the struggle of God's people to overcome (Rev. 6), and His people gathered with Him at last (Rev. 7).[92]

If Laodicea will invite the King of the universe in and give her heart completely to Him, He—the One who has conquered sin, death, and Satan—will share all the riches of His kingdom with her, for that is what the throne represents. What higher incentive could He possibly give her than to sit "beside God as equal ruler"?[93] German scholar Ernst Lohmeyer calls this "the crown" of the seven promises.[94] But as Osborne points out, we must not forget the power and authority behind this promise: "Jesus' 'victory' was the basis of his throne, and the victory of the saints as they overcome the world and its evil is the basis of their throne."[95] Christ asserts that He is ruler specifically because He was victorious—"This throne is reached through witness and death."[96] Paulien writes:

90. Fiorenza, *Book of Revelation*, 24.
91. Harrington, *Revelation*, 74.
92. Paulien, *Gospel From Patmos*, 161.
93. Roloff, *Revelation*, 66.
94. Quoted in Beasley-Murray, *Revelation*, 108.
95. Osborne, *Revelation* (BEC), 215.
96. Sweet, *Revelation*, 110.

It is the promise to end all promises. . . . That *one* promise incorporates all the 21 promises received by the other six churches. If you sit with Jesus on His throne, you have everything! Just as Laodicea is the most hopeless of the seven churches, it is also the one that gets the best promise. The church who has nothing receives the promise of everything![97] (cf. Rev 22:5).

Apparently, Jesus wanted to shock the self-sufficient Laodiceans out of their spiritual lethargy—and this would do it!

The heavenly throne—that's quite a promise. But Jesus' title, The Amen, the faithful and true witness, assures Laodicea that He is the "reliable and trustworthy one, who can be trusted to keep his covenant [agreement] with his people."[98] Let's face it, only the King of the universe, the ruler[99] of God's creation (John 1:1–3; 1 Cor. 8:6; Col. 1:15), could deliver on this.

The church of Laodicea represents the last period in church history, earth's closing years.[100] Unarguably, in many parts of the world the church has become wholly self-sufficient as its members have become immersed in materialism. Even in the early eighteenth century, Matthew Henry could say of the reformed church: "Lukewarm professors may call their lukewarmness charity, meekness, moderation, and largeness of soul; but it is nauseous to Christ. . . . Their evil tempers, unholy actions, and attachment to the world, and to its pleasures, company, and interest, dishonoured Christ more than their apostasy could do; and in the end would be equally fatal to their souls. Thus they would give [peo-

---

97. Paulien, *Gospel From Patmos*, 99.
98. Ladd, *Commentary on the Revelation*, 65.
99. The Greek word *arche* ("ruler") can refer to the first, as in the ruler of a kingdom, or the "beginning" (KJV). As the "second" Adam (1 Cor. 15:21, 22), Christ is the counterpart of the original ruler of God's creation.
100. Ladd notes that "the metaphor of Christ standing at the door [Rev. 3:19] is a familiar eschatological [end-time] concept (Mark 13:29; Matt. 24:33; Luke 12:36; Jas 5:9)." *Commentary on the Revelation*, 67.

ple] a false opinion of Christianity, as if it were an unholy religion . . . so ready to seek pleasure or happiness from the world."[101]

But the sobering fact is that there are far too many "professors" occupying space in the church pew today, people who claim to be disciples of Jesus Christ but do not *know* Him as their personal Savior and Lord.[102] Their souls not yet stirred by godly love, they lack the motivation to witness about salvation (Matt. 28:18–20). As a consequence, the church in Western society has, by and large, *hired* its "witnesses"—be it a pastor or evangelist. Where there could be hundreds of light-bearers proclaiming the everlasting gospel, there is often only one. Jesus' last message to a people who are sitting idly during the judgment hour is to *repent*—while the door of salvation is still open.

Summary

It's hard to imagine that the spiritual condition of the seven churches—loveless, compromising, apostatized, self-deceived—is an illustration of the early church. A generation had hardly passed since the Holy Spirit had been poured out on the early believers and the gospel had spread across the Roman Empire. In light of what we have read, it's a wonder that the gospel made it beyond Jerusalem!

As in Revelation 1, which made reference to a new covenant with a new Israel (Rev. 1:6), and the throne-room scene that follows (Rev. 4–5), which is built on covenant language and symbolism,[103] in Revelation 2–3 "the promises to the churches can be seen as covenant blessings, and the threats as covenant curses."[104] No different than ancient Israel, the true (spiritual) Israelite must respond to Christ in faith and obedience.

---

101. *Commentary on the Holy Bible*, 3:457.
102. LaHaye qualifies what a true member is: "If you are a member of the body of Christ—that is, if you have personally invited Jesus Christ into your heart." *Revelation Unveiled*, 140.
103. Osborne, *Revelation* (BEC), 248, 249.
104. Neall, "Sealed Saints and the Tribulation," in Holbrook, ed., *Symposium on Revelation – Book 1*, 247. "Covenant blessings." Osborne, *Revelation* (BEC), 183.

In addition to addressing the spiritual needs of the churches in Asia Minor, these seven messages tell us how the victor ought to live. Ladd writes: "The promise in each of the seven letters to the conqueror is addressed to all disciples of Christ, with the expectation that all faithful disciples will overcome."[105] But what does it mean to overcome? Lichtenwalter suggests five areas of consideration, which are worthy of mention here:[106] First, there are the "moral implications" involved, like faithfulness, truthfulness, a forgiving spirit, and loyalty to and worship of God alone. "Overcoming thus encompasses very concrete and observable dimensions."[107] Second, it is "the ability to discern and hold on to God-given truth in the face of masterful delusion and unprecedented coercion."[108] But in order to avoid becoming "spiritually disoriented," we must know what God's Word says. Third, overcoming means "choosing right values and associations."[109] As Revelation reveals, "the city of Babylon depicts the complete control of the political, religious, commercial, and cultural apparatus of society . . . [with a] self-indulgent value system."[110] Overcoming, then, is "consciously and publicly disassociating one's self" from her; "the ultimate value is identifying with God and His principles as well as honoring His commandments (Rev. 14:12; cf. Rev. 18:4)."[111] Fourth, ironically, while we are not expected to conquer Babylon but rather to withdraw from her (Rev. 18:4), we are to overcome Satan himself—as Revelation repeatedly shows, he "actively wars against God's people." Fifth, we are to overcome as Jesus did. That is, "*in the same way that Jesus did . . . through suffering and weakness rather than by either human or divine might*."[112] In this, Christ is our model—"Overcoming is

---

105. Ladd, *Commentary on the Revelation*, 69.
106. Lichtenwalter, *Revelation's Great Love Story*, 98–104.
107. Ibid., 100.
108. Ibid.
109. Ibid., 101.
110. Ibid., 101, 102.
111. Ibid., 102.
112. Ibid.

to be like Jesus in the world. . . . Denying self for the sake of Jesus and for the sake of others is what overcoming is all about. Death to self is both the greatest battle and the most profound victory."[113]

But Christ doesn't stop there. He wants us to know that we can overcome through Him: "In this world you will have trouble. But take heart! I have overcome [*nike*] the world" (John 16:33, NIV). Paul says, "Overwhelming victory [*huper-nike*] is ours through Christ" (Rom. 8:37, NLT); "we are more than conquerors through Him" (NKJV). In a strong summary statement on the topic of victory, John tells us what is the key: "For everyone born of God overcomes [*nike*] the world. This is the victory [*nike*] that has overcome [*nike*] the world, even our *faith*" (1 John 5:4). And true faith is having complete trust in Him and accepting His will entirely.

Every victor in the church is a prize for Jesus, considering that what the believer does not overcome will overcome him! As Caird writes: "The conqueror is one in whom Christ wins afresh his own victory, which is also God's victory."[114]

---

113. Ibid., 104.
114. Caird, *Revelation of Saint John*, 58.

Chapter 3

Heaven's Throne Room: Revelation 4–5

"There before me was a throne in heaven. . . .
'Do not weep! See, the Lion of the tribe of Judah,
the Root of David, has triumphed.
He is able to open the scroll and its seven seals.'
Then I saw a Lamb."

After this I looked, and there before me was a door standing open in heaven." At the end of the previous vision, we saw the Savior knocking at the door of people's hearts and pleading to be allowed in and have close fellowship with them (3:20). And to show how much He loves them, He promised them everything, including a seat on His throne (3:21)—the supreme position in the universe.

In contrast to that scene, John sees an open door leading into the heavenly throne room/sanctuary. Christ appears to be saying, "I will open my entire kingdom to all who will open their heart to me!" That is a glorious promise, conveyed here through pictures and symbols.

Like chapters 2 and 3, which highlighted Jesus' relationship with His churches, chapters 4 and 5 are one unit, and they reveal the relationship between God the Father and the Son. The two chapters are also separate scenes: a celebration of creation and redemption respectively.[1]

---

1. Harrington, *Revelation*, 82.

But this is not the end of Revelation's opening story. As Trafton observes, "There is a sense in which chapters 4-5 form a complete unit introducing the Lamb (and what he has done), *but not really*; *the seals still need to be opened*, which leads into chapter 6."[2] And even then, there's still chapter 7, where we see all of the victors standing with the Lamb before God's throne.

Once again, John hears a voice like a trumpet (1:10), and presumably it is Christ's. "Come up here," comes the heavenly command, "and I will show you what must take place after this."[3] And then suddenly, John is in the Spirit.[4] Consumed in a visionary trance,[5] John finds himself peering into the command center of the universe—God's throne room. This is the object of universal authority and power, and the very seat that Christ promises to share with all who are victorious in Him. John now sees that Christ's promise is true; the reward is real (22:12).

Raptured or enraptured?

Before we examine the contents and details of the heavenly throne room, we need to address a long-standing debate regarding chapter 4:1–2. The differences of opinion on this passage are great (along with 6:1–2, where we see a rider on a white horse). This text is the fork in the road to interpreting and understanding the book of Revelation. The primary question that divides Bible students is this: was John's experience of being "in the Spirit" just his own, or does it represent a pre-Tribulation rapture of the church?

Only a few hundred years ago, the Protestant Reformers held that Revelation was primarily about Jesus Christ and His people. It was commonly understood that believers living at the time of the end would pass through

---

2. Trafton, *Reading Revelation*, 55, italics added.
3. Some Bible students believe that the words "after this" suggest that the remainder of Revelation does not concern the church. Wilcock addresses this: "In itself, the phrase 'what must take place after this' does not necessarily mean anything but 'events from now on.'" *Message of Revelation*, 67; cf. Keener, *Revelation*, 178.
4. The author uses the same words to introduce three more visions in 1:10; 17:3; 21:10.
5. Beasley-Murray says, "Transported in his ecstasy." *Revelation*, 112.

the final tribulation, just as ancient Israel lived through the plagues that fell on Egypt. Christians, both Jews and Gentiles, considered themselves to be "spiritual Israel." But over time, this view subtly changed.

The popular teaching today is that the command to "Come up here" and John's subsequent experience ("I was in the Spirit") represent a pre-Tribulation "rapture" of the church. According to this teaching, true believers will suddenly disappear and meet Jesus in the air, escaping the Tribulation. Because this event will not be visible to those who are left behind, it has been labeled the "secret rapture."[6] This view, it must be pointed out, changes the focus of Revelation from Jesus Christ and His church to a future antichrist, who will make a pact or covenant with the Jewish nation. This view has had enormous momentum in recent years, due, in large part, to Christian media productions (e.g., the Left Behind series).

Why have Protestants in particular accepted this drastic reversal in their theology of eschatology (the study of the end of the world)? And how could such a momentous change occur without any accounting for it? As incredible as it may seem, not one book has been written to explain why the church has all but abandoned its Christ-centered view of Revelation 4–6, giving unwarrented attention instead to the antichrist and the temporal Jewish nation.

Hank Hanegraaff tells us, "For nineteen hundred years [all of church history], the idea of a pretribulational rapture was completely foreign to mainstream Christianity."[7] But a Bible teacher by the name of John Nelson Darby changed all of that. Considered the "father of dispensationalism,"[8]

---

6. The phrase *secret rapture* may have come from the fact that some proponents call it "a secret thing" (LaHaye, *Revelation Unveiled*, 140).

7. Hanegraaff, *Apocalypse Code*, 55. "No one—including historical luminaries . . . had any concept of the pretribulational rapture that LaHaye claims is so 'clearly taught' in Scripture." Ibid., 47.

8. Ibid., 17. Dispensationalists believe that Israel's prophetic "clock" stopped at the time of Pentecost, when the Spirit was poured upon the New Testament believers and the "Church Age" began. After the believers are suddenly raptured from the earth, they say, the focus of Bible prophecy will return to literal Israel, which must then pass through the Great Tribulation and the antichrist's reign.

his theories were dependent on an extremely literal interpretation of Bible prophecy,[9] even those passages that are clearly symbolic. Contending that there remains a distinction between Israel and the church, proponents of dispensationalism broke up Bible history into eight dispensations of time, separating the age of Israel's Mosaic law from the church's age of grace,[10] and teaching that believers will escape the final Tribulation. Rejecting the long-held view that the seventieth week of Daniel 9:26–27 pointed to the Messiah's sacrifice, the new teaching said that this text was still unfulfilled, awaiting a future antichrist who will make a covenant with the nation of Israel. As Hanegraaff explains, "History [in their view] hinged on herding Jews back into Palestine . . . [to] die in an apocalyptic Armageddon."[11]

In a special issue entitled *Mysteries of Faith*, *U.S. News & World Report* magazine ran an article called "The Rapture: A New Invention," which sheds light on this history:

> Certain cheerful Christians in 19th-century America, however, *refused to believe* that they would be called upon to endure such afflictions [the final Tribulation] . . . Christians who are worthy of salvation, they *preferred to believe*, will be miraculously plucked up and elevated to heaven before the Tribulation begins in earnest. . . . Their *theological innovation* came to be called the Rapture.[12]

No one is better prepared to defend this modern teaching than Tim LaHaye, co-author of the best-selling Left Behind book series. This series

---

9. "Dispensationalism has evolved into the poster child for biblical literalism." Hanegraaff, *Apocalypse Code*, 45.
10. The eight ages include: innocence, conscience, civil government, promise, Mosaic law, the church/age of grace, tribulation, and the millennium.
11. Hanegraaff, *Apocalypse Code*, 42. C. Marvin Pate puts it more subtly: "It seems that the purpose of the Great Tribulation is to win the nation of Israel to its Messiah." Gentry et al, *Four Views*, 165.
12. *Mysteries of Faith*, US News & World Report, special issue (2006), 84, italics added.

is built squarely upon the rapture theory. He writes, "[John's] elevation to heaven is a picture of the Rapture of the Church just before the Tribulation begins."[13] And yet, in his commentary on Revelation, entitled *Revelation Unveiled*, which is self-described as the "Biblical Foundation" for the fictional series, LaHaye makes this astonishing admission:

> "*None of the above [cited] reasons is sufficient in itself* to insist that Revelation 4:1-2 refers to the Rapture of the Church. . . . Most prophecy scholars are reluctant to say that Revelation 4:1-2 are a direct teaching of the Rapture because *it does not specifically say so or give us any additional details* about that event."[14]

Though it's probably safe to say that many conservative evangelical pastors and the "masses"[15] in the pews now hold the dispensationalist view, LaHaye's teachings are not in line with most Bible scholars, as we'll come to see. Ladd writes: "The entire question of a so-called pre-tribulation rapture is an assumption which does not command the support of explicit exegesis [credible biblical scholarship] of the New Testament."[16] Osborne adds, "[Some] see a veiled reference to the rapture . . . But the text [4:1–2] indicates that John alone was commanded to be transported in the Spirit."[17] Tenney says, "There is no convincing reason why the seer's

---

13. LaHaye, *Unveiling Revelation*, 99.

14. LaHaye, *Unveiling Revelation*, 100–101, emphasis mine. "However, three major dispensational commentators (Walvoord, Johnson, Thomas) agree that there is little reason to posit this as the rapture of the church." Osborne, *Revelation* (BEC), 243. As Keener notes, "Most [Dispensational] interpreters who use 4:1 to portray the Rapture of the church before the Tribulation admit that the text does not actually *prove* their position." *Revelation*, 177; cf. John F. Walvoord, *The Revelation of Jesus Christ* (Chicago: Moody, 1966), 103.

15. Pate notes the differences in opinion between Bible scholars and those taking in the message from the pulpit and media: "The futurist reading is the preference of choice among the masses. . . . The preterist has dominated among scholars." Gentry et al., *Four Views*, 18.

16. Ladd, *Commentary on the Revelation*, 72.

17. Osborne, *Revelation* (LABC), 53; Gaebelein, ed., *Hebrews Through Revelation*, 461.

being 'in the Spirit' and being called into heaven typifies the rapture of the church."[18] And why should it? John has this same experience on three other occasions (1:10; 17:3; 21:10), and none of those occurrences are interpreted in this manner. Nor is 11:12 considered a rapture verse, where the same command—"Come up here"—is heard again. Knowing all of this, Hendriksen goes straight to the point: "The Bible knows *nothing* about an invisible or secret second coming. *Nowhere* is this taught."[19] In light of the scholars' statements, we can understand why the *NIV Study Bible* states that only "*some* interpreters find the rapture of the church in this verse [Rev. 4:1–2]."[20]

A favorite argument among dispensationalists (those who believe in a pre-Tribulation rapture of the church) is that "the Church cannot be found in Revelation 6 through 18."[21] According to them, only chapters 1–3 are concerned with believers. But clear evidence in support of this position seems to be lacking, considering that the word *rapture* is found nowhere in the book of Revelation. Just because the name *Jesus* is not mentioned in the messages to the seven churches, or in the seven seals or seven trumpets, doesn't mean that the first half of the book is not about Him. The absence of the word *church* is "no sure proof that the church is not to be identified with any of the groups [i.e., "saints," "brethren," "martyrs," "my people"] mentioned in the context."[22] "To be sure, the 'church' is not mentioned on earth by that name during Revelation's Tribulation, but neither is it mentioned by that name in heaven,"[23] or in the new earth (see chapters 21 and 22). On the other hand, the New Testament identifies the "saints"—who are mentioned throughout Revelation (e.g., 13:7; 14:12; 16:16; 19:8)—as Christ's church: "To the church of God . . . called to be saints" (1 Cor. 1:2, NKJV; Acts 26:10;

---

18. Tenney, *Interpreting Revelation*, 141.
19. Hendriksen, *More Than Conquerors*, 54, italics added.
20. Kenneth Barker, ed., *The NIV Study Bible* (Grand Rapids, MI: Zondervan, 1985), notes on Rev. 4:1–2, italics added.
21. Van Impe, *Revelation Revealed*, 50.
22. Tenney, *Interpreting Revelation*, 140.
23. Keener, *Revelation*, 178.

Rom. 1:7; Eph. 4:12; Col. 1:2).[24] Finally, we will note that John never uses the word *church* to speak of the church generally, even before 4:1, but only in relation to one of the seven local churches.[25]

We need to pause here and address the heart of that Christian who believes in the rapture. Such a believer lives with the imminent return of Jesus on his heart. Knowing that Christ may take him at any moment, he seeks to walk in God's will, moment by moment.[26] What we have been addressing about the rapture is a problem with a system of beliefs, not with the sincere relationship to God of true believers.

Why must we take the time to address the rapture theory? Because there are inherent theological dangers in it. First, if one accepts that the call in Revelation 4:1–2 for John to "come up" represents a secret, pre-Tribulation rapture of the church, then chapters 4–18 become somewhat irrelevant to the reader, not having a direct application to him or her, and this goes against the grain of both Jesus' counsel and His blessing in 1:3. Second, if one ignores the warnings about Satan's deceptions found in Revelation 4–18, one is ill-prepared to defend oneself against spiritual error, now or in the future. Third, a belief in the rapture theory doesn't necessarily promote spiritual readiness. According to this teaching, anyone who is not ready at Jesus' second coming will have a second chance, a position the Bible does not teach.

There's a great deal of comfort in the notion that a believer will be snatched from the earth before the final Tribulation. Even in the best of times it can be a challenge to live within God's will. But the only question worth asking is, "What does God's Word say?" According to the Bible, God's

---

24. Osborne, *Revelation* (BEC), 243: "The term *ekklysia* always refers to the seven churches of 2:1-3:22, and the believers are called 'saints.' "

25. Keener, *Revelation*, 178. Gaebelein says, "But the word 'church' or 'churches' always stands in Revelation for the historic seven churches in Asia and not just for the universal body of Christ." *Hebrews Through Revelation*, 461.

26. To be honest, we must point out that many professed Christians are waiting to see more spectacular signs of Jesus' return and have become spiritually lackadaisical or have succumbed to the world's temptations.

people endure tribulation and have done so from the beginning (Gen. 4:8; cf. Matt. 23:35; Heb. 11:4). Jesus, who is our example in all things, endured tribulation even to the Cross. Paul's ministry was filled with painful trials. Even John, the beloved disciple, suffered for his faith (Rev. 1:9). Likewise, the early Christians suffered, and millions of later believers were persecuted during the Dark Ages. In Matthew 10, Jesus explained that this is the anticipated lot for the believer.

If the revelator's experience is truly representative of the church, then believers should anticipate a life that is given to self-sacrifice and service. Regardless of what may come, God has promised that the Christian can have victory over every trial, even in martyrdom (Rom. 8:35–39; Heb. 11:32–38; Rev. 6:9–11; 12:11). As Harrington put it, "We must look for no miracle [e.g., a pre-Tribulation rapture], apart from the abiding miracle of our God's loving care."[27]

The throne room

As he peers into the command center of the universe, John sees a throne in heaven with Someone sitting on it. The throne is a symbol of sovereignty and judgment (cf. Dan. 7:26–27). Seeing that the throne was included in the promises to the victors, Hamilton notes, "This vision says that 3:21 is correct."[28] The throne is central to this vision—it is mentioned more than a dozen times in chapter 4, and forty-seven times in Revelation. Everything in the vision is related to it.[29] Like the themes of victory and repentance, the throne is threaded throughout Revelation's opening story (1:4; 3:21; 4:2–10; 5:1, 6, 13; 6:16; 7:9, 15, 17).

Taking in the splendor of the throne room, John is struck by the display of colors. A celestial rainbow, symbol of God's eternal covenant

---

27. Harrington, *Revelation*, 99.
28. Mark W. Hamilton, ed., *The Transforming Word: A One-Volume Commentary on the Bible* (Abilene, TX: Abilene Christian University Press, 2009), 1071.
29. " 'Throne' is the key word. . . . A series of prepositions signals the various actions . . . around . . . upon . . . out from." Paulien, *Gospel From Patmos*, 103.

faithfulness (Gen. 9:13–16),[30] resembling an emerald, encircles both the throne and the one who is sitting on the throne—God the Father.[31] The emerald happens to be the fourth stone in the high priest's twelve-stone breastplate,[32] representing the tribe of Judah, which is Jesus' lineage (Rev. 5:5). The Father's appearance is likened to carnelian (or ruby) and jasper, which are the first and last stones in the priest's breastplate (Ex. 28:17, 20).[33] It doesn't seem to be a coincidence that Christ first appeared to John as a high priest (Rev. 1:13) and that one of His titles is the "First and the Last" (2:8). Though Christ hasn't actually come onto the scene yet (see 5:5, 6), the Father is described here in language that is characteristic of the Son (cf. Col. 1:19, 20).[34] Thus, the vision highlights their oneness.[35] As Christ said, "Anyone who has seen me has seen the Father" (John 14:9).

The allusions to the Old Testament sanctuary and its services, which foreshadowed the Messiah's ministry, lead Ladd to write, "Heaven is both the *throne room* of God and his *temple*."[36] Hendriksen explains:

---

30. Hamilton, *Transforming Word*, 1071.

31. "In chapter 4 the sovereignty and majesty of God is central, and worship predominates. In chapter 5 the Lamb takes the spotlight and stands 'in the center of the throne' (5:6)." Osborne, *Revelation* (BEC), 220.

32. *Expository Dictionary of New Testament Words With Their Precise Meanings for English Readers* (Grand Rapids, MI: Zondervan, 1952), 2:24: "Occupying the first place in the second row."

33. *Expository Dictionary*, 2:273. "This specific combination [emerald, jasper, carnelian] is significant . . . since the chest-piece of the high priest of Israel contains the same three stones (Ex. 28:17-19). It is the only place that Scripture mentions the three gems together. The intention is again to evoke the temple." Doukhan, *Secrets of Revelation*, 52.

34. The ties between the Father and Son are so closely linked in Revelation 4 that Van Impe writes, "The Lord Jesus Christ [is sitting] upon His throne" (*Revelation Revealed*, 52), even though he realizes that it is Christ, the Lamb, who approaches the throne in chapter 5 (see 60, 61). So closely are they connected that Beasley-Murray simply refers to both the Father and Son as "God": "A single motif [the throne] binds together the double vision of chapters 4–5, namely, that the God of creation [Creator, ch. 4] is the God of redemption [Redeemer, ch. 5]." Beasley-Murray, *Revelation*, 108.

35. Because the Father and Son are one in purpose, could it be that chapter 4 presents them as one—"Lord God Almighty" (v. 8)—as a "prelude" to chapter 5, which differentiates the two, so that we might clearly recognize Christ's sacrifice, the basis of His right to open and administer the scroll?

36. Ladd, *Commentary on the Revelation*, 103, italics added.

[The throne] stands in the Holy of holies of the heavenly
temple just as the ark of the covenant stood in the Holy of
holies of the earthly Tabernacle or Temple (Ex. 25:22). In
this vision [Rev. 4] we very definitely have a tabernacle or
temple scene. . . . The representation that His throne is in
the temple is clearly based upon biblical symbolism (Is. 6:1;
Je. 3:17; 14:21; Ezek. 1:26; 8:4; 43:7).[37]

From the throne came flashes of lightning, rumblings, and peals of
thunder. Before the throne, seven lamps were blazing. These are the sev-
en spirits of God. Also before the throne was what looked like a sea of
glass, clear as crystal. On its own, a show of nature doesn't mean anything,
but in this context, the sound and light show "are reminiscent of the theophany at Sinai"[38] and the covenant that God made with His people (Ex.
19:16ff).[39] Even the command for John to "come up" recalls God's call to
Moses,[40] when he met with God on the mountain and received the Ten
Commandments.[41] Sweet believes that the scenes here "suggest God [is
law-giver and judge] enthroned on Sinai; the *sea* [of glass] is (among other
things) the heavenly counterpart of the Red Sea."[42] The totality of this
scene leads Caird to conclude: "These reminiscences of Sinai are intended
to impress on us that the throne [or ark] of God rests upon an immutable
and inexorable moral law"[43] (cf. Rev. 11:19; 12:17).

---

37. Hendriksen, *More Than Conquerors*, 84, 85.
38. Beasley-Murray, *Revelation*, 115.
39. Mounce, *Book of Revelation*, 136; Bauckham, *Theology of the Book*, 41; Wilcock, *Message of
Revelation*, 67.
40. Keener, *Revelation*, 179.
41. "But what is primarily in the mind of John is the description of Mount Sinai as the people
waited for the giving of the law." Barclay, *Revelation of John*, 1:169.
42. Sweet, *Revelation*, 116, 118.
43. Caird, *Revelation of Saint John*, 68; Keener, *Revelation*, 173. "The ark itself was designed as
a representation of God's heavenly throne." Caird, *Revelation of Saint John*, 64. "[The throne]
stands in the Holy of holies of the heavenly temple just as the ark of the covenant stood in
the Holy of holies of the earthly Tabernacle or Temple." Hendriksen, *More Than Conquerors*,
84. "John's vision is going to take him into the heavenly sanctuary. . . . The earthly sanctuary

Allusion to the Old Testament, seen already in the first vision, "continues and increases" here in chapter 4 through a flood of symbols.[44] "No passage in Revelation," Paulien points out, "contains a larger quantity or a wider variety of allusions to the sanctuary than this introductory sanctuary scene."[45] But mindful of the context, Keener states, "The scenes of heaven are intended as scenes of worship, for heaven's furniture is the furniture of the Old Testament temple."[46]

Twenty-four elders (4:4)

Surrounding the throne were twenty-four other thrones. Twenty-four elders sat on them, dressed in white and wearing crowns of gold. The identity of the elders has also been the subject of much debate.[47] Perhaps the strongest clues are found in the items that are associated with the elders: thrones (3:21); white robes (Rev. 3:5, 18; 7:9, 14); and crowns of victory (Greek, *stephanos*; see 2:10). They all have one thing in common—they are the rewards promised to the victors in the seven churches, suggesting that the elders ought be equated with the saints who have already been redeemed.

There is also a connection to the priesthood. The word *elder* is translated from the Greek word *presbuteros*, which carries the notion of priestly service. The number *twenty-four* reminds us of the twenty-four orders of priests who served in the Old Testament sanctuary (1 Chron. 24:4–19). Believers are said to serve God as "priests" (Rev. 1:6, RSV; 7:15; 1 Pet. 2:9).

[is] where the ark in the Holy of Holies represents the throne of God." Wilcock, *Message of Revelation*, 34.

44. Earl E. Palmer, *1, 2, 3 John, Revelation*, The Preacher's Commentary 35, ed. Lloyd Ogilvie (Nashville: Thomas Nelson, 2002), 152.

45. Jon Paulien, "The Seven Seals," in Frank B. Holbrook, ed., *Symposium on Revelation – Book 1* (Silver Spring, MD: Biblical Research Institute, 1992), 208.

46. Keener, *Revelation*, 91.

47. Ladd suggests that they are "angels." *Commentary on the Revelation*, 75. Similarly, Charles says, "The most reasonable interpretation is that which identifies them with the angelic representatives of the twenty-four priestly orders." *Critical and Exegetical Commentary*, 1:131. However, as Ranko Stefanovic points out, "Angels are never called elders in either the Bible or Jewish literature." *The Revelation of Jesus Christ* (Berrien Springs, MI: Andrews University Press, 2002), 185.

Like most numbers in Revelation, the number *twenty-four* is presumably symbolic. It is divisible by twelve, which is used to identify God's covenant people—twelve tribes of Israel and twelve apostles (Rev. 21:10–14). The number *twelve* (4 = earth; 3 = number of God) is also a building block for the number *144,000* (12 x 12 x 1,000) (cf. 7:4; 14:3). When viewed in this way, "there is a beautiful merger of old and new, the new Israel coming right out of the trunk of the ancient Israel."[48]

This leads us to believe that the elders are glorified saints. They have been redeemed from the earth, "*representing*, probably, the whole church of God,"[49] or the saved of all history.[50] These probably include Enoch, Moses, and Elijah, as well as those who were resurrected at Christ's crucifixion (Matt. 27:50–53; Eph. 4:8).[51] If this is the case, these individuals may be assisting Christ in His affairs with the saints who are still on earth.[52]

Four throne creatures (4:6)

At the center of the throne room, and standing around the throne, are four living creatures. The Greek word *zoon* literally means "a live thing" ("living creatures," NKJV). Unfortunately, the KJV translates this word as "beasts," leaving the reader with the impression that they are akin to the beastly creatures (*therion*) in Revelation 13:1–2, 11, 18; 17:3.

The four throne creatures have faces like a lion, an ox, a man, and an eagle. Each has six wings and is covered with eyes all around. Positioned

---

48. John Randall, *The Book of Revelation: What Does It Really Say?* (Locust Valley, NY: Living Flame Press, 1976), 53.
49. Henry, *Commentary on the Bible*, 3:460, italics added. Harrington, *Revelation*, 79. Keener says, "Most likely they represent all believers." *Revelation*, 171. Osborne: "Probably represent all the redeemed . . . Jews and Gentiles." *Revelation* (LABC), 15. Barclay: "We think that the most likely explanation is that the twenty-four elders are the symbolic representatives of the faithful people of God." *Revelation of John*, 1:168.
50. Paulien, *Gospel From Patmos*, 105.
51. Wilcock writes, "We can scarcely doubt . . . [that they represent the] whole church of God, both before and since the time of Christ." *Message of Revelation*, 61. Building on this vision, I believe that the righteous in the seven seals, including the 144,000 and the great multitude, also represent the whole church.
52. "They function as a jury." Phillips, *Exploring Revelation*, 83.

beside God's throne, these creatures are probably cherubim or archangels (Ezek. 1:5–10; 10:1–22). The four throne creatures may well be the most captivating figures in all of God's creation.

A number of suggestions have been posited as to what the four faces symbolize. One popular view is that they represent the domains of creation.[53] H. B. Swete writes, "The four forms suggest whatever is noblest, strongest, wisest, and swiftest in animate Nature."[54] Thus, the lion is seen as the king of the wild, the ox represents the domesticated world, the man has dominion over the earth, and the eagle is the king of the air. Since Revelation 4 and other sections (14:7; 16:1–9; 21:1) contain allusions to Creation, this view has merit.[55] The throne creatures have also been equated with the four gospels,[56] Matthew, Mark, Luke, and John. But scholars are divided over which creature goes with which gospel.[57]

There's another view that seems to fit better with the scriptural evidence. That is, the faces of the throne creatures are a reflection of Christ's person and ministry,[58] or the "highest expression of God's attributes."[59] The lion represents Christ's lineage, "the Lion of the tribe of Judah" (Rev. 5:5); the ox or calf, a sacrificial animal, foreshadowed Jesus' sacrifice; the "face like a man" reflects Jesus' humanity; and the eagle symbolizes, among other things, the Lord's protection (Rev. 12:14; Matt. 23:37).

---

53. Ladd, *Commentary on the Revelation*, 77. Beasley-Murray: ". . . the entire animate creation." *Revelation*, 117.

54. Swete, *Apocalypse of St. John*, 71.

55. In his book, Caird entitled Revelation 4, "THE CREATOR." Doukhan highlights the relationship between the number four and the created world: "In the Bible, as in the rest of the ancient Near East, the number 4 symbolizes the terrestrial dimension. We recall the four cardinal points and the four corners of the earth." *Secrets of Revelation*, 53.

56. Barclay: "The earliest and the fullest identification was made by the Bishop of Lyons, Irenaeus, in about AD 170. He held that the four living creatures represented four aspects of the work of Jesus Christ, which in turn are represented in the four gospels." *Revelation of John*, 1:175.

57. Mounce has concluded, "All attempts to equate the living creatures with the four gospels . . . are groundless." *Book of Revelation*, 138.

58. Phillips: ". . . reflects an aspect of the likeness of the Lord." *Exploring Revelation*, 86.

59. Osborne, *Revelation* (LABC), 57; also see Walvoord, *Revelation of Jesus Christ*, 944. "[It] suggest[s] qualities that belong to God." Gaebelein, ed., *Hebrews Through Revelation*, 463.

The last view became fortified in my mind while I was touring the countryside of England. Stopping in a small, quaint town, I entered a very old church with an equally old pulpit. The uppermost portion, where the pastor laid his Bible, was supported by four wooden carvings of the four living creatures. The four, together, supported the Word, which is Christ (John 1:1, 14).

The relationship between the four throne creatures and Jesus doesn't end there. After the deliverance from Egypt, God instructed Israel to build a tabernacle so He could dwell with them (Ex. 25:8). The twelve tribes of families were divided into four groups, and they erected tents to the north, south, east, and west on each side of the wilderness sanctuary. According to Numbers 2:2, four "standards" or flags, each bearing an emblem, flew at each side of the sanctuary.[60] The renowned Old Testament commentators Keil and Delitzsch explain: "According to rabbinical tradition, the standard of Judah bore the figure of a lion . . . [and] the *four living creatures* united in the cherubic forms described by Ezekiel were represented upon these four standards."[61] Just as the entire tabernacle and its services prefigured the Lord Jesus Christ,[62] so too did the four standards that were raised above the children of Israel. In light of the above, Seiss writes: "It was thus that Israel was marched through the wilderness, under the four banners. . . . These were their ensigns, their guards, their coverings, the symbols of powers by which they were protected and guided. They were parts of that divine and heavenly administration."[63] Possibly it was this background that influenced Solomon to place four—not just two—

---

60. Osborne, *Revelation* (BEC), 234.
61. Carl F. Keil and Franz Delitzsch, *Bible Commentary on the Old Testament*, Vol. 1: *The Pentateuch* (three vols. in one) (Grand Rapids, MI: Eerdmans, 1983), 3:17, italics added.
62. "Every detail of the tabernacle, therefore, points to some aspect of the person and work of our Saviour. . . . It is not only a picture of the Lord Jesus, and the believer, but it is a complete picture of the plan of salvation. . . . The tabernacle God commanded Moses to build in the wilderness . . . was a perfect type and a figure of the Lord Jesus Christ." DeHaan, *The Tabernacle*, 8, 9, 27.
63. Joseph A. Seiss, *The Apocalypse: Lectures on the Book of Revelation* (Grand Rapids, MI: Zondervan, 1957), 106.

covering cherubs above the ark in the Most Holy Place of the temple in Jerusalem (1 Kings 6:23–28).[64]

Roy C. Naden has summarized the four throne creatures in the best way:

> These are living creatures, the throne room's *living* royal coat of arms. Each creature has a characteristic that points us to an important aspect of our Lord's character, and grouped together reveal the salvation Jesus offers universally ([as demonstrated by the use of] 4) to all who live in the world.[65]

We'll gain a greater appreciation for the relationship between the four throne creatures and the Lord Jesus Christ when we come to Revelation 6, where they take a role in calling forth the four horsemen.

Worshipping the creator (4:9)

It may seem incomprehensible to human beings that the four throne creatures never stop praising God. We're told that they are continually crying out, "Holy, holy, holy is the Lord God Almighty! Who was, and is, and is to come!" What a scene of praise! Add to this the act of homage, as the twenty-four elders fall down and worship the Lord God and lay their crowns before God's throne. The NKJV uses the word *cast*, as if they throw down their crowns (the word *ballo* [Greek] carries intensity) like vassal kings showing homage to an emperor.[66] From the beginning to the end, worship dominates the vision.

We have noted a number of allusions to Creation in Revelation 4, and

---

64. "[Solomon] had some artists carve a pair of covering angels from olive wood. They towered over the ark 15-17 feet high. . . . This made a total of four cherubim or covering angels associated with the ark in the Most Holy Place. So the four living creatures probably allude to the four cherubim in Solomon's Temple [1 Kings 6:23-28]." Paulien, *Gospel From Patmos*, 106. "Two smaller angels on the ark and two larger ones spreading their wings over the ark . . . " Paulien, *Deep Things*, 128.
65. Naden, *Lamb Among the Beasts*, 98.
66. Harrington, *Revelation*, 80; Barclay, *Revelation of John*, 1:179.

there are more. For example, the seven-fold Spirit (4:5) was "the active agent of Creation."[67] In the Hebrew mind, the sea of glass is a "symbol of Creation."[68] The four throne creatures represent "the whole of creation."[69] In light of all that the Creator has made, the four throne creatures and the twenty-four elders praise God with a "song of creation"[70]:

> "You are worthy, our Lord and God,
>
> to receive glory and honor and power,
>
> for you created all things,
>
> and by your will they were created and have
>
> their being."[71]

The Lord God is worthy of worship and praise because He is the Creator.

The scroll of destiny (5:1)

"Then I saw in the right hand of him who sat on the throne a scroll with writing on both sides and sealed with seven seals." As we go into chapter 5, there's a shift in the midst of the vision. Our attention is now drawn to a scroll that is rolled up and secured with seven seals. The scroll is similar to a Roman document sealed by seven witnesses,[72] the customary way of sealing a Roman will.[73] The scroll of Revelation 5 is believed to be "the

---

67. Doukhan, *Secrets of Revelation*, 53. "Here, the Holy Spirit is mentioned probably . . . [for] his work in the creation and preservation of the natural world." Ladd, *Commentary on the Revelation*, 76.

68. Doukhan, *Secrets of Revelation*, 53. The sea may be an allusion to the laver (a basin of water) in the sanctuary or the "Sea of cast metal" (1 Kings 7:23) that stood before Solomon's temple. Ladd, *Commentary on the Revelation*, 76.

69. Doukhan, *Secrets of Revelation*, 53–54.

70. Hendriksen, *More Than Conquerors*, 88.

71. In some translations, the repeated word *create* is set on each side of God's "will," thereby emphasizing the existence of life: "Thou didst create all things, and because of thy will they were, and were created" (ASV). Osborne notes that there is a chiasm here, which serves as a mechanism to highlight the fact that we exist by and for God's "will." *Revelation* (BEC), 241.

72. Mounce, *Book of Revelation*, 142.

73. "A Roman prescription demanded that a will should be sealed with seven seals." Har-

testament assuring the inheritance reserved by God for the saints,"[74] fre-quently referred to as the "scroll of destiny"[75] and containing the "secret purposes of God."[76] "The easiest identification of John's scroll," according to Ladd, "is that it contains the prophecy of the end events, including both the salvation of God's people and the judgment of the wicked. It is God's redemptive plan."[77] Since it cannot be opened until the last seal is broken (8:1), Revelation 8 and following should be understood as the outworking of the gospel.

John hears a mighty angel cry, "Who is worthy to break the seals and open the scroll?" There is utter silence as all of heaven waits for the an-swer—but none comes. Reality begins to sink in. No one in heaven or on earth or under the earth could open the scroll. As John begins to compre-hend the magnitude of the situation and what this means for the faithful on earth, he begins to weep bitterly. But then, just when it seems as though all hope is gone—as on the day John saw Christ yield up His last breath—one of the elders points to the center of the heavenly courtroom and cries, "See, the Lion of the tribe of Judah, the Root of David, [He] has triumphed [*nike*].

---

rington, *Revelation*, 84. "Roman wills were sealed by six witnesses and the testator." Paulien, "The Seven Seals," in Holbrook, ed., *Symposium on Revelation – Book 1*, 218. "So the most simple member of the Asiatic churches knew that a *biblion* made fast with seven seals was a testament. When a testator died the testament was brought forward." Guthrie et al, *New Bible Commentary*, 1288. "The breaking of the seals was preliminary to the opening of the will and disclosing who would inherit and who would not." Kenneth A. Strand, *Interpreting the Book of Revelation* (Worthington, OH: Ann Arbor, 1976), 48. See Stefanovic, *Revelation of Jesus Christ*, 197–198. Ladd sees a "major difficulty" connecting the scroll with a will because "the seals [chapter 6] as well as the trumpets [chapters 8–9] do not have [anything] to do with the Christian's inheritance but with the plagues of judgment." *Commentary on the Revelation*, 80. We could argue that this "difficulty" is resolved, however, if we understand that the seals (6:1–8:1) are the preliminary steps for opening the scroll, and not the content of the scroll.

74. W. Robertson Nicoll, *The Expositor's Greek New Testament* (Grand Rapids, MI: Eerdmans, 1983), 383.

75. It contains "the destiny of the world." Mounce, *Book of Revelation*, 142. Speaking from the preterist view, which considers the Revelation to be fulfilled in the first century AD, Kenneth L. Gentry states, "The covenantal nature of the transaction suggests that the seven-sealed scroll is God's *divorce decree* against his Old Testament wife." Gentry et al, *Four Views*, 51, emphasis mine.

76. Henry, *Commentary on the Bible*, 3:461.

77. Ladd, *Commentary on the Revelation*, 81.

He is able to open the scroll and its seven seals."

Intimately familiar with the Old Testament Scriptures, John instantly recognizes the messianic descriptions (Gen. 49:9; Isa. 11:1) and begins to scan the throne room for a mighty one who is adorned in royal garb, "the Lion from Judah, the Davidic Warrior."[78] Instead, his eyes settle on something wholly different, wholly unexpected: "Then I saw a Lamb, looking as if it had been slain, standing in the center with the throne." Like the first vision (in which the voice like a trumpet was combined with the figure of a high priest; 1:10–13), the description of royal authority is blended with a lamb, one that was slain. In a book fraught with symbols this poses no problem, because in the revelator's eyes, the two are one and the same.

Though the passage takes only a moment to read, John is taking in a "breathtakingly exalted picture of Jesus."[79] Similar to Daniel 7, where the "son of man" approaches the heavenly throne to receive "everlasting dominion,"[80] the once slain but now resurrected Lamb is "the centerpiece"[81] of the vision. This is made further evident by the vision's chiastic structure (4:4–5:14).[82] Chapter 4 mentions the twenty-four elders, then the four throne creatures, and finally the two together (5:9–10), like steps ascending the side of a pyramid. Descending the other side, we find the opposite order: they are described together (v. 8), then the four throne creatures, and then the twenty-four elders (v. 14). The vision's literary structure places the Lamb at the center of the action (5:7).

A slain lamb reminds us of the first altar, set up outside of Eden (Gen. 3:21; 4:3–4), and of the Passover lamb, whose shed blood led to Israel's exodus from servitude in Egypt (Exod. 12:21–27). It is also a reminder of

---

78. Hans K. LaRondelle, *Chariots of Salvation: The Biblical Drama of Armageddon* (Hagerstown, MD: Review and Herald, 1987), 73.
79. Trafton, *Reading Revelation*, 68.
80. "Daniel 7, however, provides the most prominent *structural* parallel. . . . Revelation 5:9-14 seems to be structured on major movements in Daniel 7:13-27." Paulien, "The Seven Seals," in Holbrook, ed., *Symposium on Revelation – Book 1*, 209–210.
81. Ladd, *Commentary on the Revelation*, 88.
82. Trafton, *Reading Revelation*, 58.

the sanctuary with its services (Deut. 16:6). From Eden to Calvary, every offered sacrifice prefigured the one true Lamb, Jesus Christ. He is our Passover lamb and the central figure of the sanctuary (1 Cor. 5:7; John 1:29; 1 Pet. 1:19). This scene reveals the centrality of the Cross, and "[it] transforms the Hebrew terms and images into Christological categories."[83] Just as ancient Israel was liberated from bondage, the blood of Christ sets the believer free from the bondage of sin and the curse of eternal death (John 1:29; Rev. 1:5).

From here forward, the Lamb dominates the Revelation (mentioned almost thirty times). And it should! Christ overcame Satan while on earth, and He conquered death through His sacrifice. This is why John uses the word *nike* ("prevailed," KJV) to describe the Lamb (5:5). In so doing, he ties Jesus' appeal to "overcome" (3:21) directly to His enthronement in the heavenly throne room/sanctuary. In Revelation 3:21, the Christian is called to overcome (*nike*), but now we can see *how* to overcome—through self-sacrifice. Committed to His Father's will, Jesus emptied Himself daily, surrendering all to the Father's will (Matt. 26:42). As contrary as it may seem to us, self-sacrifice is the path to victory.

The Lamb is pictured as a conquering ram with seven horns. The horns symbolize Christ's strength, power, and authority (Deut. 33:17; Ps. 18:2; Dan. 7:7, 8, 24). The lamb represents both dominion and sacrifice. Christ's victory was made possible only because of His suffering and apparent defeat. The lamb's slain condition is highlighted in a small chiasm:[84] *lion— slain lamb—conquering ram.*[85]

This is wonderful news for the faithful who, down through the ages, have been looking for the Messiah. The images of the lion and the root "sum up the totality of the Old Testament messianic hope."[86] By His victo-

---

83. LaRondelle, *Chariots of Salvation*, 144.
84. Osborne, *Revelation* (BEC), 255.
85. Osborne, *Revelation* (BEC), 255.
86. Ladd, *Commentary on the Revelation*, 83.

ry, Christ "fulfills the hope of Judaism that a Warrior-Lamb should arise and redeem Israel from her enemies."[87]

The lamb has seven eyes, which are the seven spirits of God sent out into all the earth. The seven-fold nature reflects the fullness of the Spirit's being and ministry. The Spirit is Christ's eyes on the earth. Christ's coronation in heaven was confirmed on earth by the fullness of the Spirit's outpouring at Pentecost (Acts 1:4–5, 8; 2:1–4). As Peter explained to those then present: "Exalted to the right hand of God, [Christ] has received from the Father the promised Holy Spirit and has poured out what you now see and hear" (Acts 2:33; see also Acts 16–17, 24–25). With Christ's earthly ministry complete, the Holy Spirit would now empower the gospel by making the Lamb's "victory effective throughout the world."[88]

Worthy is the lamb (5:7)

John watched the Lamb take the scroll from the right hand of Him who sat on the throne. The action is similar to the coronation of a king in ancient Israel (Deut. 17:18–20). John is witnessing the inauguration of the heavenly sanctuary following Christ's ascension in AD 31.[89]

The Greek language (*epi tēn dexian*) has led scholars to believe that the scroll was probably lying on the throne at the Father's right side, rather than in His hand.[90] Ancient thrones were often designed like a small couch or

---

87. Guthrie et al, *New Bible Commentary*, 1288.
88. Bauckham, *Theology of the Book*, 112.
89. "This scene . . . follows the traditional ritual of enthronement found throughout ancient Near Eastern culture. . . . Likewise, in Israel, the newly crowned king inaugurated the enthronement ceremony by reading the 'book of the covenant'." Doukhan, *Secrets of Revelation*, 55. "The enthronement imagery . . . At the coronation of a new Israelite king, the scroll of the covenant (Deuteronomy) would be presented to him . . . demonstrated the right to rule and to deal." Paulien, "The Seven Seals," in Holbrook, ed., *Symposium on Revelation – Book 1*, 218. See Stefanovic, *Revelation of Jesus Christ*, 161–163; Hendriksen, *More Than Conquerors*, 90.
90. Ranko Stefanovic, "The Backgrounds and Meaning of the Sealed Book of Revelation 5" (doctoral dissertation, Andrews University, 1996). Stefanovic, *Revelation of Jesus Christ*, 96; compare Hendriksen: "On the right hand of the Father lies a scroll." *More Than Conquerors*, 89.

loveseat. By accepting the scroll, the "Root of David" is assuming His rightful messianic place upon the throne (Isa. 11:10), at the Father's right side,[91] the same seat that Christ has promised to share with all who overcome (Rev. 3:21). The acceptance of the covenant scroll represents transference of sovereign authority. The Father has elected to govern the universe through His Son: "Through the Lamb, God is at work in history."[92]

The will and rulership are combined here. Tenney explains:

> A will could be opened only by the heir and executor of the estate, . . . [so here it] would show that Christ was the heir of God, worthy to assume rulership over the universe by right of redemption and ready to exercise the authority necessary to reclaim for God the inheritance that had been usurped by Satan and his minions.[93]

The scroll is the "last will and testament containing the inheritance of the saints."[94] As a will, the seven seals cannot be broken or the scroll opened until *after* the Lamb has been slain.[95] In other words, "the [seven] seals are preparatory to the opening of the scroll."[96]

We saw that chapter 4 contained allusions to the Exodus, the sanctuary, the Lord's covenant with Israel, and the priesthood. Building on these, chapter 5 introduces the key image—the Lamb (John 1:29). "What was promised to the Israelites at Sinai," Mounce explains, ". . . is fulfilled in the establishment of the church through the death of Christ."[97] The choice of symbols is intentional: "That John has this Passover typology in mind follows from

---

91. "He will reign on David's throne." Isa. 6:7. "One like a son of man . . . was given authority, glory and sovereign power." Dan. 7:13–14; see Luke 1:32.
92. Gaebelein, ed., *Hebrews Through Revelation*, 468.
93. Tenney, *Interpreting Revelation*, 191.
94. Osborne, *Revelation* (BEC), 248.
95. Keener, *Revelation*, 188.
96. Gaebelein, ed., *Hebrews Through Revelation*, 466.
97. Mounce, *Book of Revelation*, 148.

the observation that he describes the lamb as 'slaughtered' [Gk, *sphazo*]."[98] Christ's victory on the cross is "the new organizing principle of history in Revelation"[99]—we find a new Passover and Exodus theme in Him.[100] And yet, what we see in this vision is only a foretaste of the final, antitypical Exodus (see Revelation 15). To summarize, "Revelation 5 takes up the language of Israel's commissioning as a nation."[101] Through Christ, Israel's experiences are a model for the Christian experience (cf. 1 Cor. 10:1–4).[102]

In response to the Lamb's presence and actions, the four throne creatures and the twenty-four elders fell down before the Lamb, the Co-ruler of heaven (Matt. 26:64; Heb. 8:1). Henceforth, the plan of salvation will be administrated through the Lamb, who has "all authority in heaven and on earth" (Matt. 28:18).

The twenty-four elders are now seen holding golden bowls full of incense, which, we're told, contain the prayers of the saints. Prayer is the link between weak, finite man and supernatural Divine power. Let's be clear: *prayer is the key to victory*. There is no secret to spiritual power; after all, our Lord modeled prayer for us (see Matt. 14:23; Mark 1:35; Luke 6:12; 11:2; 18:1; also Col. 1:9; 1 Thess. 5:17).

The elders appear to have a role of some type in human salvation. Their intercession, whatever that may be, reveals a close relationship between those who overcame and are in heaven (the Bible mentions some of these cases, like Elijah, Moses, and those raised at Christ's death) and those who are still gaining the victory on earth (cf. Rev. 6:9–11.) The elders in our churches would do well to meditate on the divine model demonstrated here in the fourth chapter of Revelation.

The Father received praise in the first half of the vision (4:11). But in

---

98. Jürgen Roloff, *Revelation: A Continental Commentary* (Minneapolis: Fortress Press, 1993), 79.
99. Jon Paulien, *Decoding Revelation's Trumpets: Literary Allusions and Interpretation of Revelation 8:7-12* (Berrien Springs, MI: Andrews University Press, 1988), 50.
100. Bauckham, *Theology of the Book*, 71; Keener, *Revelation*, 187.
101. Paulien, *Deep Things*, 164.
102. Paulien, *Gospel From Patmos*, 119.

the second half, we hear a new song, "new because it is a response to the new covenant, of which the Lamb has now become the mediator."[103] But this is no typical song. LaRondelle writes, "The new doxology is a cosmic victory shout"![104]

> "You are worthy to take the scroll
> and to open its seals,
> because you were slain,
> and with your blood you purchased men for God
> from every tribe and language and people and nation.
> You have made them to be a kingdom and priests to serve
> our God,
> and they will reign on the earth" (Revelation 5:9–10).

Because He is both God and man (Heb. 2:14), Christ alone is worthy to open the scroll. Being human was a prerequisite to opening the scroll; as a man, He redeemed humanity through His sacrifice. Humanity succumbed to temptation in Eden, altering allegiance to God and forfeiting the perfect nature. But Christ has freed the human race from the bondage of sin and restored the ability to choose.

"Worthy" is the Lamb (5:12). Notice how Christ is addressed with the same term as the Father (see 4:11; Gk, *axios*).[105] The stage was already set for this announcement: "Who is worthy . . . ? No one was found who was worthy" (5:2, 4). As Bauckham notes, "A close study of this pattern [that is, a comparison of verses that describe the Father and Son] can reveal the remarkable extent to which Revelation identifies Jesus Christ with God" (see 1:8 and 1:17; 21:6 and 22:13).[106]

---

103. Caird, *Revelation of Saint John*, 76.
104. LaRondelle, *Chariots of Salvation*, 73.
105. Sweet, *Revelation*, 130.
106. Bauckham, *Theology of the Book of Revelation*, 55.

Borrowing language from Israel's covenant (Ex. 19:6), the church is now called a "kingdom of priests" (Rev. 1:6). But things are quite different now. Because of what the Lamb has done, the saints have the privilege of being able to "approach the throne of grace with confidence" (Heb. 4:16). But this comes with great responsibility. "To be a Christian is to be both king and priest," notes Caird. "In and through his faithful followers he [Jesus] continues to exercise both his royal and his priestly functions."[107] The weight of such responsibility should be sobering for anyone who calls him- or herself a Christian.

How can it be said that believers "have [been] made" a kingdom, when they do not yet "reign on the earth"? It has been noted that Christians live with a tension described as the "already" and "not yet." Though Christ is "*already* king . . . the subjugation of all rebellion has *not yet* taken place, however, but belongs to the future judgment."[108] As Ladd explains, "The church is already a kingdom in the sense that believers have been raised up to be seated in the heavenly places with Christ (Eph. 2:6). . . . [However,] what [Christ] did on the cross remains forever unfinished until the ransomed enter into their kingly reign with Christ and until faith is changed to sight."[109] Thus, "The message of this book [Revelation] is that the victory over evil has already been achieved at the cross. The eschaton is simply the final manifestation of that victory."[110]

Progression through the scenes (5:11)

As the vision reaches its apex, the heavenly choir expands to include an innumerable number of angels, numbering thousands upon thousands, and ten thousand times ten thousand. The voices come together with a seven-fold hymn of praise for the Son of God: "Worthy is the Lamb, who

---

107. Caird, *Revelation of Saint John*, 77.
108. Stefanovic, *Revelation of Jesus Christ*, 164. He also speaks of the "inaugurated [launched] and consummated [accomplished] eschatology." Ibid.
109. Ladd, *Commentary on the Revelation*, 92–93.
110. Osborne, *Revelation* (BEC), 266.

was slain, to receive power and wealth and wisdom and strength and honor and glory and praise!" And, if that were not grand enough, all of creation joins in! Every creature in heaven and on earth and under the earth and on the sea, and all that is in them raises its voice, praising both the Father and the Son in a four-fold tribute: "To him who sits on the throne and to the Lamb be praise and honor and glory and power, for ever and ever!" Morris writes: "The Two are joined. . . . There cannot be the slightest doubt that the Lamb is to be reckoned with God and as God."[111] To punctuate the entire scene, the four throne creatures cry out with an affirming "Amen"!

Heaven's praises have not gone unnoticed on earth. We can hear the saints joining in the heavenly choir with glorious hymns:

> Holy, holy, holy! Angels adore Thee,
> Casting down their bright crowns around the glassy sea;
> Thousands and ten thousands worship low before Thee,
> Which wert, and art, and evermore shalt be.
>
> Holy, holy, holy! Lord God Almighty!
> All Thy works shall praise Thy name in earth and sky and sea;
> Holy, holy, holy! merciful and mighty!
> God in three persons, blessed Trinity!

Summary

We have seen how the first two visions (Revelation 1–3 and 4–5) in the opening story are linked by the theme of victory (*nike*). In the first vision, Christ has called every Christian to overcome (*nike*), just as He did (3:21). The second vision has shown us that Jesus prevailed (*nike*) (5:5, 6) through the daily surrender of the will to the Father and through

---

111. Morris, *Book of Revelation*, 102.

self-sacrifice, which led to the Cross. This is how Christ, our example, conquered (*nike*) temptation and the accuser.

The throne is another key motif, and it is tied to victory. After conquering death, Christ took His rightful place on the heavenly throne as co-Ruler with the Father. One day soon Jesus will return as "KING OF KINGS" (19:16) in all of His royal splendor.

The good news is that the throne-reward is God's promise to His people. Because of what the Lamb has done, we, too, can overcome (*nike*) through His power and have a share in His eternal reign. The next vision (Revelation 6) will show us how we can overcome.

Chapter 4

The Four Horsemen: Revelation 6

"I watched as the Lamb opened the first of the seven seals. . . .
The great day of their wrath has come, and who can stand?"

We have arrived at the heart of Revelation's "opening story"—the breaking of the seven seals and the introduction of the legendary four horsemen of the apocalypse. Let's begin by reviewing the highlights of the previous visions.

The story began in Revelation 1 with a vision of Jesus Christ. He was garbed as a high priest and walking among seven lamp stands, which represent the church. The story is solidly situated in the heavenly sanctuary. In Revelation 2 and 3, Jesus appealed to every member of His Church to overcome (*nike*) just as He has done (3:21). The emphasis throughout the seven messages was on victory and achieving the promised throne. In chapters 4 and 5, John was taken up in vision into the heavenly sanctuary/throne room. There we saw the Father surrounded in covenant imagery. Next, we saw the once slain but now victorious Lamb. Jesus' victory is founded on His sacrifice (5:5–6). Upon receiving the seven-sealed scroll from the Father, the Lamb assumed His rightful place on the heavenly throne.

As the story continues in Revelation 6, we see the Lamb breaking the seals in order to unroll the scroll and reveal its contents. As He does, four cosmic horsemen charge onto the scene on four colored steeds—white, red, black, and pale green. As we examine the symbolism, it's critically important that we not forget the backdrop and context of the seals—the sanctuary, sacrifice, victory, the throne-promise, and, above all, Jesus Christ.

It's important that we understand that the Lamb must break *all* seven seals in order to open the scroll and reveal the contents. Though some commentators use the word *open*, the seals are not opened as though they contained something. Thus, Revelation 6 is not the content of the scroll. In all likelihood, these seals are like those used in John's day—pressed wax that holds the scroll shut. The scroll cannot be opened until all seven seals are broken.

Many commentators refer to the seals (particularly the first four) as "plagues,"[1] and they believe that the "dreaded period of time known as the Tribulation begins" with the first seal.[2] But Beasley-Murray reminds us that the scenes associated with the breaking of the seals are but "the precursors of the salvation of the world."[3] Though there is warrant for using the word *plague* with the fourth seal (as we'll see later), the seal "judgments," as they are often referred to, are not the same as the seven trumpets (chapters 8 and 9) and seven bowl-plagues (chapter 16). Accordingly, John uses the word *plague* (Greek, *pleegai*) with the seven trumpets (9:20) and the seven bowl-plagues (15:1), but not with the seals. Even a cursory review of the trumpets and bowls will show that they, unlike the seals, are parallel in both pattern and content[4]—both are rooted in the plagues of Egypt and

---

1. "A series of plagues." Harrington, *Revelation*, 90. "The symbols [in the seals] that follow are negative." Keener, *Revelation*, 201.
2. LaHaye, *Revelation Unveiled*, 132.
3. Beasley-Murray, *Revelation*, 129. "The seven seals are preliminary judgments on the earth that prepare for the trumpets and bowls . . . The contents of the scroll are concerned with the trumpets, bowls, and ensuing events." Osborne, *Revelation* (BEC), 269. Fiorenza points out that the seals reflect "the events traditionally expected in the End-time" while the trumpets and bowls "picture God's day of wrath." "The Book of Revelation" in *Hebrews, James, 1 and 2 Peter, Jude, Revelation*, ed. Gerhard Krodel (Minneapolis: Fortress Press, 1977), 105.
4. The first trumpet/bowl is directed at the earth; the second, the bloody sea; the third, rivers and springs; the fourth, the sun; the fifth, darkness; the sixth, the Euphrates; and the seventh, divine wrath in the form of hail.

the days of creation. Holding the word *plagues* (or even *judgments*) like an umbrella over the seals creates a negative impression that goes further than was intended. The challenge for every student of Revelation is to suspend any judgment on the passage before examining the textual evidence.

The great debate

Bible scholars are divided over who or what the first horseman represents. Most now assume that he is evil, representing a future antichrist.[5] On the other hand, many scholars hold that the first seal represents something righteous, such as the gospel[6] or Jesus Christ.[7] Christ versus antichrist—could there be two views more diametrically opposed to each other in the entire universe? Acknowledging that only one of these teachings is true, and realizing that our interpretation of the first rider determines how we will interpret the three that follow, and the entire book, we will devote a great deal of attention to the evidence in and surrounding the first seal.

---

5. "Woe upon woe and disaster upon disaster, any picture of the victorious Christ is quite out of place in it." Barclay, *Revelation of John*, 2:4. "All four riders represent evil." Caird, *The Revelation of Saint John*, 81. "[He] can be identified with the man of sin of Second Thessalonians 2:3-4." W. A. Criswell, ed., *The Criswell Study Bible* (Nashville: Thomas Nelson, 1979), 1487. "Fierce images of terrifying judgment." Keener, *Revelation*, 199. "Four dreadful horses of tragedy." Palmer, *1, 2, 3 John, Revelation*, 176. "Unfolding series of disasters." Morris, *Book of Revelation*, 104. "[The] dread horsemen . . . [have a] career of destruction." Wilcock, *Message of Revelation*, 79. "The servant of tyranny . . . There is probably no picture of terror as frightening as these four horses of the Apocalypse and their riders." Palmer, *1, 2, 3 John, Revelation*, 170. It's interesting that similar language may be found among those who believe that the first seal represents either the gospel or Jesus Christ (generally, historicists): "Ravages of the horsemen." Strand, " 'Victorious-Introduction' Scenes," in Holbrook, ed., *Symposium on Revelation – Book 1*, 63. "In Revelation 6 all of humanity is subject to the plagues unleashed by the horsemen." Jon Paulien, *Armageddon at the Door: An Insider's Guide to the Book of Revelation* (Hagerstown, MD: Review and Herald, 2008), 86. "The four horsemen symbolize the judgments of God on those who claimed to be God's people." Stefanovic, *Revelation of Jesus Christ*, 248. "The ravages of the three evil horsemen." C. Mervyn Maxwell, *God Cares* (Nampa, ID: Pacific Press, 1985), 2:180.
6. Ladd, *Commentary on the Revelation*, 99.
7. Hendriksen, *More Than Conquerors*, 93. "This rider on the white horse, then, is more likely the influence Jesus wields on this earth, the power of his Word." Wayne D. Mueller, *Revelation*, People's Bible Commentary (Saint Louis, MO: Concordia, 1997), 76.

A WHITE HORSE

I watched as the Lamb opened the first of the seven seals. Then I heard one of the four living creatures say in a voice like thunder, "Come!" I looked, and there before me was a white horse! Its rider held a bow, and he was given a crown, and he rode out as a conqueror [nike] bent on conquest [nike] (Rev. 6:1–2).

Of the four, the first rider, on the white horse, has been the primary subject of most debates. This is because His activity—whether righteous or wicked—appears to have a direct impact on the next three riders, the seals as a whole, and the rest of book. As we have already discussed, the rapture teaching (see Rev. 4:1–2) is built on the assumption that the first horseman is the antichrist and that the four horsemen are a collective portrayal of demonic devastation during the final tribulation. If, on the other hand, the first horseman represents Jesus Christ, the four horsemen may be bearing life-saving messages for the church.

In short, the first seal is the crucial fork in the road.

The Antichrist?

Let's first examine the "antichrist" view of the horsemen. Similar to the way they see the rapture itself, the adherents of this view believe that the antichrist is due to arrive on the world scene at any moment. They interpret the first rider's actions—"bent on conquest" (6:2)—as "hell bent," overcoming through deception and force, which are Satan's primary methods (Rev. 13:11–17). But no matter how popular this view may be, a student of Scripture must ask, "Is this what the author intended for us to believe?"

Some have labeled the rider in the first seal a "counterfeit,"[8] "imposter,"[9]

8. Van Impe, *Revelation Revealed*, 67.
9. Edward Hindson, *The Book of Revelation: Unlocking the Future* (Chattanooga, TN: AMG,

or "deceiver,"[10] because, as they contend, he resembles the rider on the white horse in Revelation 19:11, whom all agree is Jesus Christ. True, the first horseman is wearing a victor's crown and not a royal *diadema* (19:12). But does this prove that the rider is an imposter? Let's take a look at the reasons given for the antichrist position.

Wholly different missions. First, just as their crowns are different (victor's wreath vs. royal *diadema*), as are the instruments in their hands (bow vs. sword), the riders are on two different missions (compare 19:15). The headwear and weapons correspond with the type of mission. While the former is a victor, conquering some kind of territory, the latter is the "KING OF KINGS," coming to execute judgment.

Three horsemen follow. Some conclude that the first horseman is the antichrist because the three that follow are associated with murder, famine, and plague (6:3–8).[11] The assumption is based on the notion that if the last three riders are evil, then the first rider must be evil also. But the Bible contains numerous examples of divine judgments being carried out by heavenly beings (e.g., the angelic messengers in Sodom and Gomorrah; the angel of execution in Ezekiel; and the angels who pour out the seven last plagues in Revelation). But what's more of a concern is that arguing backwards can overshadow the facts! Phillips gives us an example of this: "The context provides the clue [to the first horseman's identity] . . . For the Holy Spirit Himself interprets the

---

2002), 81.

10. Graham, *Approaching Hoofbeats*, 78. Graham adopts the antichrist position but admits at the start, "I am an evangelist, not a scholar." "My major emphasis," Graham clarifies, "was not necessarily to interpret these passages as much as to make them relevant." Ibid., 19, 10. To this end, his work has proven a blessing.

11. "[There being] three other horsemen who wreak havoc . . . suggests . . . [the first rider has a] lust for conquest." Osborne, *Revelation* (LABC), 71. "This [Christ] view, however, founders on the strict parallelism of this first rider with the three that follow: like them, he must also represent a plague." Roloff, *Revelation*, 86. "[The] gospel [in the first seal seems] . . . more plausible, but in view of the similarity of the four riders it seems more natural to interpret all as portraying the last judgments." Guthrie et al, *New Bible Commentary*, 1289. "[The four] . . . must surely be taken together, and they all indicate destruction, horror, terror." Morris, *Book of Revelation*, 102. "Since the other three are evil powers . . . the victorious coming of Christ is out of place in this context." Ladd, *Commentary on the Revelation*, 97.

symbolism of the fourth horseman: he is Death, and Hades follows . . . The [first, second, and third] horsemen, therefore, are . . . things most unpleasant indeed."[12] Of course, we need to consider the activity of all four horsemen as a whole. But an interpretation of the first seal should stand on its own if the evidence can support it.

Revelation 4:1–2. If one approaches the seals with the assumption that the church has already been raptured at this point (a theory we have already shown to be incorrect), one is almost forced to believe that the first rider is the antichrist, despite any textual evidence to the contrary. But the entire argument has no foundation, because the rapture theory [4:1–2] is based on the assumption that the first rider is the antichrist! This is a circular argument.

Lamb and horseman. Some have argued that Christ, the Lamb, cannot be opening the first seal and also riding upon the horse of that seal. Nicoll writes:

> [The first horseman is] by no means to be identified with that of the Christian messiah or of the gospel. It would be extremely harsh and confusing to represent the messiah as at once the Lamb opening the seal and a figure [the horseman] independently at work.[13]

At first glance, his point seems logical. But Beasley-Murray reminds us that we are dealing with an apocalyptic book: "Such questions should not be asked . . . [The author] should not be expected to preserve an undeviating consistency in his pictures."[14] Apocalyptic thought and language

---

12. Phillips, *Exploring Revelation*, 96.
13. Nicoll, *Expositor's Greek New Testament*, 389. "It would be pretty difficult for the Lord Jesus, who is the one opening the seal, now to make a quick change, mount a horse, and come riding forth." J. Vernon McGee, *Revelation Chapters 6–13*, Thru the Bible Commentary Series (Nashville: Thomas Nelson, 1975), 39. "As for the Lamb, he opens the seals and would not be one of the riders." Gaebelein, ed., *Hebrews Through Revelation*, 473.
14. Beasley-Murray, *Revelation*, 11. The author is actually speaking to 4:1–2, where, in a visionary state, John is viewing the heavenly throne room while still on earth.

are "fluid," allowing for the most "unimaginable spiritual realities."[15] For example, in the Revelation, Christ is both priest and sacrificial lamb (1:12, 13; 5:6). Thus, it really is not difficult to imagine that Christ is revealing the outworking of His ministry through the horseman's activities. Wilcock concurs: "Neither is it a serious objection to say that if Christ is the Lamb opening the seals, he cannot be one of the riders as well."[16]

Unloaded bow. Another argument is the one suggesting that the rider must be a politician[17] because the verse mentions a bow but no arrows. Assuming there must be a deeper meaning behind the absence of the word *arrow*, some have conjectured that the rider must be a political figure, probably of European descent, who will establish a deceptive agreement with the nation of Israel, after the church has been raptured.

But think about the reasoning here. If John had described the rider as a gunman, would we assume that the gun had no bullets simply because the author didn't mention them? No. Nor would we assume that David had no arrows because he wrote, "I will not trust in my bow" (Ps. 44:6). This argument attempts to prove a negative from silence. As students of God's Word, we must be careful to avoid making the author say more than he intended.

The rider is not identified. It's true that the first rider is not specifically identified, as is the rider in Revelation 19. But the same argument could be made for other key passages in which Christ is believed to be the subject. For example, the reader assumes that the Lamb in 5:6 is Christ. Likewise, the man-child in chapter 12 is believed to represent Jesus.

As we can see, strong evidence is lacking for the antichrist position. Now we'll turn our attention to the case for Jesus Christ as the rider of the

---

15. Ladd, *Commentary on the Revelation*, 102.

16. Wilcock, *Message of Revelation*, 170.

17. "He will conquer by diplomacy." LaHaye, *Revelation Unveiled*, 142. "Future world leader." Walvoord and Zuck, *Bible Knowledge Commentary*, 947. "The Antichrist comes to power through an international peace pact. . . . [He] conquers through diplomacy as a king, hence the crown." Van Impe, *Revelation Revealed*, 71. Note that the first rider is not adorned as a king—he's wearing a victor's *stephanos* wreath, which should not be confused with a king's *diadema* (cf. 19:12).

first horse, the white horse under the first seal (6:1-2).

Jesus Christ

The opening words of Revelation are clear. First and foremost, this book is the "revelation of *Jesus Christ*" (1:1). Jesus is the central subject of the book. Revelation is about Him and not about the antichrist. It reveals aspects of Christ that are not found elsewhere in Scripture. Thus it's not surprising that "the oldest opinion was that the first horse represented the cause of Christ. This was taught by Victorinus, and right on down through the centuries until comparatively recent years."[18] This was also the position of the Protestant forefathers, who, as devout students of Scripture, guided the faithful remnant in the church out of theological darkness during the Middle Ages. In his *Commentary on the Bible* (1792), Matthew Henry tells us that "*most* [religious teachers of his day] believe [the first horseman] is Jesus Christ."[19] Later, Hendriksen (1940) would write that it shouldn't come as a surprise that "many eminent interpreters"[20] believe the conqueror on the first horse is a symbol for Jesus Christ. And despite the overwhelming voices being raised in the Christian church today for the antichrist view (and a pre-Tribulation rapture), this message is still being heralded by many, and by historicists in particular.[21]

---

18. Desmond Ford, *Crisis* (Newcastle, CA: Desmond Ford Publications, 1982), 2:353.

19. Henry, *Commentary on the Bible*, 3:464. Emphasis mine. "Supposed to represent Jesus Christ." Adam Clarke, *Commentary on the Bible* (1831), http://www.sacred-texts.com/bib/cmt/clarke/rev006.htm. "Expressive of Christ's regal power and authority, of his honour and dignity, and of his victories and conquests." John Gill, *Exposition of the Old and New Testament* (1746–1763), http://www.sacred-texts.com/bib/cmt/gill/rev006.htm. "Evidently Christ, whether in person, or by His angel." Robert Jamieson, A. R. Fausset, and David Brown, *A Commentary, Critical, Practical, and Explanatory on the Old and New Testaments* (1882).

20. Hendriksen, *More Than Conquerors*, 93. These include Irenaeus (*Adversus Haereses* 4.21.3), Victorinus of Pettau, Grotius, Henry, Alford, Bachmann, Bede, Ladd, Hodges, Allo, Giet, Wordsworth, J. P. Lange, R. C. H. Lenski, W. Milligan, A. Plummer, Ramsey, Hoeksema, Sweet, Williams, and more. Though McGee acknowledges that "the preponderate [prevailing] interpretation among commentators is that he represents Christ [though "most of the contemporary Bible scholars" say he's antichrist]," he contends that "this is an *imitation* of Christ, this is one who *pretends* to be Christ." *Revelation Chapters 6–13*, 39, 40.

21. "Christ wears the diadem in 19:12 because His conquering activity is complete. He

Now we'll examine the evidence for this position.

White

The first piece of evidence is the color white, the color of the first rider's horse. White is consistently used in Revelation to represent what is godly and pure, and there are no exceptions. As George E. Ladd notes, "[White is] always a symbol of Christ . . . or of spiritual victory."[22]

Four horses

While we're on the subject, the inclusion of four horses here is significant for many reasons. First, the number four is often used in Bible prophecy to suggest universality, or the totality of something (cf. Rev. 7:1; 20:8). In Daniel 4 and 7, four kingdoms represent the world. In the next chapter, we read about the "four corners of the earth" (Rev. 8:1). Based on Zechariah 1 and 6, some Bible scholars believe that there is a link between the four horses in Revelation 6 and the "four winds of the earth" in Revelation 8.[23]

Second, when we speak of four horses, particularly in the context of the first century, we think of a quadriga, "a chariot drawn by four horses harnessed abreast."[24] Found on ancient coins and reliefs (like the one found in the palace of Sargon II in Khorsabad, Assyria), the quadriga also adorns world-famous sites like the Brandenburg Gate in Berlin, St. Mark's Basilica in Venice, the Arc de Triomphe du Carrousel in Paris, and other places. In Roman times, the chariots of triumphant Roman generals were pulled by

---

wears the victory crown (stephanos) in 6:2." Paulien, "The Seven Seals," in Holbrook, ed., *Symposium on Revelation – Book 1*, 229. "And the one riding that horse, wearing a crown is Jesus. He goes out 'conquering and to conquer.'" Mark Finley, *Revelation's Predictions for a New Millenium* (Fallbrook, CA: Hart Books, 2000), 325. "The symbolism is clear; the rider of this white horse can be none other than Jesus Himself." Loren M. K. Nelson, *Understanding the Mysteries of Daniel and Revelation* [self-published manuscript, 2010], 199.
22. Ladd, *Commentary on the Revelation*, 98.
23. Osborne, *Revelation* (BEC), 305; Paulien, "The Seven Seals," in Holbrook, ed., *Symposium on Revelation – Book 1*, 224.
24. *Oxford Universal Dictionary*, s.v. "quadriga."

four horses.[25] In Zechariah 6:1–8, a background source for the seals, God sends out four chariots (called "spirits" [or "wind," Hebrew *ruwach*]), drawn by horses of four different colors, to patrol "all the earth." A similar scene is found in Habakkuk 3:8, where Yahweh's horses are referred to as his "chariots of salvation" (see Psalm 104:3).

Third, like the victor's wreath,[26] the horse is a military symbol. J. Massyngberde Ford points out that "in the OT the horse is primarily a war animal."[27] For example, in Psalm 45:4 we find a prophecy about the Messiah riding forth victoriously.

With this in mind, we might ask, "Is it possible that these four colored horses are all under the direct control of Jesus Christ?"

The bow

Some commentators assume that the bow, an instrument of battle, must be "connected with the enemy of God's people, . . . forces opposed to Christians."[28] But a Bible concordance demonstrates otherwise. In the Old Testament the bow is not only indicative of military power[29] but also a common symbol for divine judgment (see Ps. 7:11–13).[30] It's interesting to note that in Psalm 45:5—a "royal wedding psalm"—the king, mounted on his horse, carries a bow. The Ryrie Study Bible[31] notes the following about the bow-warrior: "The king is addressed to God . . . but ultimately refers to Jesus

---

25. "The general in a Triumph . . . was borne like the god in a four-horse car." Ramsay, *Letters*, 58.
26. "The image is that of triumphant warfare." Harrington, *Revelation*, 89.
27. Massyngberde Ford, *Revelation*, 97.
28. Gaebelein, ed., *Hebrews Through Revelation*, 473.
29. Barclay, *Daily Study Bible*, 2:4; Morris believes that "John's mind is on more than the Parthian king or the Roman emperor. . . . [Rather] any nation that embarks on a career of conquest[,] . . . especially in the last days." *The Book of Revelation*, 105.
30. "God using his bow in his role as judge is a common Old Testament symbol." Trafton, *Reading Revelation*, 73. "In an even greater number of cases, bows and arrows represent Yahweh's weapons." Paulien, "The Seven Seals," in Holbrook, ed., *Symposium on Revelation – Book 1*, 228.
31. The prophecy notes are of the dispensationalist persuasion.

Christ."[32] We naturally think of Christ's royal wedding in Revelation 19, when He rides forth on a white horse for His bride (19:7, 11).

Conquer *(nike)*

Like the white horse and the bow, the word *conquer* (Greek, *nike*) also implies warfare: "That the image of conquering is a militaristic one should be unmistakable."[33] Some Bible commentators argue that there is "*no point of similarity* between Christ [in 19:11] and this [first] rider other than the color of the horse."[34] But is this really the case? John has already used the word *nike* twice with Christ [3:21; 5:5], and now he uses it again with emphasis, repeating it—"conquering and to conquer." Because most Bible translations use two or three different English words to translate *nike*, many Bible students (ministers included) are unaware that the author has used the word *nike* to link the opening visions together. For example, the King James Version translates *nike* as "overcome," "prevailed," and "conquered" in the three opening visions (3:21; 5:5; 6:2).[35] Unless the Bible student is using a Bible concordance that shows the Greek words that lie behind the translation, he or she will probably be unaware of the fact that John has used the word *nike* in all of the opening scenes.

Even more troubling for the student is how a translator's choice of words can influence theology. For example, the Darby and NASB versions use the

---

32. Charles C. Ryrie, *The Ryrie Study Bible* (Chicago: Moody Press, 1976), note on Psalm 45. Looking narrowly at the New Testament only, Sutton misses this important Old Testament passage, stating: "The Scriptures always describe Jesus as using the two-edged Sword (the Word of God), *never a bow* and arrow." Hilton Sutton, *The Book of Revelation Revealed: An In-Depth Study on the Book of Revelation* (Tulsa, OK: Harrison House, 2001), 91, italics added.
33. Bauckham, *Theology of the Book*, 69.
34. Edward Hindson, *The Book of Revelation: Unlocking the Future*, Twenty-first Century Bible Commentary Series (Chattanooga, TN: AMG, 2002), 81, italics added. As Paulien has correctly observed, "The imagery in both cases has to do with conquest." "The Seven Seals," in Holbrook, ed., *Symposium on Revelation – Book 1*, 205.
35. Because the KJV is a product of the early Protestant era, when most Christians believed the first horseman was Jesus Christ, I contend that the translators used a plurality of words—overcame, prevailed, conquered—to simply illustrate the breadth of Christ's victorious attributes.

word *overcome* with Christ (3:21; 5:5) but change the word to "conquer" for the rider in the first seal (6:2). This creates an artificial separation between Christ's activity in the first two visions and what many assume is the work of the antichrist in the first seal.[36] Fortunately, a few translations translate the word *nike* consistently. The Revised Standard Version uses the word *conquer* throughout, while the Contemporary English Version, New Living Translation, and the Holman Christian Standard Bible use the words *victory* or *victorious* consistently.

Victory (*nike*) is the golden thread that connects all the visions in the opening story: the seven churches (ch. 1–3), the heavenly throne room (ch. 4–5), and the breaking of the scroll's seals (ch. 6). But the theme of victory doesn't stop there. As the opening story comes to a close, the redeemed are found before the throne in heaven "clothed with white robes" and waving "palm branches" (Rev. 7:9), which are emblematic of victory.[37] In Revelation, the reward for victory is God's throne.

Up to this point, John's Greek-speaking audience has come to associate the word *nike* with Christ alone. Certainly they would see the *nike* activity of the first horseman as something positive. This is the most natural way to interpret the first seal. Sweet rightly argues, "The 'Satanic parody' [Rev. 12–13] has not yet been set up. The imagery [in the first seal], if interpreted by what has gone before rather than by what is yet to come, points unequivocally to something heavenly. This rider's function is simply *conquering*, which must be interpreted by the Lamb's [*nike*] conquest (5:5)."[38] Paulien concurs, noting that "the more immediate context of 6:2 is the 'conquering' [*nike*] of Christ on the cross (5:5, 6, 9; cf. 3:21)." And Trafton comes right to the point: "The obvious answer is that the rider is Jesus. After all,

---

36. We should note that the doctrine of the secret rapture was first conceived by John Nelson Darby of the Plymouth Brethren in 1827. He is known as the father of dispensationalism, allegedly inventing it.

37. Keener, *Revelation*, 243–244; Osborne, *Revelation* (BEC), 319, 320.

38. Sweet, *Revelation*, 138; Paulien, "The Seven Seals," in Holbrook, ed., *Symposium on Revelation – Book 1*, 228; Trafton, *Reading Revelation*, 73.

Jesus has already been identified in terms of his having 'conquered' (5:5)."

In light of what we have discovered, we can summarize Revelation's opening scenes as follows: because of Christ' *victory* on Calvary (5:5), every believer may have the *victory* over Satan (12:11) and participate in the victory of the gospel (Matt. 24:14).

A crown-wreath

Although the crown is generally used as the single most important piece of evidence for labeling the first horseman as an evil "deceiver,"[39] it actually serves as the "crowning" touch in the case *for* Jesus Christ. As we know, the overcomers in the churches and the twenty-four elders all wear a wreath (*stephanos*), the emblem of victory (2:10; 3:11; 4:4; cf. 12:1). But does Christ wear a *stephanos*?

In his commentary, *Revelation Unveiled*, Tim LaHaye makes clear that "it is important that we identify this first rider, as a key to understanding the three that follow him."[40] But in the very next sentence he concludes: "The Antichrist and his kingdom are obviously what is symbolized." LaHaye is correct, however, when he agrees with other scholars that the "One sitting on the white cloud [Rev. 14:14] with a crown of gold on his head . . . [is] none other than the Lord Jesus Christ appearing in judgment."[41] But LaHaye does not mention the fact that Jesus is wearing a victor's wreath (*stephanos*), a fact that scholars have long been aware of.[42] It's the very same wreath that "He shares with His fellow victors, the saints (see 4:4)."[43] Consequently, he seems to have concluded that since Jesus wears the crown

39. Relying on the scholarship of others, Billy Graham writes, "You will note that [the first horseman] is wearing a crown of victory. . . . The crowns Christ wears in Revelation 19, on the other hand, are diadema, or the crowns of royalty." *Approaching Hoofbeats*, 78.
40. Ibid., 142. "Chapter 6 is one of the most important and pivotal chapters of the entire book." Walvoord and Zuck, *Bible Knowledge Commentary*, 949.
41. LaHaye, *Revelation Unveiled*, 242.
42. Hendriksen, a renowned scholar, notes that the Son of Man wears a "wreath of victory, the golden stephanos." *More Than Conquerors*, 155.
43. Mueller, *Revelation*, 148.

(*diadema*) in 19:12, the first rider, wearing the *stephanos*, must be the anti-christ: "That he [the first seal rider] will be ultimately victorious is seen by the fact that he has a crown on his head."[44]

However, did John really intend for his readers to see the first rider as a counterfeit of Christ? Let's consider the textual implications. In order to deceive, one must create an imitation of the original.[45] This means that the first horseman should appear to be like Christ the king (Rev. 19). But some scholars contend that there is "no point of similarity apart from the colour of the horse."[46] The first rider is wearing a *stephanos* wreath, not a royal *diadema* crown (19:12). In addition, the first rider is carrying a bow, not a sword (19:15). Make careful note: a victor is not necessarily a king. The first horseman isn't trying to deceive anyone.

John seems to have taken steps to ensure that his audience would not become confused over the crowns. For example, the dragon in Revelation 12:3 (which is a parody of the Father[47]) is wearing many royal crowns (*diadema*) like Christ (19:12). But John goes on to explain that this demonic king is none other than "that serpent of old, called the Devil and Satan, who deceives" (12:9). A better example is seen in Revelation 9: "A star [that's] fallen from heaven" releases a mass of bizarre locusts that are wearing victor's wreaths (*stephanos*) of gold (9:1–7). Because the "star" comes down from heaven and the gold crowns are similar to those worn by the twenty-four elders, John intentionally adds the Greek word *hos*, meaning "something like." In other words, the locusts only appear to be victors, but are not; they're evil pawns. So, like the saints (2:10; 3:11), the twenty-four elders (4:4), the woman who represents God's people (12:1), and the Son of Man on the clouds (14:14), the first horseman is a *true* victor in the eyes of John's original audience. Remember, Revelation was read aloud in church. The members were listening to a story, not poring over the

---

44. LaHaye, *Revelation Unveiled*, 142.
45. "I personally take the viewpoint that this is Antichrist, this is an imitation of Christ, this is one who pretends to be Christ." McGee, *Revelation Chapters 6–13*, 40.
46. Morris, *Book of Revelation*, 104.
47. The second or sea beast is a parody of Christ, and the land beast, a parody of the Spirit.

details as you and I do. If the author intended to switch gears and suddenly introduce an evil character, it's safe to assume that he would have made such an abrupt transition in the story quite clear.

The truth is that the differences in the crowns (6:2; 19:12) reveal the progression in Christ's ministry. At the onset, He's wearing a *stephanos* wreath emblematic of His early victories (5:5; 6:2).[48] He overcame Satan and death and continues to conquer through His people—the church. To this day, the gospel of Jesus Christ continues to conquer the hearts of men and women around the earth. But at the end, when He returns as "KING of kings," Christ will be wearing many *diadema* crowns.

Divine attributes

Even the finer details of the first seal point to Christ as the rider. For example, we're told that the crown "was given" (*edothe*) to the rider. Scholars point out that this word is "a divine passive pointing to God's control of the process"[49] and is "frequently used euphemistically when God is the agent."[50] Just as the Lamb was worthy to receive the scroll from God the Father (5:2, 7), so the first horseman is granted permission and authority to go forth "conquering and to conquer" (see John 5:27).

Grant Osborne notes that "the one who sat" on the white horse "is described with the unusual expression" *ho kathemenos*, which is "a direct parallel to the description of God 'sitting on' the throne in 4:2, 3, 9, 10."[51]

---

48. Confusing the difference in the crowns in Revelation, J. Van Impe writes: "The Antichrist conquers through diplomacy as a king, hence, the crown." *Revelation Revealed*, 71. Similarly, the *Clear Word* Bible paraphrase states incorrectly, "crown of a king" (Hagerstown, MD: Jack J. Blanco, 1994). The 2003 edition removed the "crown" altogether! Unfortunately, mistranslations like these fuel the misconception that the first horseman is a counterfeit of Jesus Christ, who is the "KING of kings" and wears a royal *diadema* in Revelation 19:16 (cf., Glen Walker, *Prophecy Made Easy: Experience the Future Now!* [Fort Wayne, IN: Prophecy Press, 2001], 231.

49. Osborne, *Revelation* (BEC), 277.

50. J. Massyngberde Ford, *Revelation*, 101.

51. Osborne, *Revelation* (BEC), 277. Since Osborne believes that the riders relate to "human lust for war," he holds that the first "rider then represents humankind setting themselves up in the place of God." Ibid.

J. Massyngberde Ford goes further, explaining that John could have used "the usual Greek word for cavalier or rider, *hippeus*," but did not. She reasons, "This may have been done deliberately to associate the riders on the horses with 'he who sat upon' the throne."[52] But that's not all. In addition to the linguistic link between the first horseman and the former throne-room scene, Trafton points out that the description for the first horseman is identical to the "nine Greek words: *kai idou hippos leukos kai ho kathemenos ep' auton* (lit., 'and behold a white horse and one sitting upon it')" in Revelation 19:11.[53] "Such extensive verbal agreement between the two passages can hardly be accidental; surely John intends at 19:11 for the reader to remember 6:2."[54] In light of all the evidence we have uncovered, it seems that John's "unusual expression" is definitely intended to highlight Christ's ministry, given that He is the central figure of Revelation.

Finally, John uses the word *erchou*, the throne-creature's command for the horses to "come" forth (NIV).[55] As Ford notes, "In Revelation it [*erchou*] refers to the coming of God or the Christ."[56]

It's no wonder Trafton concludes that if one does not get caught up in "circular reasoning"—that is, reading *back* into the first seal the negative connotations that many so quickly attribute to seals two, three, and four—"the first seal is not necessarily 'bad' at all. What should strike any sensitive reader of the book are the positive traits [e.g., white, victor's crown, conquering] associated with this [first horseman]."[57]

The living creatures

The evidence for the Christ-centered view extends beyond the confines

---

52. Massyngberde Ford, *Revelation*, 101. Keener suggests that the four riders may in fact be "angels of judgment." *Revelation*, 200.
53. Trafton, *Reading Revelation*, 73.
54. Ibid.
55. The KJV adds "and see," leading the reader to assume that it is John who is being told to "come and see."
56. Massyngberde Ford, *Revelation*, 97.
57. Trafton, *Reading Revelation*, 72.

of the text as well. The first horseman, we're told, is called out by one of the throne-creatures, which has "a voice like thunder." Earlier, John listed the four creatures in the following order: a lion, calf, man, and eagle (4:7). It so happens that the lion, the first of the four, is the only creature that has a thunderous voice. Even more significant is the fact that the throne-creatures are *always* associated with God (4:6, 8–9; 5:6, 8; 7:11; 14:3; 15:7; 19:4), never with evil. The close relationship between the four horsemen and the four throne-creatures suggests that these horsemen are godly characters, and not demonic ones.

The x factor

In recent decades, scholars have come to realize that the book of Revelation, like many Old Testament writings, is written in a poetic Hebrew form called a chiasmus or chiasm.[58] This isn't surprising, since John was a devout Jew and the book of Revelation is heavily imbued with Old Testament words, symbols, people, ideas, and themes. The chiasm's name is derived from a likeness to the Greek letter *chi* (X), and is seen in the document's structure.

    Prologue (1:1–8)
        Seven Churches (1:9–3:22)
            Seven Seals (4:1–8:1)
                Seven Trumpets (8:2–11:18)
                    The Great Controversy (11:19–15:4)
                The Wrath of God (15:5–18:24)
            The Judgment (19:1–20:15)
        The Reward (21:1–22:5)
    Epilogue (22:6-21)

This literary device serves two primary purposes: first, it allows the author to split his story-work into two halves, so the second mirrors the first. With this,

---

58. Strand, *Interpreting the Book of Revelation*, 43–52.

the author can build on key elements of the first half. Second, having mirrored halves creates a center point in the book, where the true heart of the story can be found (see the illustration below, where D is the center point):[59]

A B C D C' B' A'

Revelation's chiastic structure is important here because a rider on a white horse appears in both halves of the book (6:2; 19:11), strategically located in the opposing sections.[60]

Notice the striking similarities between the two sections that contain the white horses, as outlined by Mervyn Maxwell:

- o Heaven opened (4:1; 19:11)
- o Rider on a white horse, riders following (6:2–8; 19:11–16)
- o Souls of martyrs (6:9, 10; 20:4–6)
- o White robes (6:11; 7:9–14; 19:14)
- o Kings and other leaders killed (6:15, 16; 19:17–21)[61]

Though some contend that the two horsemen on the white horses represent two different persons—the antichrist and Jesus Christ—Revelation's very structure leads us to believe that the two horsemen are the same person, Jesus Christ, Conqueror and King. He is worthy to be called King because of His sacrificial victory (5:1–9).

---

59. Chiasms can also be very small. The *Harper Collins Study Bible* illustrates how the author of Genesis used a chiasm to develop the story of the fall of humanity in the Garden of Eden (Gen. 2:4–4:1). Notice how the two flanks (ABC/A'B'C') parallel each other:
(A) humanity is given *life*
   (B) the couple experiences *companionship*
      (C) the *serpent promises* a better life
      (C') their eyes are opened to the *serpent's deception*
   (B') the couple experiences *shame*
(A') humanity is separated from the *Tree of Life*
Sin is found at the center of the chiasm above (3:6), which explains why the second half of the story is altogether different from the first, though written in parallels.
60. God is working for man's salvation in the first half (Rev. 4:1–8:1) and completing His work for man's salvation in the second half (Rev. 19:11–21:8).
61. Adapted from Maxwell, *God Cares*, 2:54–62.

Conquering and to conquer

As we have seen, the evidence lends itself to seeing Jesus Christ as the conqueror on the white horse. Massyngberde Ford opened our eyes to this possibility: "In the light of this passage, and the acknowledged OT influence on Revelation, might not the first rider be the angel of the Lord?" Hendrickson quotes S. L. Morris as saying that "the church . . . in all the ages has been practically unanimous in interpreting it [the first seal] as the conquering Christ entering upon His militant world career."[62] With Christ as the central figure in each chapter leading up to Revelation 6, and in chapter 7 as well, we shouldn't be surprised to learn that He is also the conquering figure of chapter 6. But bear in mind that the first seal only reveals the initial stage in Christ's ministry: "Yeshua is merely victorious, not yet king. He has won a battle [Calvary], but the war is not over."[63]

Thus, the antichrist theory is either a case of mistaken identity or a desperate attempt to make the first rider fit a particular teaching (e.g., a pre-Tribulation rapture). Revelation's opening visions are focused exclusively on Christ's victory and His church. To interject the antichrist here in the opening story is scripturally and contextually unjustified. Just as two negatives, when added together, do not create a positive outcome, two erroneous teachings—the secret rapture (4:1–2) and the antichrist (6:1–2)—result in a total misunderstanding of the Revelation.

There's a looming question that should concern all Bible students: How did the church come to abandon, or reject, the Christ-centered view? One would think that volumes would be written on such a monumental change in church teachings—the antichrist replacing the Lord Jesus Christ in this chapter. And yet, not one book has been written to explain this change. This may be the devil's best deception yet.

---

62. Hendriksen, *More Than Conquerors*, 26.
63. Doukhan, *Secrets of Revelation*, 59. "In Rev 6 the victory is predicted, in ch. 19 it is realized." Massyngberde Ford, *Revelation*, 105.

A historical application

"In general, the seals, trumpets, and bowls . . . [are all seen to be] climaxing in the second coming of Christ."[64] Similar to the seven churches, the seals span "the entire [Christian] dispensation,"[65] beginning with the commencement of the gospel and closing with the great Day of the Lord (6:12–17). As such, the seals "express the *historical principles or trends* that bring judgment upon the world."[66] This view coincides with Christ's general outline of church history, as recorded in Matthew 24 (cf. Mark 13; Luke 21). As Wilcock observes, "In fact we do not have to strain the text in any way to postulate that Christ is not only expounding the same subject, but expounding it in the same order, in both places [Matthew 24 and Revelation 6]. The two chapters engage at point after point like two sides of a zip[per]."[67]

And so, just as Matthew 24 and its parallels speak of the gospel's advances,[68] Christ the victorious Warrior of the first seal now leads His church "conquering and to conquer" (6:2, KJV); to "conquer in many battles" (TLB). Sweet writes: "The first unsealing, on its own, suggests the triumphant progress of God's cause in the gospel. . . . [We're] shown Christ's victory taking effect in the world in ch. 6," which is accomplished through the church's witnessing.[69] Paulien writes: "[Christ] wears the victory crown

---

64. Walvoord and Zuck, *Bible Knowledge Commentary*, 947. "As in the rest of Scripture, the imminent return of Jesus and the final judgment is a recurring theme in Revelation." Mueller, *Revelation*, 23.

65. Hendriksen, *More Than Conquerors*, 17. "The vision of the seven seals runs parallel to that of the seven letters. They recount the same story but with a different emphasis." Doukhan, *Secrets of Revelation*, 59.

66. Tenney, *Interpreting Revelation*, 81, emphasis added.

67. Wilcock, *Message of Revelation*, 74. Osborne is less convinced: "The thematic parallels are striking . . . I am not as certain as they are, however, that John here shows direct literary dependence on the Olivet discourse. The language of Rev. 6 does not show sufficient similarities to Mark 13 and its parallels to have a direct literary connection." *Revelation* (BEC), 270.

68. "If we then ask what Christ is doing here [in the first seal] . . . we are referred back to Mark 13:10 and its parallels, which tell us to expect in the course of this age not only the spread of evil [verse 6; Matt. 24:5] but also the spread of the conquering gospel [verse 10; Matt. 24:14]." Wilcock, *Message of Revelation*, 70.

69. Sweet, *Revelation*, 135.

(stephanos) in 6:2. . . . It seems best, therefore, to understand the white horse to symbolize Christ's kingdom and its gradual conquest of the world through the preaching of the gospel by His church."[70] Maxwell writes: "The rider on the white horse is still riding! In fact, he is today conquering more hearts in more places around the world than ever before, in fulfillment of Matthew 24:14 ['And this gospel of the kingdom will be preached in all the world']."[71]

Like the first church (2:1–7), then, the first seal aptly represents the onset of the gospel during the Apostolic Age.[72] Following Jesus' ascension, the Holy Spirit was poured out in special measure upon the infant church (Acts 2:1–4; 2:33), empowering it to fulfill Christ's great commission (Matt. 28:19–20; Acts 1:8). On the first seal, Matthew Henry notes:

> [Christ] enters upon the great work of opening [the seals] and accomplishing the purposes of God towards the church and the world. . . . [These are the] *beneficent victories of Christ* by his word and Holy Spirit, in the conversion of sinners to the obedience of faith. . . . The convictions impressed by the word of God are sharp arrows. . . . As long as the *church continues militant,* men go on opposing, and *Christ goes on conquering; he conquers his enemies in his people.* . . . The [C] hristian religion, preached in purity by its apostles, overcame

---

70. Paulien, "The Seven Seals," in Holbrook, ed., *Symposium on Revelation – Book 1,* 229. Paulien also notes the problems that can arise from a strictly historical approach: "It is possible, however, to pay so much attention to history that we miss the literary dynamics of the biblical text on which the historical applications must be based." Jon Paulien, *What the Bible Says About the End-Time* (Hagerstown, MD: Review and Herald, 1998), 111. "It is not a bad thing to try to understand the implications of Revelation for Christian history. But what often happens is that we get so absorbed in history that we fail to follow the *story* of Revelation itself." Paulien, *Armageddon at the Door,* 63–64.
71. Maxwell, *God Cares,* 2:185. "[In Revelation 6] Christ has begun the expansion of his kingdom by conquering and winning human hearts." Stefanovic, *Revelation of Jesus Christ,* 228.
72. Preterists hold that the first rider symbolizes the Parthian army that came from the east of Rome. See Harrington, *Revelation,* 91; Randall, *Book of Revelation,* 61.

the powers of darkness and all human opposition.[73]

And as we will soon see, the Christ-centered view is perfectly in keeping with the view held by most scholars that the 144,000 represents Christ's church.

Personal victory

Revelation's opening story is about Christ and His victories. Jesus overcame Satan through His sacrifice on the cross, prevailed over death through His resurrection, and His gospel is continuing to gain victories throughout the earth (Rev. 1:18; 5:5; 6:2). Wilcock notes the tie between the previous visions and what comes to view in chapter 6:

> Many commentators note that it is his redeeming death which qualifies Christ to break the Seals . . . and infer, thinking of the cross primarily as a great achievement, that the events to be described in chapter 6 are also in some sense 'achieved' by Christ, and not merely revealed by him.[74]

The good news is that Christ's victory is ours! The apostle Paul wrote, "Thanks be to God, who gives us the victory [nike] through our Lord Jesus Christ" (1 Cor. 15:57). Paulien writes: "What is exciting about this is that the value that He has by right [having become human, died and paid the price of sin, and offered up a perfect and worthy sacrifice] can also become ours by redemption."[75] Barclay describes Christ's victory for us this way: "He gave us *triumph*. . . . In Christ, there is victory over self, victory over

---

73. Henry, *Commentary on the Holy Bible*, 464, emphasis added. "Through the Holy Spirit and through the preaching of the gospel by His faithful people, Christ has begun the expansion of His kingdom by conquering and winning human hearts for Himself and bringing the gospel into their lives." Stefanovic, *Revelation of Jesus Christ*, 228.
74. Wilcock, *Message of Revelation*, 69.
75. Paulien, *Gospel From Patmos*, 124. "The conquest of Christ is his power to win men and women to the love of God," Barclay, *Revelation of John*, 1:104.

circumstances and victory over sin."[76] Christ overcame through His blood, and we can overcome through the same blood (Rev. 12:11). And since Jesus has already gained the victory for us, His command to "overcome" is actually a promise (Rev. 3:21). "The decisive victory of Christ on the cross becomes the basis for the victory that human beings win over Satan throughout history."[77] Keeping the words "conquering and to conquer" in mind, Hewitt explains, "In the confessions and moral actions of the faithful, the Lamb again and again conquers."[78] Paul ratchets up this point when he writes, "In all these things we *overwhelmingly conquer* [*huper nike*] through Him who loved us" (Rom. 8:37, NASB; cf. 2 Cor. 2:14).

There's a condition for receiving Christ's victory as our own: "For everyone [who is] born of God overcomes [*nike*] the world. This is the victory [*nike*] that has overcome [*nike*] the world, even our faith" (1 John 5:4). But for some, this raises the question, how can I be born again? To be "born of the Spirit" from above (John 3:8), the self-centered nature, or "old man," as Paul calls it (Rom. 6:6), that rules our heart must be surrendered at the Cross, "crucified" and buried. Jesus told His disciples, " 'If anyone desires to come after Me, let him deny himself, and take up his cross daily, and [then] follow Me' " (Luke 9:23–24). Before Jesus can be the Lord of my life, I must first be willing to surrender my heart to His complete rule. In Romans 6, Paul describes this surrender process, this renouncement of self, as a literal crucifixion of the "old man":

> Don't you know that all of us who were baptized [immersed] into Christ Jesus were [spiritually] baptized into his death? We were therefore buried with him through baptism into death in order that, just as Christ was raised from the dead

---

76. Barclay, *Revelation of John*, 1:196.

77. Lichtenwalter, *Revelation's Great Love Story*, 106.

78. C. M. Kempton Hewitt, *Revelation*, Genesis to Revelation Series (Nashville: Graded Press, 1987), 17.

through the glory of the Father, we too may live [even now] a new life.

If we have been united with him like this in his death, we will certainly also be united with him in his resurrection. For we know that our old self was crucified with him so that the body of sin [our sinful nature] might be done away with, that we should no longer be slaves to sin—because anyone who has died [to self] has been freed from [the power of] sin. . . .

In the same way [trusting in God's power], count yourselves dead to sin but alive to God in Christ Jesus (Rom. 6:3–7, 11).

In order for us to overcome, then, Christ's Spirit must dwell *in* us (1 John 3:9; 4:4; Rom. 8:10). Likewise, our life—our overcoming—is *in* Him (1 John 3:6), through prayer and feeding on His Word. When we are born again, with Christ's Spirit dwelling in us, "there is no need and no excuse to fail in obtaining God's objective in us."[79]

Living in a sinful world, the Christian is being continually attacked by temptation; he is ever at battle with Satan and self. "Do not be overcome [*nike*] by evil, but overcome [*nike*] evil with good" (Rom. 12:21). This is not a battle that we can ignore: *what we do not overcome will overcome us!* But Henry explains the good news in this way: "Their sins are their enemies, and [Christ's] enemies. When Christ comes with power into their soul, [H]*e begins to conquer these enemies.*"[80] A true believer, then, is not powerless. Rather, he or she has been equipped with "the whole armor of God" (Eph. 6:11, 12), which includes the "shield of faith" and the "sword of the Spirit," God's Word (6:16, 17). With Christ as Commander, the believer has been empowered to "fight the good fight of faith" and gain

79. Epp, *Practical Studies*, 202.
80. Henry, *Commentary on the Holy Bible*, 1:464, italics added.

the victory (1 Tim. 6:12). As Warren W. Wiersbe states, "It is possible to be victorious over the 'the beast' and be an overcomer!"[81] But as true champions—for that is what *nike* implies—we must talk, live, and act out our faith, for faith is the key to the victorious life (Rom. 14:23).

How exactly does one overcome? In a chapter entitled "He Helps Me Win," which is built on Revelation 3:21 and the word *nike*, Larry Lichtenwalter shares four specific steps for overcoming "existentially"— in our daily experience.[82] First, you must claim Jesus' substitutionary atonement as your own. The key to victory is found in death—His death. Second, you must participate in His cross by bearing public witness to it. Your testimony of faith should reveal what Christ's victory means to you and how it has changed your life. Third, a true victor will cling to the foot of the cross, depending wholly on His will, no matter what comes. Finally, we must be "continually dipping our robes in the white-bleaching blood of the Lamb." These practical steps show us "*how* we receive both forgiveness and moral power to be different from the world."[83]

Reminding us of our present salvation in Jesus, W. W. Prescott draws the following inspiration from Revelation's promises: "His righteousness is mine. His victory is mine. His throne is mine. He is mine, and I am His."[84] Or as evangelist Joe Crews writes, there is a "sweet, triumphant infilling of a new spiritual power."[85] This power, which enables us to go from victory to victory, is available to the true believer. As Peter so wonderfully put it, "You are now a 'partaker of the divine nature' " (2 Pet. 1:4).

THE RED HORSE

When the Lamb opened the second seal, I heard the second living

---

81. Wiersbe, *Be Victorious*, 119.

82. Lichtenwalter, *Revelation's Great Love Story*, 109.

83. Ibid.

84. W. W. Prescott, *Victory in Christ* (Hagerstown, MD: Review and Herald, 1987), 27–28.

85. Joe Crews, *The Surrender of Self* (Roseville, CA: Amazing Facts, 2006), 25.

creature say, "Come!" Then another horse came out, a fiery red
one. Its rider was given power to take peace from the earth and
to make men slay each other. To him was given a large sword
(Rev. 6:3–4).

It's not hard to see why most Bible students assume that the second horseman is "evil."[86] After all, this blood-red scene depicts a sword-wielding rider and masses of people dying. But as we just discovered in the first seal, it's easy to jump to the wrong conclusions—especially if we ignore the author's original language, which most Bible students do here. Samuel Johnson wrote, "Language is the dress of thought." Nowhere is this perhaps more true than in the second seal. So, once again, we'll begin by examining what the Revelator actually wrote.

A great knife

Most Bible students are surprised to discover that the horseman's "large sword" (*megas machaira*) is more akin to a knife.[87] This instrument is shorter than the longer *rhomphia*-sword,[88] which is used by the fourth horseman (6:8). It's noteworthy that John usually uses the word *megas*, translated as "large" or "great," to denote emphasis rather than size.[89] Similarly, Paul was not referring to size when he wrote, "Great [*megas*] is the mystery of godliness" (1 Tim. 3:16, NASB). In short, the word *large* can be misleading, and in this case the word *great* should be preferred.

What makes this particular knife great? According to the *Theological*

---

86. "The other three are evil powers of destruction and death." Ladd, *Commentary on the Revelation*, 97. "All four riders represent evils." Caird, *Revelation of Saint John*, 81. "The ravages of the three evil horsemen." Maxwell, *God Cares*, 2:180.

87. James Strong, *The Exhaustive Concordance of the Bible* (1890). *Greek Dictionary of the New Testament*, 46. "A relatively short sword or other sharp instrument . . . *dagger*." Walter Bauer, Frederick W. Danker, William Arndt, *A Greek-English Lexicon of the New Testament and Other Early Christian Literature* (Chicago: University of Chicago Press, 2000), 622.

88. "Short sword." Mounce, *Book of Revelation*, 156.

89. Cf. 1:10; 2:22; 6:17; 11:8; 12:1; 17:5.

Dictionary of the New Testament, the *machaira*-knife was used by the priests to slay animals for sacrifice.[90] Hendriksen elaborates on this fact: "Yet [the *machaira*] signifies strictly the sacrificial knife, the natural instrument of the slaughter mentioned. It is the word used in the LXX [Septuagint, the Greek translation of the Old Testament] of Genesis 22:6, 10, in the story of Isaac's sacrifice."[91]

We'll come back to the *machaira* shortly.

Sacrifice

Machaira isn't the only sacrificial term in the second seal. Instead of using the word *apoketeino* ("kill"), which is "the normal word for death,"[92] John uses the word *sphazo*.[93] According to the *Expository Dictionary of New Testament Words* this word means "to slay, to slaughter, *especially victims for sacrifice*."[94] In other words, it is known to be a "ritual term."[95] But was the author of Revelation familiar with the "normal" word *apoketeino*? He most certainly was. As with the long *rhomphia*-sword, John reserves *apoketeino* ("kill") for the fourth seal. As you may have surmised by now, the fourth seal possesses its own unique message about death.

Because John chose the words *machaira* and *sphazo*, his first-century, Greek-speaking audience caught the underlying topic of *sacrifice*. Unfortunately, many English translations of the Bible use the word *kill* indis-

---

90. *Theological Dictionary of the New Testament*, s.v. *"machaira."*
91. Hendriksen, *More Than Conquerors*, 100.
92. Mounce, *Book of Revelation*, 155.
93. "This is not the ordinary term which John uses to indicate the act of killing or warfare. Everywhere else in the writings of the apostle John, with only one exception (Rev. 13:3), this term refers to the death of Christ or the execution of believers." Hendriksen, *More Than Conquerors*, 99. "It is not the normal word for death in battle." Mounce, *Book of Revelation*, 155.
94. *Expository Dictionary of New Testament Words*, s.v. *"sphazo,"* italics added. See also, *Theological Dictionary of the New Testament*, s.v. *"sphazo."* Morris notes that the word *kill* is "not the usual one, and has a meaning like 'slaughter' (NEB) or 'butcher' (Berkely)." *Book of Revelation*, 105. "*Slain is esphagmenon*, a word used for the slaughter of a sacrificial victim." Sweet, *Revelation*, 124.
95. Keener, *Revelation*, 203. "The sacrificial sense was prominent in secular Greek and predominant in LXX." Sweet, *Revelation*, 128.

criminately in the wording of the second and fourth seals, destroying the distinction that John created (see KJV, NKJV, TLB). Some translations are more accurate and consistent, using the word *slay* in the second seal (NIV, RSV; "slaughtered" in AMP) and *kill* in the fourth.

What about the second throne-creature that introduces the second horseman? Does its ox-face (4:7) fit the context of the second seal, just as the lion did with the first? Yes, it does! Of all the creatures surrounding God's throne, the ox, "the most expensive victim", is the only one that was offered in the Old Testament sacrificial services.[96]

As you can see, the entire blood-red seal is drenched in *sacrifice*—a theme that flows throughout Revelation (cf. 5:6; 13:8; 18:24).

Christ our high priest

Like the first, the second horseman has many features that suggest a commonality with Jesus Christ.[97] John used the word *sphazo* repeatedly in the previous scene to describe Christ's substitutionary death (5:6, 9, 12). Its use here in the second seal is no coincidence. In fact, John uses it again in the fifth seal, where the faithful martyrs are likened to the sacrificial blood that was poured out at the base of the altar by the priest (6:9).[98] Christ has already revealed Himself to John as the heavenly High Priest of the new cov-

---

96. Roy Gane, *The NIV Application Commentary: Leviticus, Numbers* (Grand Rapids, MI: Zondervan, 2004), 102.

97. "On the basis of the Old Testament passages it would not surprise us if here, too, the second, third and fourth riders are subservient to the first; Christ's instruments for the refining and strengthening of His people." Hendriksen, *More Than Conquerors*, 98. Wilcock points out that "the repeated 'given' of 6:1-8 indicates that the first rider's authority is of the same sort as that of the other three." *Message of Revelation*, 74. "If the first horseman is Christ and the conquering gospel, does the second stand for . . . divisions between men that are caused when the gospel is accepted by some and rejected by others (Mt. 10:34-36); or for persecution of the church by the world?" Ibid., 70. Massyngberde Ford in *Revelation* concludes that the second horseman is a divine messenger: "The four horsemen in Rev 6 are therefore angels" (104); "Might not the first rider be the angel of the Lord and the other riders lesser angels who affect the earth?" (106); "The second rider, therefore, must be an angel of Yahweh" (107).

98. "The word 'slain' (verse 9) means 'put to death like a sacrificial animal.'" Mueller, *Revelation*, 80.

enant (cf. Rev. 1:12, 13; Heb. 8:1–2). Accordingly, in the New Testament, believers offer up their lives as "living sacrifices" to Jesus daily (Rom. 12:1; Luke 9:23). By reserving the word *apoketeino* (kill) for the fourth horseman (who is on a mission of execution), John has created a link between Christ's sacrifice in chapter 5 and the second rider's ministry in the second seal. But we should have seen this all along.

Because of the similarities between features of the second horseman and Christ's ministry, many Bibles include Matthew 10:34 in the margin beside the second seal ("I did not come to bring peace, but a sword").[99] After speaking about the proclamation of the gospel (which is the message of the first seal), and subsequent persecution, Jesus said: "I did not come to bring peace, but a [*machaira*] sword" (verse 34). When they assume that the church is raptured in 4:1–2 and that the first horseman is the antichrist, many Bible students fail to note the specific words John chooses or the linguistic connections between Christ's sacrifice and the second horseman's activity. As a result, they seek after things like "Red Russia" as the fulfillment of the second seal.[100]

Tying the messages together

Under the first seal, Christ rode forth as a mighty Victor on a white horse. By His Spirit He is conquering hearts for God through the power of the gospel. The true overcomers in the church are His medium to accomplish the great worldwide mission (Matt. 28:18–20). The first seal also represents the onset of the Christian age, when the gospel initially spread across the then known world. No less powerful now, the gospel continues to reach the most remote regions of the earth.

---

99. Cf. *The Ryrie Study Bible* (Chicago: Moody Press, 1976), a dispensational study tool.
100. "One of the nations that marches during this period of time is Red Russia." Sutton, *Book of Revelation Revealed*, 72. "The [horseman's] first action is . . . sending Russia from the north." Van Impe, *Revelation Revealed*, 93. LaHaye is less dogmatic here: "One of the mysteries of prophecy is whether Russia is destroyed before the Rapture or after it occurs." *Revelation Unveiled*, 143.

The backbone of the second seal is the sacrificial life and death of Christ. Jesus demonstrated by His death that "true victory comes in sacrifice and weakness. . . . [This is] the Lamb's path to victory."[101] Many readers err in assuming that the second rider is evil and is killing masses of people.[102] As the text specifically states, it is the "*men* [who will] slay each other" (NIV) in the name of religion. The "sacrificial" slayings come as the direct result of accepting the gospel and daily submitting one's life to the Lord.

Jesus warned His disciples that strife and persecution would follow in the wake of the gospel. While such trials may come to the individual anytime, they were borne out especially in the lives of church members in the second and third centuries (see notes on Smyrna).[103] But persecution did not deter the early Christians from their Lord's great commission. Accepting that this life is temporal, their eternal hope was in Christ. Trusting their lives to Jesus ("Do not be afraid of those who kill the body but cannot kill the soul" [Matt. 10:28]), martyrs were often heard offering up prayers for their persecutors as they were burned alive at the stake. The raging fires of Rome were no match for the flames of love that burned within their hearts. Instead of quenching the church's voice, persecution only fueled the gospel's advance. In Romans 8, which speaks of the faithful as "sheep to be slaughtered," Paul describes the persecuted as being "*more* than conquerors" (*huper-nike* in the Greek) (8:37)! On this point, Tertullian wrote these immortal words: "The blood of the martyrs is the seed of the church." Just as Christ's death brought forth life eternal, so victory sprang up from the deaths of the faithful.

---

101. Paulien, *Gospel From Patmos*, 125.

102. This has been the assumption of many in the historicist camp as well. Referring to the last three riders, Maxwell speaks of "the ravages of the three *evil* horsemen" (*God Cares*, 2:180, emphasis added). In the self-published 2004 pocket edition of *The Clear Word*, Jack Blanco paraphrases the second seal as follows: "Its rider had a sword in his hand. He waged war against God's people who refused to compromise."

103. "The seals offer a general progression of history rather than a detailed chronology; their interpretation, therefore, is not bound specifically to the prophecy of the seven churches . . . The seals are a parallel development of Matthew 24 and 25 (the Synoptic apocalypse)." Holbrook, ed., *Symposium on Revelation – Book 1*, 179.

True sacrifice

Addressing His followers, Jesus explained that a true disciple must be willing to "deny himself, and take up his cross daily" (Luke 9:23), just as Jesus did. The cross, of course, is a symbol for death. Keener writes: "Jesus' conquest through his self-sacrifice (5:5-6) provides a model for believers. . . . Thus, 'conquering' in both cases, that of Christ and that of Christians, means no more or less than dying."[104]

In His statement, Jesus is referring to the crucifixion and death of *self*—surrendering the self-centered and sinful nature that each of us was born with. Paul explains that this death is necessary in order to live a new life in Christ: "I have been crucified with Christ; and it is no longer I that live, but Christ living in me: and that life which I now live in the flesh I live in faith, the faith which is in the Son of God, who loved me, and gave himself up for me" (Gal. 2:20, ASV).

The word *deny* (*arneomai*) means to refuse or to reject. The force of this word can be seen in Peter's firm and thrice repeated renouncement of Jesus (John 18:25–27). This sheds light on what it means to reject my self-centered nature, so that I can claim Jesus as the "Lord" of my life. The death of self is the greatest battle any of us will ever endure, because it calls for nothing less than decisive self-denial.

Dietrich Bonhoeffer (1906–1945), a German pastor and martyr, seems to have captured the essence of this subject:

> The cross is laid on every Christian. . . . When Christ calls
> a man, he bids him come and die. It may be a death like
> that of the first disciples who had to leave home and work
> to follow him, or it may be a death like Luther's, who had to
> leave the monastery and go out into the world. But it is the
> same death every time—death in Jesus Christ, the death of

---

104. Keener, *Revelation*, 191.

the old man at his call . . . dead to his own will.[105]

To encounter the cross "daily" is to offer up my life daily—a total surrender of my will—to God, as a "living sacrifice" (Rom. 12:1). As Christ did, I submit my will to the Father's ("Thy will be done" [Matt. 26:42, KJV]).

Only through Christ's indwelling presence can self remain dead and buried (see Rom. 6:6–11). As illogical as it may seem, *total surrender is the key to victory*. It is only by constant surrender to the Spirit that the believer is able to live the life of faith, a life exemplified by self-sacrificing love. It is the daily tests that determine whether we will achieve victory or suffer defeat in the greater crisis.

With self deposed, Jesus reigns on the throne of my heart. Through the transforming power of Christ's Spirit my "inward man" is "renewed day by day" (2 Cor. 4:16). A true believer, I am a "new man" in Christ (Eph. 4:22–24). *Self*—self-centeredness, self-dependence, self-righteousness—is washed from my heart and mind. Matthew Henry seemed to comprehend the depth of meaning behind the first two seals, explaining: "When Christ comes with power into their soul, he begins to conquer [first seal] these enemies [i.e., sins], and he goes on conquering in the work of sanctification [second seal]."[106]

In other words, we have received divine power to overcome temptation and sin. As Paul said, "Consider yourselves to be dead to sin, but alive to God in Christ Jesus. Therefore do not let sin reign in your mortal body that you should obey its lusts" (Rom. 6:11, 12, NASB).

In his book, *How to Be a Victorious Christian*, Thomas A. Davis shares an insightful allegory that summarizes the life of the victorious Christian. I paraphrase: A tyrant ruler (self) and his followers (evil habits and tendencies) have long ruled a very special kingdom (the sinner's heart). Tired of

---

105. Dietrich Bonhoeffer, *The Cost of Discipleship* (New York: Touchstone, 1995), 89–90.
106. Henry, *Commentary on the Holy Bible*, 3:464.

living under oppression and bondage, and unable to overcome the ruler, the citizens (sinners) of the realm turn to the kind and gracious ruler (God) of another kingdom, appealing to him for help. In turn, he only asks for their complete surrender and obedience. He then sends his son (Jesus Christ) to overcome the tyrant ruler and assume the throne (of the heart). Going further, he builds a fortress around the kingdom to protect the citizens from guerilla warfare and admonishes the citizens to keep vigilant watch, never letting their guard down. The tyrant ruler (self) makes numerous attempts to retake the kingdom, and at times it appears that he may even succeed. But with each attack the citizens immediately turn to their new king, who immediately routs him. Weakened, the tyrant ruler begins to lose nearly every fight, until he is unable to achieve any further success. Though he's still alive, harassing the citizens at times, he's a defeated foe.[107]

THE BLACK HORSE

When the Lamb opened the third seal, I heard the third living creature say, "Come!" I looked, and there before me was a black horse! Its rider was holding a pair of scales in his hand. Then I heard what sounded like a voice among the four living creatures, saying, "A quart of wheat for a day's wages, and three quarts of barley for a day's wages, and do not damage the oil and the wine!" (6:5–6).

Bible students generally agree that the third seal highlights the onset of a famine. Some believe that the text is alluding to a severe famine in the first century, in the Mediterranean region. Others believe that the symbolism pertains to the end of the world and a worldwide famine. Still others

---

107. Thomas A. Davis, *How to Be a Victorious Christian* (Ukiah, CA: Orion Publishing, 2003), 132–134.

hold that the crops—wheat, barley, oil, and wine—are symbols for spiritual realities (e.g., wheat represents Christ's body, oil is a symbol for the Holy Spirit). As we consider the content of the third seal, it's imperative that we keep the context of the seals in mind—the gospel, the church, the sanctuary, and the Old Testament background.

A covenant relationship

To begin, the crops listed here—wheat, barley, olives, and grapes—were staples in the days of the Bible (2 Chron. 2:15; Joel 1:10). In many areas, they still are. In Bible times the Mediterranean peoples had two harvest seasons. They harvested the shallow-rooted grains in the spring and the deeper-rooted vines and trees in the fall. These harvests coincided with Israel's annual religious festivals and were an integral part of Israel's covenant with Yahweh. With that in mind, let's step back in time and see why the famine was a critical sign for God's people.

After God delivered the Israelites from Egyptian bondage, He entered into a covenant relationship with them. This pact or agreement contained specific blessings for obedience, as well as consequences—also called "curses"—for disobedience (see Lev. 26; Deut. 11, 28). It was God's desire to bless Israel and hold her up before the nations as the token of His love for all humanity. If Israel strayed from the covenant, through spiritual infidelity or rebellion, God reserved the right to recapture her attention through the use of "curses," which would lead her to repent. Famine was one of God's tools (Lev. 26:26; Ezek. 14:21; Jer. 15:2).

But a famine was more than just an indicator of Israel's spiritual condition. It had an impact on Israel's salvation. As the book of Joel explains, the sanctuary's services would cease to function without grain, oil, and wine.[108] *The means of sacrifice for sin were cut off* (Joel 1:9, 13–15; 2:12–18).

---

108. "These products were sacrificial elements in the temple especially for the daily burnt offerings." Massyngberde Ford, *Revelation*, 98.

And that's not all. If Israel suffered from the effects of a spring famine, there was opportunity to repent before the fall harvest, which ushered in the close of Israel's religio-agricultural year and the annual Day of Atonement—the day of judgment (Lev. 23:27). On this day the high priest entered into the Most Holy Place of the sanctuary and cleansed it from all of the sins that had accumulated there throughout the year (cf. Heb. 9:7).

The original recipients of Revelation would have readily discerned the natural division of the two harvests in the text. They would see that the first harvest had already suffered a covenant curse, and that only a voice from heaven was staying the anticipated destruction of the second harvest. Thoughts of the covenant, spiritual waywardness, rebellion, and judgment must have run through their minds.[109]

With that background in mind, we see that it's no coincidence that the third horseman is carrying a pair of balances or scales (Greek, *zugon*). In addition to their use for the weighing of food for commerce, the scales have always been a symbol for judgment from Bible days to the present (cf. Dan. 5:27: Job 31:6; 1 Samuel 2:3).

A couple of "man"-ly details

The third throne creature, which ushers out the third rider, is described as having "a face like a man" (4:7). As we have already noted, the throne creatures reflect aspects of Christ and His ministry. In Revelation 5, Christ's sacrifice was declared "worthy" because He is both man and God.[110] As a man, He stands out from all other men (Rev. 5:5, 9). He has received from the Father "authority to execute judgment also, because He is the Son of Man" (John 5:26, 27).

---

109. Osborne notes that Mathias Rissi sees here some type of "limitation on the judgment." *Revelation* (BEC), 281.

110. "It is the combination of Jesus' divinity and His vulnerable humanity that is the key. . . . [O]nly Someone who is both God and man, who is both human and divine, can open the scroll. . . . There is only one Person in the entire universe who can resolve this universal problem, and that is Jesus Christ." Jon Paulien, *Seven Keys: Unlocking the Secrets of Revelation* (Nampa, ID: Pacific Press, 2009), 66.

This Man is also our heavenly High Priest. As time rapidly draws to a close, many people are self-deceived, playing church. They have never been born again and sealed with God's Spirit (2 Cor. 1:22; Eph. 1:13; 4:30). Thus it's not surprising to hear Christ's voice crying out from the heavenly sanctuary, from "in the center of the four living creatures"[111] (6:6, NASB): "Don't hurt the final harvest! Spare it a little longer!"[112] On the Day of Atonement, loyal Israelites were separated from those who did not repent and were rejected by God. The great antitypical "day of judgment" (Rev. 6:16, 17), echoing the Old Testament type, is fast approaching. And yet a divine delay is reflected in the fact that the last two horses do not "go out" (Greek, *exerchomai*) like the first two.

What does it all mean?

Many students of Revelation have recently come to assume that Christ and His sanctuary, which are prominent in chapters 1–5, suddenly drop from view in chapter 6. But our examination of the passage has shown otherwise. The first horseman revealed Christ's conquering power. The good news of the gospel is that through Him we can overcome lives of temptation and sin. The second horseman's message went further, showing that we must surrender our lives to Christ daily. Now, under the shroud of darkness, the third horseman's message is a warning to all who are resisting God's Spirit or clinging to sin. Let's look at a couple of examples.

Daniel 5 records the story of King Belshazzer's final party at the palace in Babylon. Defying the God of Israel by drinking wine from the golden

---

111. Compare Rev. 14:14–15, 19; Matt. 13:27–30. Coming from the "midst," this "seems to be the voice of the Lamb." Doukhan, *Secrets of Revelation*, 61 (see Rev. 5:6). "Operations seem to be directed from the throne room itself . . . By the four repetitions of edothe, 'it was granted' or 'given,' the impersonal passive frequently used euphemistically when God is the agent." Massyngberde Ford, *Revelation*, 101.

112. "Hurt [KJV, *adikeo*] is a curious verb to be used" for the oil and wine, notes Morris. "All this adds up to a famine which is not yet a disaster. It is in the nature of a warning." *Book of Revelation*, 106. Stefanovic notes that the term *harm* (NKJV) is "used elsewhere in the book of Revelation repeatedly for judgment on evildoers (see 2:11, 9:10, 19)." *Revelation of Jesus Christ*, 231.

cups seized from Jerusalem's temple, Belshazzar is suddenly struck with terror when a disembodied hand appears and inscribes the following words on the palace wall: "MENE, MENE, TEKEL, PARSIN" (5:25). The word *tekel* is interpreted by Daniel to mean, "You have been weighed on the scales and found wanting" (5:27).

And then there is the apostle Paul.

> Years previously, Paul had been at the height of his determined service of the law when Christ had interrupted his life on the road to Damascus. His efforts were weighed and found lacking. Seeking to pursue "spiritual justice," in reality he had been persecuting God's Son.[113]

As we saw in the seven letters, there are many "professors" in the church (i.e., the Balaamites, Nicolaitans, Jezebels), those who profess to follow Christ but do not know Him as their personal Lord and Savior. Though they claim to believe the "good news" of the new covenant, they have not committed their lives to Christ unconditionally (Matt. 26:28; Heb. 12:24). Because of their unfaithfulness to the covenant relationship, Christ permits a "famine" to awaken their slumbering souls.[114]

Earlier, in the seven letters, Christ pleaded with the wayward, backslidden, and rejecters of His grace to repent and return to Him (cf. 2:5, 16, 22; 3:3, 19). Later, under the judgments of the seven trumpets, the wicked are shown to be unwilling to repent (9:20, 21), which explains in part why the seven trumpets are parallel to the seven plagues (Rev. 16). The vision of the four horsemen lies between the visions of the churches and the trumpets. It's here, just before the trumpet judgments, that Christ is judging His

---

113. Osborne, *Galatians*, Life Application Bible Commentary (Wheaton, IL: Tyndale, 1994), 75.

114. "Both pagans and Jews also understood that such hardships often represented divine judgments, and they called for repentance (Lev. 26:26; Jer. 11:22; 21:6; Ezek. 4:16; 33:27)." Keener, *Revelation*, 203.

church. As Wiersbe notes, "Before Christ judges the world, He must judge His own people (1 Peter 4:17; Ezek. 9:6)."[115]

Billy Graham rightly observed that the seals are "primarily a call to repentance."[116] God is loving and long suffering. He doesn't want any of His creation to perish (Mt. 18:14; John 3:16; 2 Pet. 3:9). But intercession for sin is about to end (Rev. 8:3–5; 15:5–8; Heb. 8:1–2), and our heavenly High Priest is taking every possible step to warn the unrepentant "professors" about the eternal consequences of their choices (Rev. 6:10; 14:7; 19:11).

Just as the first two seals paralleled the character of the church during the opening centuries of church history, so the third seal reflects the changes that occurred in the church beginning in the fourth century. As Constantine undertook to "Christianize" Roman society, the church began to fall away from the pure truths of Scripture, and spiritual compromise set in. Soon, the teachings of men were elevated above the Scriptures, and man-made traditions became the means of salvation.[117] Despite the fact that the Old Testament priesthood found its fulfillment in Christ, and that He is our heavenly High Priest, a new priesthood was set up on earth. As the world would soon see, the church would be transformed from a white beacon of light into a dark institution of human engineering. A famine of the Bread of Life would soon result in spiritual death, as described under the fourth seal.

THE PALE-GREEN HORSE

When the Lamb opened the fourth seal, I heard the voice of the fourth living creature say, "Come!" I looked, and there before me was a pale horse! Its rider was named Death, and Hades was

---

115. Wiersbe, *Be Victorious*, 25.
116. Graham, *Approaching Hoofbeats*, 11.
117. This included prayers for the dead; the worship of saints and Mary; the institution of the Mass; a new priesthood; the doctrine of purgatory; and more. See LaHaye, *Unveiling Revelation*, 59.

following close behind him. They were given power over a fourth of the earth to kill by sword, famine and plague, and by the wild beasts of the earth (6:7–8).

Under Knute Rockne, Notre Dame's football team, a small unit of men—composed of the quarterback, half backs, and the fullback—were immortalized in 1925 when they achieved the victory over Army's football team. They became forever known as the "Four Horsemen of Notre Dame."

However, the four horsemen, and particularly the fourth horse, have gained a negative character in the eyes of the public. We're not surprised to find four horses featured on the cover of *Armageddon*, the eleventh book in the Left Behind series, where all four horses are painted black. In a similar vein, the following words are found on the inside of the jacket of Helen MacInnes's book, *Ride a Pale Horse*: "A gripping novel of suspense involving political assassination, blackmail, forgery, violence and murder, espionage and counterespionage." The author quotes Revelation 6:8 in her foreword.

Because the seven last plagues of Revelation—where the word *Armageddon* is mentioned—parallel the seven trumpet judgments in Revelation 8 and 9, and not the four horsemen, we must approach the fourth seal in the same manner as we did with seals one through three. We must begin with the text itself.

The New Testament

As the student of the Scriptures will readily note, the fourth horseman's arsenal—sword, famine, plague, and wild beasts—has been taken straight out of the Old Testament (Lev. 26:21–26; cf. Deut. 32).[118] Referred to in ancient Israel as the "four dreadful judgments"[119] (Ezek. 14:21, NIV; "punishments,"

---

118. The covenant curses in Lev. 26:21–26 "contain many parallels" to the four horsemen. Paulien, "The Seven Seals," in Holbrook, ed., *Symposium on Revelation – Book 1*, 222.
119. These are considered to be "the four worst forms of punishment by God." Roloff, *Revelation*, 87.

TLB), these were God's covenant response—or "curses"—to unfaithfulness and rebellion and were intended to bring about repentance.[120] Notice what Ezekiel 14 says: the "children of Israel" purposed to "set up idols in their hearts and put wicked stumbling blocks before their faces" (verse 3); participated in "detestable practices" (verse 6); behaved as an "unfaithful" wife (verse 12; cf. chapter 16); and "defiled [the Lord's] sanctuary" with their gross sins (5:11; 8; compare Isaiah 28:15, 18, where unrepentant Israel is described as covenanting with death and hell). When it became clear that Israel would not repent of her ways, "the glory of the Lord departed" from the temple (10:18–20).

Lying here in the heart of Revelation's opening story, these judgment symbols now apply to the unrepentant of spiritual Israel—the church (Jer. 31:31–33; Rom. 2:29; Gal. 3:29; Heb. 12:24). Already in Revelation 2 and 3 there was warning: "Christ announces the covenant curses against the churches if they continue in disobedience."[121] As Christians, our responsibility to the "better" covenant (Heb. 7:22; 8:6) is of no less importance than was the ancient Israelites', since it is conceived out of the Lamb's own blood (Heb. 12:24). Osborne sums it up this way: "When a people transgress the laws of God, they are in effect denying the covenant and bringing the wrath of God on themselves."[122]

A reversal of fortune

An interesting phenomenon in the fourth seal has gone unnoticed. Some of the key elements in the first three seals—i.e., the sacrificial knife, slayings, famine—have undergone "reversals" or transformations, something that is not uncommon in Revelation.[123] For example, the seven trumpets, which

---

120. Also Jeremiah 24:10: " 'And I will send the sword, the famine, and the pestilence among them, till they are consumed from the land that I gave to them and their fathers.' " See also 14:12.

121. Richard M. Davidson, "Sanctuary Typology," in Holbrook, ed., *Symposium on Revelation – Book 1*, 110, 115.

122. Osborne, *Revelation* (BEC), 297.

123. See Massynberde Ford, *Revelation*, 134. Sweet makes note of the "striking reversal of

are usually associated with worship,[124] become warnings of impending judgment (8:6). The altar of incense, which is used in the service of mediation, becomes the source of God's punishments (8:3–5). And a chaste woman flees into the desert, only to reemerge as a harlot (12:1; 17:3–5).

Rather than a sacrificial *machaira*-knife, the fourth horseman is wielding the larger and broader *rhomphia*-sword, which is used in execution, as in chapter 19:15, 21.[125] No longer is the famine limited to the spring crops; people are now dying from hunger. Even the type of death has changed, from sacrifice-*sphazo* to execution-*apokteino*—"death, and Hades."[126] The author may have wanted his reader to envision a change in the fourth throne-creature as well. The "eagle" (*aetos*; see 4:7), which symbolizes God's overseeing protection (12:14), is translated elsewhere as "vulture,"[127] and associated with the judgment woes (Matt. 24:38; Luke 17:37; Rev. 8:13

---

roles" in 7:17, where the Lamb becomes the Shepherd. *Revelation*, 154.

124. Paulien, *Decoding Revelation's Trumpets*, 207: "The predominant usage of trumpets in the Old Testament is a spiritual one in the context of the covenant (80 times out of a total of 144, or 56%)."

125. Massyngberde Ford, *Revelation*, 99. "A large and broad sword." Bauer et al, *Greek-English Lexicon*, 907. "The long and heavy great-sword." Hendriksen, *More Than Conquerors*, 104. "In Ezek 21 the sword (*rhomphaia*) is wielded by Yahweh Himself against Jerusalem." Massyngberde Ford, *Revelation*, 106. In the LXX, the *rhomphaia*, an instrument of war, is mentioned in the covenant curses in Ezek. 14:21 (compare Rev. 2:16; 19:21). We disagree with Mounce, who states that "no significance" should be attached to the fact that the author "chooses different swords" for the second and fourth riders (*Book of Revelation*, 156; also, Osborne, *Revelation* [BEC], 282). For in another place, he concludes that the two riders on the white horses (6:2; 19:12) have nothing in common because of the fact that their crowns are different (*Book of Revelation*, 156)!

126. With regard to what follows the fourth rider, "This does not refer to Hell but, instead, to the grave." Osborne, *Revelation* (LABC), 74. "The translation hell is misleading . . . in most cases ['hades'] refers simply to the realm of the dead (cf. Matt. 11:23 . . .)." Criswell, ed., *Criswell Study Bible*, 1480, note on Rev 1:18. As for the second mention of *thanatos* in verse 8, "it is likely that in this passage Death stands first for pestilence . . . and secondly for death in its general meaning. For this reason the passage goes on to extend the scope of the activity of Death and Hades to embrace the 'four sore acts of judgment' enumerated in Ezekiel 14:21." Beasley-Murray, *Revelation*, 134. "Death" (Greek, *thanatos*), then, may also mean "pestilence" (see RSV). Sweet, *Revelation*, 140.

127. ". . . an eagle (also a vulture). . . . In Matt. 24:28 and Luke 17:37 the vultures are probably intended." *Expository Dictionary*, 2:9. Commenting on Rev. 8:13, Mounce points out that the word *aetos* "may be used for the vulture as well as the eagle," depending on the context. *Book of Revelation*, 189.

[NIV]). Thus, we believe that Mounce's observation is correct: "It may be that this fourfold plague represents an intensification of that which is represented by the first three seals."[128]

Many writers have used the words *plagues* or *curses* too loosely with reference to the horsemen, particularly the last three. But because the "fourfold formula" in Ezekiel (5:17; 14:21) is specific to the fourth seal,[129] and considering what we have discovered in seals one through three, it's most appropriate to use the word *plague* with the fourth seal alone.[130]

In short, every opportunity and blessing spurned by the professors in the church has become a covenant curse.

The fourth horseman

It's at this point of the study that I am frequently asked, "Whom does the fourth horseman represent?" In order to answer that question, we must first answer the following: Was not the new covenant borne out of Christ's blood (Heb. 12:24)? In light of His death and resurrection, is it not Christ who possesses "the keys of hell and of death" (Rev. 1:18)? Will the rejecters of the gospel not flee in that last day from "the wrath of the Lamb" (Rev. 6:16)? Is it not Christ who uses the *rhomphia*-sword to execute judgment and destroy the wicked (Rev. 19:15, 21)? And is it not Christ who ultimately determines our eternal destiny (22:11–12)?

We cannot say that the fourth horseman, whose name is Death, is Jesus Christ. As Maxwell reminds us, the riders are "not actual persons."[131] However, in light of the evidence above, it's reasonable to conclude that the fourth horseman's activity is based on Christ's authority (John 5:27) and entirely under His control[132]—since He does "hold the keys of death

---

128. Mounce, *Book of Revelation*, 156.
129. Ibid.
130. "But such a fourfold formula [Ezek. 5:17; 14:21] recurs specifically in Revelation 6:8 and may not stand behind the horsemen as a whole." Keener, *Revelation*, 200.
131. Maxwell, *God Cares*, 2:182.
132. "In John's Apocalypse all the OT promises and threats are transformed into blessings and curses of Jesus Christ." Hans K. LaRondelle, "Babylon: Anti-Christian Empire," in Frank

and Hades," He is intimately involved. It appears that Hendriksen was on the right track when he wrote, "It would not surprise us if here, too, the second, third and fourth riders are subservient to the first: [they are] Christ's instruments for the refining and strengthening of His people."[133] Just as the conqueror upon the white horse represents Christ, so it is His functions and His ministry that are represented by the three that follow. After we have demonstrated the weaknesses behind the rapture (6:1, 2) and antichrist (6:1, 2) teachings, it's no leap to see Jesus Christ represented by the last three horsemen. Trafton writes: "But the reference to Death and Hades reminds the reader that Jesus has the keys to Death and Hades (1:18)." "Death and Hades" is directly related to the Lamb's book of life, or more specifically, those whose names are not written in it (Rev. 20:13, 14). Trafton concludes: "For the attentive reader, then, the section containing *the first four seals begins and ends with Jesus.*"[134]

There's still hope

Though the symbols suggest finality, there's reason to believe that the fourth seal also serves as a foretaste of what is still to come at the end. This comes as no surprise, since Revelation is written in repeated cycles. Consider first that, unlike the first two riders who "go out" (*exerchomai*), the last two do not go out; their activity seems to be restrained or limited.[135] Second, the activity in the fourth seal only affects "a fourth of the earth." (The seven trumpets affect "a third," and the seven last plagues are worldwide in scope.) Third, to be accurate, the horse's color is actually green. The Greek word is *chloros*, from which we get *chlorophyll*, the green coloring in plants ("pale green," NLT). Translators have undoubtedly chosen the word *pale*

B. Holbrook, ed., *Symposium on Revelation – Book 2*, 158.

133. Hendriksen, *More Than Conquerors*, 98.

134. Trafton, *Reading Revelation*, 73, emphasis mine. "There is a sense in which we experience them [the last three horsemen] daily." Maxwell, *God Cares*, 2:185.

135. Intended to evoke repentance: "The third and fourth horsemen themselves are not final events. They are preliminary and partial foretaste of the great end-time collapse." Paulien, "The Seven Seals," in Holbrook, ed., *Symposium on Revelation – Book 1*, 234.

because it is a "cadaverous color,"[136] signifying sickness and death. And yet, John uses the word *chloros*, which everywhere refers to that which is living (8:7; 9:4).

The church has been sifted

The four horsemen's messages lie at the heart of Revelation's opening story. Progressing (or rather, descending) from life to death, they demonstrate how the faithful are identified and sifted from the mere professors in the church (Matt. 25:32).[137]

Four in total, the messages are universal in scope. Having "strong parallels" with the Synoptic Apocalypse (Mark 13, Matthew 24, and Luke 21), the four horsemen's messages are intended for all in the church through the whole Christian age,[138] "forces that will be operative throughout history."[139]

And yet their character, like the seven churches, seems to parallel the "progression" of church history.[140] Listen to how Howard-Brook and Gwyther summarize the Dark Ages of church history:

> Ever since Constantine's "conversion," the church has taken on the forms and mind-set of empire. Its ministry and liturgy resemble those of the imperial cult, admittedly with Jesus rather than Caesar as the focus of worship. Crusades, missionary voyages, and the Inquisition all reek of imperial rather than covenantal practice. Centuries of church history find popes and bishops arm in arm with kings, princes, and generals. The very notion of "Christendom" that prevailed

---

136. Gaebelein, ed., *Hebrews Through Revelation*, 474.
137. Gaebelein sees a sifting in the fourth seal, stating that it "represents conflict directed at Christians to test them and to sift out false disciples." *Hebrews Through Revelation*, 473.
138. Paulien, *Gospel from Patmos*, 136.
139. Ladd, *Commentary on the Revelation*, 96.
140. "[The seals] probably should be understood more as a progression of thought [the trend of history] than as a rigid historical sequence." Paulien, "The Seven Seals," in Holbrook, ed., *Symposium on Revelation – Book 1*, 233.

throughout much of the church's history as the primary goal of the church has almost nothing to do with biblical faith and everything to do with imperial power.[141]

To summarize, the first two seals contain the essentials for a victorious Christian life; the third and fourth messages are addressed primarily to those who have strayed from their covenant relationship with Christ, have rejected the gospel, and are unrepentant. These divine judgments on those who have falsely claimed to be God's people are the "consequences of their sins."[142]

Hendriksen writes: "Our Lord Jesus Christ uses these woes as instruments, for the sanctification of His Church and the extension of His kingdom."[143] Through these messages, the Lamb pleads with His people to overcome and gain the victory over the world and sin. The four horsemen's messages are a plea from the heavenly throne for repentance and total surrender.

THE SAINTS

When he opened the fifth seal, I saw under the altar the souls of those who had been slain because of the word of God and the testimony they had maintained. They called out in a loud voice, "How long, Sovereign Lord, holy and true, until you judge the inhabitants of the earth and avenge our blood?" Then each of them was given a white robe, and they were told to wait a little longer, until the number of their fellow servants and brothers who were to be killed as they had been was completed (6:9–11).

---

141. Howard-Brook and Gwyther, *Unveiling Empire*, 261.
142. Stefanovic, *Revelation of Jesus Christ*, 234. "They show us the self-defeating character of sin." Morris, *Book of Revelation*, 102.
143. Hendriksen, *More Than Conquerors*, 105.

With the mission of the four horsemen complete, the Lamb proceeds to break the fifth seal. The fifth and sixth seals are a unit and can be likened to the two sides of a coin: in the fifth seal, John sees the saints at the base of the altar in the heavenly sanctuary; the sixth seal depicts the fate of the wicked on earth. Every soul *in the church* has made a final decision—to fully accept the gospel or wholly reject it.

Living sacrifices

As the Lamb breaks the fifth seal, the altar of burnt offering comes into view. Now many contemporary commentaries on Revelation either ignore or have little to say about the temple imagery in Revelation 6. And yet, as we have found, the symbolism is sprinkled throughout the seals. We found terms and images in the second seal that were directly related to sacrifice. Under the third seal, we were reminded of how the annual religious events connected with the sanctuary ran parallel with the harvest seasons. Borrowing from imagery straight out of the Old Testament's covenant curses, the fourth seal was seen to contain one of Revelation's strongest verbal parallels. And here in the fifth seal, we find an altar, perhaps the most common and well-known article in the temple.

In the Mosaic sanctuary, this altar was located outside the tabernacle, in the courtyard. The scene reminds us of the blood that was poured out at the "foot of the altar" (6:9, AMP). As Doukhan notes, "The Apocalypse borrows language from Leviticus, which identifies the soul with the blood (Lev. 17:11), to better express the *sacrificial character* of their suffering."[144] Thus, we should understand the symbolism to mean that "their lifeblood has been poured out [at the base of the altar] as an offering to God" (Lev. 4:7).[145] Their cry, then, reflects the appeal of Abel's blood, recorded in Genesis 4:10.[146]

---

144. Doukhan, *Secrets of Revelation*, 65, emphasis added.
145. Barclay, *The Revelation of John*, 2:12. Paul uses similar language in 2 Tim. 4:6 and Phil. 2:17, where he speaks of himself as a "drink offering."
146. Massyngberde Ford, *Revelation*, 110.

But why are there souls "under the altar"? Where did they come from? The most reasonable explanation is that these are the souls who had surrendered their lives as "living sacrifices" to their heavenly High Priest under the second seal.[147] The word *slain* (*sphazo*) links these sacrificial deaths to the sacrificial slayings under the second seal (not the fourth seal). As we discovered earlier, the submitting of our lives to Jesus Christ may result in persecution or death at the hands of "the inhabitants of the earth whose names have not been written in the book of life" (17:8, NIV). Understanding what has occurred in the symbolism of the fifth seal, Caird points out that "at some time in the past they [the martyred souls] have been offered in sacrifice on [the heavenly altar]."[148] And to this point, Hendriksen writes: "Does it not seem reasonable to suppose that those who under the second seal are seen as *being* slaughtered are the same as those who under the fifth seal are described as *having been* slaughtered?" Of course! To what other scene, previous to the fifth seal, could we point? The answer, of course, is

---

147. As in the surrounding texts, the souls represent lives—not disembodied spirits that have left their bodies and gone to heaven. This understanding is "made clear by [John's] use of psuche throughout the book." Trafton, *Reading Revelation*, 75. "The use of [*psuxas*] here is interesting, for it normally refers to the whole person" Osborne, *Revelation* (BEC) 284. "[*Psuxas*] probably stands here for the actual 'lives' or 'persons' who were killed rather than for their 'souls.' " Gaebelein, ed., *Hebrews Through Revelation*, 475. Accordingly, this text has "nothing to do with the state of the dead." Ladd, *Commentary on the Revelation*, 103.

148. Caird, *Revelation of Saint John*, 84. Though Revelation begins and ends with a focus on the earth (1:12–20; 21:1-22:5), Richard M. Davidson sheds light on the fifth seal when he sets forth the hermeneutic for knowing when we are in the heavenly sanctuary or on earth, in the typology of Revelation:

> But here we note that amidst the heavenly sanctuary scenes of Revelation, there are brief shifts to *earthly* sanctuary allusions. For example, in Revelation 6:9-11 we find mention of the altar [of burnt offering]. Since this altar was in the outer court of the earthly sanctuary, and since according to Revelation 11:1-2 the outer court symbolizes earthly and not heavenly things, we must interpret this as a shift to the earthly realm. In harmony with the ecclesiological aspect of the typological fulfillment, we should interpret these earthly references in a spiritual, nonliteral way (Richard M. Davidson, "Sanctuary Typology," in *Symposium on Revelation – Book 1*, Holbrook, ed., 110, 115).

nowhere. Hendriksen goes on to state, "These are the souls which under the second seal were being slaughtered."[149]

Commenting on the dual imagery of the spiritual sacrifice and literal persecution, Ladd says:

> In fact, they were slain on earth and their blood wet the ground; but in Christian faith, the sacrifice was really made in heaven where the souls were offered at the heavenly altar . . .
>
> Here John appears to have in mind *all Christian martyrs of every age.*[150]

As Sweet points out, "The death of a martyr was conceived as a sacrifice on the altar of the heavenly temple."[151]

---

149. Hendriksen, *More Than Conquerors*, 100, 106.

150. Ladd, *Commentary on the Revelation of John*, 103–104, italics added. ". . . may represent all who *suffer in any way* for Christ's sake." Wilcock, *Message of Revelation*, 72, italics added. "The faithful, whether as martyrs or *confessors*, are sacrifices to God." Charles, *Critical and Exegetical Commentary*, 7, italics added. "It was the cry of the exiled Hebrews in Babylon [OT], . . . the early Christians [NT], . . . Christian outcasts [Church Age], . . . also the cry of the Jews [non-Christians]." Doukhan, *Secrets of Revelation*, 64.

> The question arises as to why the martyrs alone receive so much attention rather than all suffering or persecuted Christians. One solution understands John to be referring to all those who so faithfully follow Christ as to form a group that may be characterized as the slain of the Lord. They may or may not actually suffer physical death for Christ, but they have (like John) so identified themselves with the slain Lamb that they have in effect already offered up their lives (Gaebelein, ed., *Hebrews Through Revelation*, 474).

Howard-Brook expands the application beyond the church:

> There is no reason to limit this group to Christians or to specific persons killed during John's lifetime. Rather, they represent all those prophets and holy women and men throughout history who have suffered empire's reaction against them for testifying against its falsity, oppression, and injustice (Howard-Brook and Gwyther, *Unveiling Empire*, 142).

151. Sweet, *Revelation*, 142.

As Henry's writings reveal, the early Protestants saw the entire church in this text:

> There seems no reason why this [fifth] seal should be restricted to any particular body of martyrs of any particular period. . . . It may, perhaps, be most fitly understood to comprehend *all the martyrs to the [C]hristian cause*, from the [A]postolical age to the happy time when such sufferings shall finally cease.[152]

Like Jesus and His disciples, a true believer may suffer for "the word of God and for the testimony of Jesus Christ" (1:9; cf. 12:11, 17). As Roloff reminds us, "Indeed, many in the church must still reckon with the fact that they also, like so many before them, will lose their life."[153]

Patience rewarded

True to Revelation's unique manner of seeing one thing but hearing another, John hears the "haunting cry [that] reflects the anguish of the innocent of all ages"[154]: "How long . . . until you judge . . . and avenge our blood?" Some are disturbed by this plea, asking, "Doesn't this reflect a selfish desire for vengeance?" No, that would not be consistent with the character of a true saint (Rom. 12:19). These are people who have suffered unjustly for their faith and trust God to judge righteously—which He does through the seven trumpets (Rev. 8–9).[155] Their "cry does not constitute an ethical low in the book, but rather a call for divine justice" to be applied against the injustices they have endured for God's sake.[156]

---

152. Henry, *Commentary on the Holy Bible*, 3:465.
153. Roloff, *Revelation*, 88.
154. Lichtenwalter, *Revelation's Great Love Story*, 87.
155. "The cry goes out in Revelation 6:10 and receives its answer in 8:13. The trumpets of Revelation 8 and 9 are about what God is doing to judge those who have persecuted His saints. . . . Whatever else they may mean, the trumpets are clearly a response to the prayers of the saints for justice in relation to the persecutions that have taken place during the course of Christian history." Paulien, *Deep Things*, 118.
156. Osborne, *Revelation* (BEC), 286.

In this tabernacle scene, the prayers can be likened to the smoke that ascended from the altar of incense in the Holy Place and came before the mercy seat in the Most Holy Place. But in reality, the blood of the innocent has been shed across the earthen altar (cf. Gen. 4:9–11; Luke 11:50–51; Rev. 18:24).[157]

In response to their faithfulness, the saints are given "white robes" of assurance and told to wait patiently until the eternal destiny of all has been decided and the Lamb returns (cf. 6:17).[158] By faith, the saints have surrendered and exchanged their "filthy rags" of self-righteousness (Isaiah 64:6) for Christ's "robe" of righteousness (Rev. 3:18). Just as ancient military leaders paraded on white horses after a triumphant battle, the white robe is an emblem of "victory and honor"[159] and eternal life (Rev. 3:4–5; 2:10; 7:9). Robed in Christ's righteousness, the true believer is able to stand "before the throne of God" as a child of the King (Rev. 7:15; Heb. 4:16).

As with the first four seals and churches, there is some similarity between the characteristics of the fifth church, Sardis, and the fifth seal. Thus, some have applied the message of this seal to a period of time in church history. However, it's best not to press the comparisons between the seven churches and the seven seals,[160] since the seals, which are quite similar to the prophetic outline in the Olivet Discourse (Matthew 24), simply follow "the trend of [church] history."[161]

Victory by sacrifice

We would be making a mistake to think of the fifth (and sixth) seals as

---

157. "The altar is upon earth, not in heaven." Adam Clarke, *Commentary on the Bible* (1831), notes on Rev. 6:9.

158. As reflected by the italics in the KJV, the word *number* has been supplied by the translators. "John is not thinking of a predetermined number of saved; his point is that there will be many more martyrs." Harrington, *Revelation*, 94.

159. Henry, *Commentary on the Holy Bible*, 3:465.

160. A contemporary historicist, Maxwell, writes: "Rather than comparing the seven seals with the seven churches, it is better to compare them with the sequence of events outlined by Jesus in the Olivet Discourse [Mt. 24]." *God Cares*, 2:185.

161. Paulien, "The Seven Seals," in Holbrook, ed., *Symposium on Revelation – Book 1*, 233.

nothing more than just the outcome of the four horsemen's ministry. As Ford suggests, the fifth seal is "the *key* to the whole chapter for it looks backward to the concept of the 'martyred' Lamb in ch. 5 and forward to the number of those sealed [ch. 7]."[162] Building on this, Keener observes that "the martyrs do share in Christ's sacrificial suffering [Rev. 5:6] . . . and will also share in His exaltation (3:21; 20:4)."[163] This is the backbone of the fifth seal. As Dr. C. M. Kempton Hewitt states it so well, the saints are under the altar "because their lives of sacrifice are a heavenly imitation of Christ's supreme sacrifice."[164]

Oh, to be like Jesus! But the good news is that we can be! Instead of falling quickly into discouragement, and crying for God to remove every trial, we must prayerfully plead for patient endurance and the power to overcome, just as Christ our example did in the Garden.

Revelation's opening story is about victory through sacrifice. At the heart of the story we find a Lamb, victorious because of its sacrifice. Next, we see the faithful victorious because of their identity with the Lamb. Victory through sacrifice is a consistent motif in the book of Revelation[165]—founded on the Lamb's sacrifice.

THE WICKED

I watched as he opened the sixth seal. There was a great earth-quake. The sun turned black like sackcloth made of goat hair, the whole moon turned blood red, and the stars in the sky fell to earth, as late figs drop from a fig tree when shaken by a strong wind. The sky receded like a scroll, rolling up, and every mountain and island was removed from its place.

---

162. Massyngberde Ford, *Revelation*, 110, italics added.
163. Keener, *Revelation*, 219.
164. Kempton Hewitt, *Revelation*, 21.
165. Mounce, *The Book of Revelation*, 171.

Then the kings of the earth, the princes, the generals, the rich,
the mighty, and every slave and every free man hid in caves and
among the rocks of the mountains. They called to the mountains
and the rocks, "Fall on us and hide us from the face of him who
sits on the throne and from the wrath of the Lamb! For the great
day of their wrath has come, and who can stand?" (6:12–17).

As the Lamb breaks the sixth seal, John witnesses *seven* momentous phenomena associated with the end of time. Though the sun, moon, and stars are literal here, the descriptive adjectives are figurative (e.g., black as "goat hair," red as "blood," like a shaken "fig tree"). And, once again, the background for the symbolism can be found in the Old Testament, particularly in the book of Joel.

Most students of Revelation do not realize that the book borrows much of its imagery from the book of Joel. At its core is an appeal for God's people to repent, and this is a theme in Revelation as well. And similar to Revelation, the sanctuary is the backbone of Joel. It's no surprise to find striking similarities between the two books. Here's an example in Joel:

Before them the earth shakes, the sky trembles, the sun and moon are darkened, and the stars no longer shine. The Lord thunders at the head of his army; his forces are beyond number, and mighty are those who obey his command. The day of the Lord is great; it is dreadful. Who can endure it? . . .

I will show wonders in the heavens and on the earth, blood and fire and billows of smoke. The sun will be turned to darkness and the moon to blood before the coming of the great and dreadful day of the Lord (Joel 2:10–11, 30–31, NIV).

Understanding that these celestial events occur *before* the "day of the

Lord," Bible students in the nineteenth century from various denominations came to believe that certain earth-shaking cosmic events were in fact signs that the world was nearing its end. Some of the more notable events included the great Lisbon earthquake (November 1, 1755), which claimed the lives of half the city's population; the infamous Dark Day (May 19, 1780); and the great meteor shower of November 13, 1833. Noteworthy enough to be recorded by the historians of the day, these events served to further awaken the fascination with Bible prophecy, a period that has been referred to as the Second Great Awakening. Further Bible study led some to believe that these signs coincided Daniel 8:14 and 9:24–27, believed to be the longest time prophecy in the Bible. (Using the "day-for-a-year" principle, the 1,260-year period was said to extend from the fall of Rome in AD 598 to the dethronement of the pope in 1798.)

However, the events described in the sixth seal go beyond anything that mankind has witnessed to date.[166] They describe "the end of the entire universe as we know it,"[167] which occurs just before Christ's return.[168] This is good news for the believer, because this sinful planet must be destroyed before the "new earth" can be ushered in (Rev. 21:1). The de-creation language in 6:12–17 is broken down for the reader in the seven trumpets (Rev. 8) and again in the final plagues (Rev. 16).

Under the fifth seal, the righteous were described as residing under the heavenly altar. Now, in the sixth seal, we learn the fate of those who have rejected Christ's gospel and the Father's mercy. The wicked, who must face the "dreadful day of the Lord," are divided into seven social classes, which include kings, princes, generals, rich, mighty, slave, and free. This same

---

166. Stefanovic suggests that the "great earthquake" in verse 12 occurs prior to, and is separate from, the event that causes the land and islands to "move out" of their place (v. 14). The latter would be the "mighty and great earthquake" mentioned in 16:18. *Revelation of Jesus Christ*, 243.
167. Wilcock, *Message of Revelation*, 73.
168. Paulien, *Gospel From Patmos*, 142.

group is said to be killed by Christ's *rhomphia*-sword in 19:17–21. The number seven[169] suggests the thoroughness in which God acts—no injustice will get past His "seven eyes" unnoticed (5:6). The "entire godless world" is included here.[170] The passage clearly shows that social status, finances, and deeds are all meaningless when it comes to eternal salvation. The unrepentant—those who have ultimately demonstrated that they will never recognize Jesus Christ as the Lord—are described as seeking the solace of a tormented death at the Second Coming.[171]

Love and wrath

Many Christians, and even ministers, are so uncomfortable with the notion that Christ would act with divine wrath that they reject it outright.[172] This, they argue, doesn't fit Jesus' character. To this point, Warren Wiersbe of the *Back to the Bible Broadcast* says:

> We are so accustomed to emphasizing the meekness and gentleness of Christ (Matt. 11:38-30) that we forget His holiness and justice. The same Christ who welcomed the children in the temple also drove the merchants from that same temple.[173]

Many simply err in pinning divine wrath on the Father alone, as if to

---

169. Hendriksen argues that the groups more naturally break down into six, a point that is worthy of consideration:

> In this connection it is interesting to observe that this final outpouring of the divine wrath upon mankind is described under the sixth seal—six, or rather six hundred and sixty-six, being the number of man (Rev. 13:18)— and is represented as affecting six objects of creation [verses 12–14]; and as distributed among six classes of men. *More Than Conquerors*, 107.

170. Ibid., 109.
171. Stefanovic, *Revelation of Jesus Christ*, 245.
172. "Many scholars have reacted . . . as if it contradicted divine love." Osborne, *Revelation* (BEC), 296.
173. Wiersbe, *Be Victorious*, 67.

make Him appear as the "bad guy" in relation to His Son. Instead of seeing this text as further evidence that the Father and Son are one,[174] they create a false dichotomy between the two members of the Godhead and do harm to the doctrine of the Trinity.

Bearing in mind that the slain Lamb is breaking the seals, Caird notes that "the Lamb is at all times a symbol to be understood with reference to the Cross, so that the Cross itself is both the victory of God and the judgment of the world."[175] The message of the Cross, then, like a two-edged sword, cuts both ways (cf. Matt. 12:30). We must confess that there are two aspects to God's wrath: the first regarding His wrath toward sin itself, and the second toward injustice.

With regard to the first, since it was through the cross that Jesus joined us in reaping the consequences of sin, "[His] wrath represents [His] unwillingness to compromise with sin."[176] This wrath is a direct result of the sinner's choice: "When a people transgress the laws of God, they are in effect denying the covenant and bringing the wrath of God on themselves."[177] It is in light of this fact that Neall can state, "The seals unit, of which chapter seven is the climax, depicts the outcome of the blessings and curses upon the churches."[178] God's wrath is also specific: "God's wrath is the evidence of His holy love for all that is right and His holy hatred for all that is evil . . . The people [wicked] mentioned here are *impenitent*. They refuse to submit to God's will . . . [and] blaspheme Him as well! (Rev. 16:9, 11, 21)."[179]

The second regards injustice toward God's people, the saints. As Harrington explains, God's answer to "injustice . . . is the Lamb. His 'wrath' is

---

174. "Here the Lamb is again assimilated to the Father." Harrington, *Revelation*, 96.
175. Caird, *Revelation of Saint John*, 91.
176. Paulien, *Gospel From Patmos*, 144.
177. Osborne, *Revelation* (BEC), 296.
178. Neall, "Sealed Saints and the Tribulation," in Holbrook, ed., *Symposium on Revelation – Book 1*, 248.
179. Wiersbe, *Be Victorious*, 67. "The wrath of the Lamb . . . is the specific end-time judgment of Christ on the despisers of His atoning grace and the rejecters of His divine authority." LaRondelle, *Chariots of Salvation*, 172.

written on the Cross."[180] Thus, those who have "refused [the Lamb's] sacrifice, [and] mocked his name" fall into the same camp with those who have "persecuted [the Lamb's] people."[181]

Here is the bottom line: "Salvation implies justice. To save, God must judge."[182]

But let's not fail to miss the *purpose* of this prophetic scenario. "The purpose of this apocalyptic forecast is to *lead each unbeliever and half-committed Christian to genuine repentance* before God."[183] While many will be drawn to Christ through the loving illustrations in the Gospels, others are compelled to fall at His feet when they see His abundant mercy toward them as sinners. The four horsemen's messages in the seals,[184] the seven trumpet judgment-warnings that follow, as well as the whole of Revelation, have been given to us so that we may see that the Lamb is victorious in the end, and we may accept His gift of mercy and life now.

"Who is able to stand?"

"Who is able to stand?" The force of that question has brought some of the world's strongest men to their knees. Indeed, who is able to stand before God? The answer is so obvious that it is not given here. Not the greatest warrior, or the wealthiest person, or any potentate on earth can stand before God Almighty. No one will be able to stand before God on that last day unless they are robed in Christ's righteousness.

The question points us back to the opening vision: "The [seven] letters have already shown the conditions for *standing*."[185] And from there, the four horsemen have revealed the steps by which we overcome[186]—

---

180. Harrington, *Revelation*, 97.
181. Osborne, *Revelation* (LABC), 79.
182. Doukhan, *Secrets of Revelation*, 65.
183. LaRondelle, *Chariots of Salvation*, 172, italics added.
184. "The judgments of the seals are but the precursors of the salvation of the world." Beasley-Murray, *Revelation*, 129.
185. Sweet, *Revelation*, 146.
186. Paulien, "The Seven Seals," in Holbrook, ed., *Symposium on Revelation – Book 1*, 203;

sifting the true believers from the mere professors in the church. And so, the focus of the seals "is on the gospel and on the historical process within which God's people overcome just as Christ overcame."[187] "The breaking of the seals," Strand concludes, "would therefore represent *successive steps or means by which God through Christ acts* in preparing the world for judgment."[188] The fifth and sixth seals confirm what we have known all along—there is no middle ground, no fence to sit on. We are either children of God's kingdom (Phil. 3:20) or we are still among the "inhabitants of the earth." Faced with the knowledge of the gospel of Jesus Christ, the responsibility rests on each of us to either accept or reject the Cross and everything it stands for.

But the question also points us forward to the last scene in the opening story, where we find the victors of earth standing before God's throne, the entire church triumphant (Rev. 7:14–17).

Deep Things, 117.
187. Paulien, "The Seven Seals," in Holbrook, ed., *Symposium on Revelation – Book 1*, 227.
188. Strand, *Interpreting*, 48, emphasis added.

Chapter 5

The Victors: Revelation 7

"Then I saw another angel coming up from the east,
having the seal of the living God. . . .
Then I heard the number of those who were sealed: 144,000 . . .
and there before me was a great multitude that no one could count,
from every nation, tribe, people and language, standing before the throne."

Chapter 7 brings us to the close of Revelation's "opening story," and the final victory scene. Were this John's last vision, and Revelation ended here, we would have a complete picture of the New Testament age and the ultimate triumph of God's people.

Before we proceed with the final scene, let's recap what we have already seen. In Revelation 1–3, Jesus revealed Himself to John as the church's heavenly High Priest. Through seven messages to the churches, Jesus repeated appeals to every Christian to overcome and experience spiritual victory, as He did (3:21). Then, through the symbolism of the four horsemen, Christ showed us how the victors in the church are being sifted from those who merely profess to know the Lamb. And now, in response to the previous question, "Who can stand?" (6:17), John sees a multitude of conquerors standing with the Lamb before the heavenly throne (7:9, 15–17).

The timing of the scene in Revelation 7 is unique. Although it's a continuation of the sixth seal, the scene is also a flashback—the sealing of God's people as described in chapter 7 must occur before Christ's second coming (6:17). Scholars refer to Revelation 7 as an interlude because it's akin to a parenthetical thought. The interludes in Revelation (compare chapters 10–11 and 14) serve as a "spotlight on last events."[1] In chapter 7, an angel seals the people of God in order to protect them from the divine judgments that are about to fall upon the earth and those clinging to it (6:10).

Revelation 7 contains some of the most popular and controversial subjects; for example, the twelve "tribes of the children of Israel," and the renowned figure of "144,000." Christians had commonly held for centuries that both Israel and the 144,000 were symbolic and represent the church. But this long-held view has undergone a dramatic change in recent decades. Many, if not most, Christians now believe that these two subjects are to be interpreted literally, and that they pertain to the nation of Israel, particularly in the last days. (Some Christians believe that there will only be 144,000 believers ready at Jesus' second coming. But this is less than the attendance at the Daytona 500!) To be sure, one's view on these matters is undoubtedly shaped by what the minister teaches or by the most popular books on the Christian bookstore shelf. This, as we have already seen, has been the case with belief in the rapture (4:1–2) and the antichrist (6:1–2).

The seal of God (verses 1–3)

As the final scene of the story is unveiled, John sees four angels standing at the four corners of the earth, holding back the four winds. Again, the number four suggests the totality of the world, just as the words "four corners of the earth" suggest. Since the wicked are the inhabitants of the earth (Rev. 6:10, 15), these winds probably represent strife and chaos (cf. Dan. 7:2).

A number of scholars have pointed to a relationship between the four horses and the four winds.[2] This idea is supported by the fact that the four

---

1. Strand, *Interpreting*, 48, 51.
2. "The 'four winds of heaven' there [Zech. 6:5] take their place in front of each of the chariot horses and lead them in the four directions of the compass . . . [Thus many] believe that the

colored horses in Zechariah, which are patrolling the four corners of the earth, are literally "winds" (Hebrew, *ruwach*; Zech. 6:5–7). Considering the reversals that we discovered under the fourth horseman (the transformation from opportunity to judgment), Paulien is probably correct in saying, "This may indicate that the four winds of Revelation 7:1-3 are the horses of chapter 6 unleashed in a *covenant reversal*. . . . The horses apparently have their counterpart in the destroying winds of chapter 7."[3]

Who is the angel that appears from the east, having the seal of the living God? Some think that this messenger (Greek, *angelos*) represents Jesus Christ. He is elsewhere called the "Sun of righteousness" and associated with the east,[4] particularly in those scenes that are related to the end (cf. Ezek. 43:2; Mal. 4:2; Matt. 2:2; 24:27; 2 Pet. 1:19). At the very least, the messenger seems to be acting on Christ's behalf.

This scene appears to be built on Ezekiel 9:1–11,[5] where the angel of death passed through the city of Jerusalem, marking the foreheads of—and thereby *sealing*—the covenant faithful in Israel; that is, those who were repentant and grieving over their nation's sins. The divine mark would protect the faithful from destruction. As in Revelation 1 through 6, the sanctuary is in the background here (cf. Ezekiel 8–10).

The heavenly messenger is heard crying out to the four angels, "Do not harm the land or the sea or the trees until we put a seal on the foreheads of the servants of our God." This must be a flashback, since the sealing would occur before the "great day" of the Lamb (6:15–17). The phrase "do not harm" (Gk, *me adikeo*) connects the present scene with what has gone

---

four winds are identical with the four horsemen, a very real possibility." Osborne, *Revelation* (BEC), 305. Having interpreted the first four seals as judgments under the "dread horsemen," Wilcock concludes, "God's control over the horsemen/winds ensures that his church is sealed and secure *before they ride forth.*" *Message of Revelation*, 79.
3. Paulien, "The Seven Seals," in Holbrook, ed., *Symposium on Revelation – Book 1*, 224, italics added.
4. "The Messiah was expected to appear from the east (cf. Matt. 2:1ff). . . . [He's called the] dayspring . . . [also the] morning star." Sweet, *Revelation*, 148.
5. Osborne, *Revelation* (BEC), 310.

before and what is to follow; under the third seal a warning was directed toward those who would not repent (6:6), but under the seven trumpets the unrepentant become the subject of the judgments (9:4).

What exactly is this seal? "In the ancient world the seal meant owner-ship, protection, and privilege."[6] Apparently, this seal—"written on their foreheads" (14:1)—includes the Father's name.[7] This is contrasted with the beast, whose mark is set either "on their right hand or on their foreheads" (13:16). Barclay explains: "In the early Church, this picture of sealing was especially connected with two things . . . baptism . . . [and] the gift of the Holy Spirit" (cf. 2 Cor. 1:22; Eph. 1:13; 4:30).[8] Because the " 'seal' (*sphrag-is*) is already a technical term for baptism" in Paul's writings (2 Cor. 1:22; cf. Eph. 1:13; 4:30), Roloff is "certain that here John is thinking specifically of baptism."[9] Considering that Ezekiel 9 is in the background, Sweet explains that "the tau [Ezekiel's mark—the last letter of the Hebrew alphabet, writ-ten as a "+" or "x"] was soon connected with the cross, and baptism signi-fied dying with Christ (Rom 6:3ff)."[10] The connection between the sealing and baptism seems to be supported by verses 13 and 14: the redeemed, who are dressed in "white robes," have "washed their robes."

But there's something more to this seal. Osborne reminds us that Rev-elation 7 is set in "an end-time [eschatological] context," and, therefore, cannot be merely a "reference to the baptism of believers or the recep-tion of the Spirit."[11] More than just the seal that is placed on the be-liever at conversion, this is a "unique apocalyptic 'seal.' "[12] And yet, the 144,000 would not be the first to be sealed, because an end-time seal must surely follow the Holy Spirit's sealing of the heart. Unlike the end-time

---

6. Osborne, *Revelation* (BEC), 307.
7. "The hand and forehead were also the location for the phylacteries, by which God's ser-vants showed their fidelity to his law." Keener, *Revelation*, 234.
8. Barclay, *Revelation of John*, 2:27.
9. Roloff, *Revelation*, 97.
10. Sweet, *Revelation*, 148.
11. Osborne, *Revelation* (BEC), 310.
12. LaRondelle, *Chariots of Salvation*, 171.

seal, which is *visible only to God*,[13] the believer's heart can be witnessed by all around them. Charles observes: "In its deepest sense this sealing means the outward manifestation of character."[14] Accordingly, this "seal of life" probably contains the "Father's name," a sign of God's ownership (Rev. 3:12; 14:1). Whereas those who are "owned" by the beast wear its "mark."[15]

The true believers have been identified already through the ministry of the four horsemen. Gaebelein writes: "[John's] language might indicate God's selecting the true church [the sealed] out 'from' the professing church . . . [In Ezekiel's day] the seal identified the true servants of God from the false ones among the professing people of God."[16] Here, the sealed are none other than "the victors of the [seven letter] messages,"[17] "the saints of all ages."[18]

To be clear, "the sealed are exempted merely from the plague of the winds, not from martyrdom or persecution."[19] The faithful who are living at the end will endure on the same path as their Lord (cf. 1:9). In the context of tribulation, "[God] promises to protect believers and give them the strength to endure any and all tribulation."[20]

What about those who are not sealed? Under the seven trumpet judgments, there's a divine command to "[not] harm the grass of the earth or any plant or tree but *only those people who did not have the seal* of God"

---

13. "Certainly this sealing [Rev. 7] is a spiritual fact and not a visible bodily phenomenon. . . . An analogous idea is found in the spiritual sealing by the Holy Spirit of all Christians [Eph. 1:14]." Ladd, *Commentary on the Revelation*, 112.
14. Charles, *Critical and Exegetical Commentary*, 1:206.
15. Osborne, *Revelation* (LABC), 83.
16. Gaebelein, ed., *Hebrews Through Revelation*, 483.
17. Harrington, *Revelation*, 146.
18. Neall, "Sealed Saints and the Tribulation," in Frank B. Holbrook, ed., *Symposium on Revelation – Book 1*, 259. "It should not be assumed that the sealing of Revelation 7:1-3 is limited to the end-time. Revelation 7:1-3 does not explicitly limit the sealing to the end-time; it merely focuses on the significance of sealing work in an end-time setting." Paulien, "The Seven Seals," in Holbrook, ed., *Symposium on Revelation – Book 1*, 224, emphasis added.
19. Nicoll, *Expositor's Greek New Testament*, 395.
20. Osborne, *Revelation* (LABC), 84.

(9:4). As Doukhan's work demonstrates, the symbolism only makes sense if the trees represent the righteous (compare Ps. 1:3–4; 52:8; Isa. 11:1; Jer. 2:21; Mark 11:11–22),[21] and the "land" and "sea" together represent the earth, or the habitation of the wicked (Rev. 6:10).

Of interest to us is that the "earth, sea, and trees sequence" echoes the Creation week (compare Gen. 1:9–13).[22] It so happens that this comes just before the seven trumpet judgments, which, like the seven plagues (Rev. 16), are the undoing of Creation (Rev. 8, 9). Tying chapter 7's opening themes together, Doukhan writes: "The seal marks those who believe in the Creator. To confess God's ownership of our lives is to recognize Him as our Creator."[23] It should come as no surprise that there is an appeal at the heart of Revelation—the center of the book's chiastic structure—to worship the Creator (14:7).

Israel's 144,000 (verses 4–8)

John heard the number of those who were sealed: 144,000 from all the tribes of Israel. The name "Israel" and the number of 144,000 have been the subject of countless debates. Today, the most popular belief is that both the name and number refer to literal ethnic Jews. Many ministers now teach that a pre-ordained number (144,000) of Jews will be converted at the onset of the great Tribulation, which will last seven years.[24] This view[25] is promoted heavily in the Christian market by such pastors and Bible com-

---

21. "The chiastic structure (ABA') of the announcement to the angels identifies the survivors. . . . The trees are the sole survivors." Doukhan, *Secrets of Revelation*, 69. Whereas the "earth, sea, trees" are all spared in verses 1 (A) and 3 (A'), only the earth and sea are threatened in verse 2 (B). Thus, as the Greek grammar reveals, "the winds relate differently to the earth and the sea [genitive] than they do to the trees [accusative]. . . . The trees represent persistence. Their roots, growing deep into the earth, protect them from the winds." Ibid.

22. Doukhan, *Secrets of Revelation*, 70.

23. Ibid.

24. "[God will have] sealed a remnant of believing Jews." Phillips, *Exploring Revelation*, 109.

25. The view that relegates the book of Revelation as a whole to the future has been soundly challenged all along. For example, H. Grattan Guinness wrote in 1887, "Futurism is *literalism*, and literalism in the interpretation of symbols *is a denial of their symbolic character.*" *Romanism and the Reformation* (London: Hoddar and Stoughton, 1887), 298.

mentators as Hal Lindsey, Tim LaHaye, John Walvoord, John Hagee, Grant Jeffrey, and others.

It comes as a surprise to many, then, to learn that most Bible scholars agree that Israel and the 144,000 are *symbolic*, that they represent the New Testament church (and by extension, the faithful of God in the Old Testament). Obviously, both of these views cannot be correct.

As in the debate over the horseman in the first seal, the two views are as far apart as light is from darkness. While one has Christ and His church in focus, the other sees everything through the lens of the antichrist, and the Jews who must suffer under him. Not only that, but the two views lead the reader down different paths on how the remainder of Revelation is interpreted. We need to examine each of the terms to find out where the two views will take us.

Israel

Generally speaking, those who believe in the pre-Tribulation theory and the secret rapture (4:1–2) also hold that "Israel" must be interpreted *literally*. According to this view, Israel refers to the Jewish nation and the ethnic Jews who are living at the end of time. It's believed that the Jewish leaders will create a pact with an individual who is actually the antichrist (presumably of European or Middle Eastern Muslim descent). This will occur at the beginning of the seven-year great Tribulation, a "terrible period of trial"[26] for the Jewish people. But as John MacArthur puts it: "Finally, Israel will be the witness nation she refused to be in the OT."[27] This view is founded, in part, on the now-popular teaching that the last prophetic "week" in Daniel 9:27 must be fulfilled with the Jewish people in the future. But our examination of the rapture (Rev. 4:1–2) and the antichrist (6:1–2) found this entire theory to be lacking credible biblical evidence.

---

26. Phillips, *Exploring Revelation*, 109.
27. John MacArthur, *The MacArthur Bible Commentary* (Nashville: Thomas Nelson, 2005), 2008.

Just as we saw that the book of Revelation is symbolic (1:1; "signified"), I contend that the name "Israel" is symbolic, based on the following:

- The name "Israel" has represented spiritual victory over sin from the beginning (Gen. 32:28).

- The New Testament writers have applied the very language of ancient Israel to the church, or "spiritual" Israel (cf. Rom 2:26–29; 4:11; Phil. 3:3; Gal. 3:29; James 1:1; 1 Pet. 2:9, 10). The Christian, whether Jew or Gentile, is the true Jew. The church is the Israel of God in Christ.

- Though Walvoord states that there is "no justification whatever for *spiritualizing*" either the name or the number of the twelve tribes "to make them represent the church,"[28] we have noted how Christ used ancient characters (i.e., Jezebel, Balaam) as representative of individuals in the New Testament church. It's only reasonable that Israel's name would be used in the same manner (inconsistency would have only confused the original readers).

- Because each of the twelve tribes of Israel are *exactly* twelve thousand in number, one could rightly argue that 144,000 literal Jewish converts would lack *free will*, which is contrary to the biblical view of salvation.

- The original twelve tribes no longer exist. As Van Impe acknowledges: "Presently the Jews are not certain of their tribal heritage . . . Actually, no one today really knows what his stock is. As a result of migrations, most people are a hodgepodge of differing nationalities."[29] The northern kingdom of Israel, composed of ten tribes, was attacked and scattered by the Assyrians in 722 BC.

---

28. Walvoord and Zuck, *Bible Knowledge Commentary*, 949, italics added.
29. Van Impe, *Revelation Revealed*, 85–86. Though they acknowledge the historical facts, some literalists believe that God has maintained a genealogical record through time: "Israel's tribal divisions are no longer known. But God knows them." Phillips, *Exploring Revelation*, 110. "The 12 tribes are not 'lost' as some contend. . . . God knows." Walvoord and Zuck, *Bible Knowledge Commentary*, 949.

Later, the southern kingdom fell to Babylon around 586 BC (during the time of Daniel and Ezekiel). And then, some forty years after Christ's ascension, the Romans razed the city of Jerusalem, killing about a million Jews. In this last attack against the Jewish nation, "the records of who belonged to most tribes had disappeared with the destruction of the Temple."[30]

- The list of Israel's tribes in Revelation 7 is unlike any other list in the Bible, and for good reasons. Judah is now in the first or head position, due, no doubt, to the fact that Jesus is the central subject of Revelation—He's called the "Origin and Beginning" (3:14; AMP). Furthermore, Christ's lineage is of the tribe of Judah (5:5). In addition, the tribes of Dan and Ephraim have been removed, due, it would seem, to their history of spiritual rebellion—they do not rightly represent spiritual victory.[31] By the very "irregularities" of this list, as Ladd points out, "John intends to say that the twelve tribes of Israel are not really literal Israel, but the true, spiritual Israel—the church."[32]

It's only reasonable to conclude that the first-century Christians understood the name *Israel* to mean the church, the spiritual Israel of God. Though this view has been weakened over the past century, it remains the view of most Bible scholars today:

- **Matthew Henry**: "Here the *universal church* secured by the seal of God, is figured under *the type of Israel*."[33]
- **William Barclay**: "One of the basic ideas of the New Testament is that the Church is the real Israel . . . the new Israel, the Israel of God."[34]

---

30. Doukhan, *Secrets of Revelation*, 71.
31. "In Old Testament history, both of those tribes were prominent for their connection with idolatry." Phillips, *Exploring Revelation*, 110.
32. Ladd, *Commentary on the Revelation*, 114, 115.
33. Henry, *Commentary on the Holy Bible*, 3:467.
34. Barclay, *Revelation of John*, 2:28.

- **G. B. Caird**: "In the Revelation John has already applied to the church so many descriptions of the old Israel that it would be perverse to treat the present case as an exception to the general rule."[35]
- **Frank Gaebelein**: "Already in Revelation there has been the distinction between Jews who were Jews in name only and not true Jews because they did not acknowledge Jesus as Lord (2:9; 3:9)."[36]
- **Wilfred Harrington**: "In early Christianity 'Israel' represents the Church as the continuation of Israel . . . John portrays the Church as the Israel of God." "[The Church is] a royal house of priests, inheriting the privilege of the chosen people."[37]
- **William Hendriksen**: "In the church Israel lives on, . . . spiritual Israel, the Church of God."[38]
- **George Eldon Ladd**: "The New Testament [i.e., Rom. 2:28, 29; 4:11; Phil. 3:3; Gal. 3:29] clearly conceives of the church as the true, spiritual Israel."[39]
- **Leon Morris**: "The Christian appears to be the true Jew (Ro. 2:29) and the church 'the Israel of God' (Gal. 6:16) . . . There is thus good reason for seeing a reference here to the church as the true Israel."[40]
- **W. Robertson Nicoll**: "This interpretation of Christians as the real Israel or twelve tribes is favoured not only by early Christian thought . . . but by the practice of John himself (e.g., 18:4)."[41]
- **Grant Osborne**: "However, there are many indications that John does mean the church, not the least of which is the centrality of the church throughout the book. . . . Throughout the book, the emphasis is on one group, the faithful overcomers, and they are linked inextricably with the believers in the seven churches of chapters

---

35. Caird, *Revelation of Saint John*, 95.
36. Gaebelein, ed., *Hebrews Through Revelation*, 480.
37. Harrington, *Revelation*, 98, 48.
38. Hendriksen, *More Than Conquerors*, 53, 111.
39. Ladd, *Commentary on the Revelation*, 115, 116.
40. Morris, *Book of Revelation*, 114, italics added.
41. Nicoll, *Expositor's Greek New Testament*, 395.

2-3, composed of Gentile (probably predominant) and Jewish Christians. Moreover, the NT as a whole has a great deal of material on the church as the new or true Israel."[42]

- **John Sweet**: "All Christians, not some, constitute the true Israel already." "For John, as for the other NT writers, all Christians, whatever their origin, now constitute 'the Israel of God.' "[43]

To be sure, it has been argued that a symbolic interpretation of Israel is tantamount to suggesting that the "Church has taken the place of [or replaced] Israel," thereby negating God's promise in Romans 11 to restore Israel.[44] Such an interpretation, some contend, rises out of an "anti-Semitic theology."[45] But this is simply not true. Wohlberg addresses this matter:

> For those familiar with the term, this is not "replacement theology," which teaches that "the Church" has categorically "replaced" Israel. Neither is it "separation theology" (dispensationalism's opposite error), which teaches the unbiblical notion that God's Israel and God's Church are two distinct entities—and never the twain shall meet. Rather, the truth is an "Israel of God" theology (Galations 6:14-16), which sees God having one faithful Israel throughout history composed of true Israelites and true Gentiles who believe in the Messiah (either looking forward to His cross in

---

42. Osborne, *Revelation* (BEC), 311.
43. Sweet, *Revelation*, 147, 150.
44. Sutton, *Book of Revelation Revealed*, 103. According to Sutton, "Paul distinctly distinguishes between the natural seed of Abraham—the nation of Israel—and the spiritual seed—the Church."
45. Hagee, *In Defense of Israel*, 52. Hagee contends that "Scripture plainly indicates that the church (spiritual Israel) and national Israel exist side by side." Ibid., 146. But is it really that "plain"? This was not the position held by the Protestant Reformers, and though it may be popular today on Christianity's "Main Street," it is not the view of most contemporary scholars either. As Keener points out, "most contemporary commentators" still hold that Revelation's references to Israel and the 144,000 represent "all believers" (Keener, *Revelation*, 231).

the Old Testament days or looking back to His all-sufficient atonement). . . . He loves us all.[46]

Two clarifying statements help us understand the transformation of Israel from nation to church:

- **Craig Keener**: "This does not mean that God 'replaced' Israel with Gentile Christianity; it means that Gentile Christians have been grafted into the heritage of Israel and can speak of Abraham as 'our father.' "[47]
- **Hank Hanegraaff**: "The faithful remnant of Old Testament Israel and New Testament Christianity are together the one genuine seed of Abraham and thus heirs according to the promise. . . . And all clothed in Christ constitute *one* congruent chosen covenant community connected by the cross."[48]

144,000

If one interprets the name *Israel* literally, that no doubt means interpreting the number 144,000 literally as well. Many[49] Bible teachers believe that exactly 144,000 Jews will be converted after the church is secretly raptured. This group will become "Jewish Christian witnesses"[50] to fellow Jews during the great Tribulation,[51] and to professed or nominal Christians who were "left behind." According to this teaching, the "Jewish evangelist" will win over a "great multitude" (7:9) of "converts."[52]

Hanegraaff challenges this theory head on, stating, "Historic Christianity

---

46. Wohlberg, *End Time Delusions*, 170–171. See also the chapter titled "The Christian Replacement" in Doukhan, *Israel and the Church*, 55–72.
47. Keener, *Revelation*, 241.
48. Hanegraaff, *Apocalypse Code*, 50.
49. Only a few decades ago (1977), Mounce could say that only a "few" interpreted the number literally. *Book of Revelation*, 168.
50. LaHaye, *Revelation Unveiled*, 45.
51. Van Impe, *Revelation Revealed*, 88.
52. Sutton, *Book of Revelation Revealed*, 99.

has always believed in one people of God based on *relationship* rather than race. In sharp distinction, LaHaye divides people. . . ."[53] And most scholars agree that "for the followers of Jesus all such sectarianism is broken down" (cf. Eph. 2:14).[54]

Here are some of the key reasons for interpreting the number 144,000 *symbolically*:

- **Hear/see**. John says he *heard* only the number of those who were sealed—he never *saw* 144,000 souls. In verse 9 he sees a "great multitude which no one could number" (7:9). John continually uses this literary pattern (he hears one thing and sees another),[55] but "the two images depict the same reality."[56]

- **Symbolic figures**. In the book of Revelation, numbers usually have a symbolic meaning (e.g., seven represents perfection or completeness; three is the Trinity; four means worldwide, universal, or totality; ten represents complete or completely tested). The 144,000 must be symbolic, according to Hanegraaff, because the number is "exactly 12,000—not 11,999 or 12,001—[which] must surely stretch the credulity of even the most ardent literalist beyond the breaking point."[57] (And the exact number of 12,000 is repeated twelve times for each tribe!)

- **God's family.** The number 144,000 is built on the number 12 (12 x 12,000), which represents God's people in the Bible. Thus, 144,000 would represent "the full number of the people of God."[58] In the Hebrew mind, the number 12 is also "the number of the covenant

53. Hanegraaff, *Apocalypse Code*, xx. According to LaHaye, believers are broken down into three categories: Old Testament saints, the church, and Tribulation saints. "Each group has its own relationship to Christ." *Revelation Unveiled*, 161.
54. Gaebelein, ed., *Hebrews Through Revelation*, 481.
55. John hears a trumpet but sees a priest and candlesticks (1:10, 12); he hears something about a lion but sees a slain lamb (5:5–6); he hears about the "many waters" but sees a beast (17:1, 3); he hears about the Lamb's bride, but he sees the holy city (19:7; 21:2).
56. Bauckham, *Theology of the Book*, 76.
57. Hanegraaff, *Apocalypse Code*, 126.
58. Ladd, *Commentary on the Revelation*, 117.

between God and His people (4 [number of the earth] x 3 [number of God])."[59] The Israelite nation was composed of twelve tribes, from the twelve sons of Jacob, and the church was built on twelve apostles (see Rev. 21:12, 14). In the ancient Hebrew culture, families and the military (both of these concepts fit the present context) were cast in units of a thousand.[60] The number 144,000 seems to represent all of God's covenant people: 12 tribes x 12 apostles = 144 x 1,000 = 144,000.[61]

- **Military.** The 144,000 are also likened to "12 battle units of 12,000 warriors, similar to Moses' special legion of consecrated warriors" (Num. 31:1–7).[62] The repeated number has the ring of a regimented cadence (12,000, 12,000, 12,000, etc.).[63] Before Israel marched into the Promised Land, a census was taken of its warriors to assess military preparation (Num. 1:3). This is "holy war imagery."[64] The fact that abstinence was mandated[65] during wartime probably explains why the 144,000 are described as spiritual "virgins" (14:3, 4).[66] As

---

59. Doukhan, *Secrets of Revelation*, 71.

60. "In Hebrew, the word *elef* (thousand) stands for the tribe, the crowd, the clan, or even the regiment. . . . The rhythmic regularity of the list—like that of a parading army—reinforces the impression of completeness and perfection. The word *ochlos*, rendered in verse 9 by 'multitude,' also means 'army.' " Doukhan, *Secrets of Revelation*, 71. See Kittel and Friedrich, eds., *Theological Dictionary of the New Testament*, 750, 751.

61. Just as the 144,000 is based on the numbers 3, 4, 12, and 1,000 and represents the Israel of God in totality, we should understand the destruction of the wicked (14:20), described as the flowing blood of pressed grapes over a space of 1,600 furlongs (based on the mathematical sum: 4 x 4 x 10 x 10), to be universal and complete—with emphasis (Rev. 14:20)!

62. LaRondelle, *Chariots of Salvation*, 166. See David E. Aune, *Revelation 6-16*, Word Biblical Commentary 52b (Waco, TX: Thomas Nelson, 1998), 443.

63. "It was a military roll-call, like the census." Caird, *Revelation of Saint John*, 178.

64. Hamilton, *Transforming Word*, 1073. Revelation contains a number of military scenes and terms, including Michael's battle with the dragon and Christ leading His army into battle (12:7, 11; 19:11–16).

65. "The much misunderstood reference to the virginity of the 144,000 (14:4a) belongs to the image of an army . . . the ancient requirement of ritual purity for those who fight in holy war (Deut. 23:9-14; 1 Sam. 21:5; 2 Sam. 11:9-13; 1 QM 7:3-6)." Bauckham, *Theology of the Book*, 78.

66. "These [Rev. 14] are the same as the 144,000 in 7:4-8, i.e. the spiritual Israel, the entire Christian community, alike Jewish and Gentile." Charles, *Critical and Exegetical Commentary*, 2:4. "The 144,000 in this vision [Rev. 14] are surely to be identified with the similar company

we saw under the first seal (6:1, 2), the church—marching under the standard of the Lion of Judah (5:5)—is militant in its cause for the gospel (6:1, 2; Eph. 6:10–20). Jesus Christ is her Commander. The 144,000, then, is "the totality of Israel ready to enter the battle of the great day of God Almighty."[67]

- **New Jerusalem**. Knowing that the victors are part of God's family, it is no coincidence that Revelation uses the identical mathematical description to describe the eternal home of the victors, the "Holy City, the new Jerusalem" (21:2, 17).[68] As Keener points out, "the 144,000 represent all those destined for the new Jerusalem!"[69]

The following statements, taken from a broad array of Christian scholars and commentators, serve to confirm what we discovered above:

- **Craig Keener:** "The view, shared by *most* contemporary commentators, [is] that the 144,000 represent all believers." "The symbolic interpretation [144,000] is also not impossible, and on the whole probably better fits the nature of Revelation, which revels in insightful symbolism and reinterpreting traditional Jewish end-time symbols."[70]
- **R. H. Charles**: "The number of the sealed is purely symbolical . . . [It] connotes perfectness and completion."[71]

---

in chapter 7." Beasley-Murray, *Revelation*, 222. Though the numbers are identical, some contend that the 144,000 in chapters 7 and 14 are not the same group of people, and contend that the word *virgin* must be literal. But further proof that the 144,000 in Revelation 7 and 14 are the same group is found in the fact that both are mentioned only in the "interludes," lying parallel to each other. As Massyngberde Ford states, "It would be surprising if John had a different symbolic meaning for the same number in Ch. 14." *Revelation*, 245.

67. Stefanovic, *Revelation of Jesus Christ*, 262.

68. "New Jerusalem is [described as] a *cube* . . . the symbol of perfection par excellence. The cubic structure of New Jerusalem likened it to the 'Holy of Holies' of the Jerusalem temple." Howard-Brook and Gwyther, *Unveiling Empire*, 187. One thousand is 10 x 10 x 10, which indicates a perfect cube. See Hendriksen, *More Than Conquerors*, 111.

69. Keener, *Revelation*, 232.

70. Ibid., 231, 238, italics added.

71. Charles, *Critical and Exegetical Commentary*, 1:206.

- **Grant Osborne**: "Most likely, it is a symbolic number . . . [representing] all God's true followers—the 'true Israel,' which is the church (Romans 2:29; 9:6; Galatians 3:29; 6:16; 1 Peter 2:9)."[72]

- **Bruce Bickel and Stan Jantz:** "The number probably symbolizes all of God's true followers, Jews and Gentiles alike."[73]

- **Robert Mounce**: "The number is obviously symbolic. . . . They [the 144,000 in Rev. 14] are to be taken as the entire body of the redeemed. In chapter 7, 144,000 were sealed against the woes that lay ahead (7:4-8). Now the same number stands secure beyond that final ordeal. . . . They are the overcomers upon whom the risen Christ has written his own new name (3:12)."[74]

- **Elisabeth Fiorenza**: "[The 144,000 may point to] the church to be the restored 'Israel of God' (Gal. 6:16)."[75]

- **George Eldon Ladd**: "There is good reason to believe that by the 144,000 John means to identify spiritual Israel—the church."[76]

- **Hans LaRondelle**: "[John] uses the twelve (tribes) multiplied by twelve (the apostles), multiplied by ten (the number of completeness) raised to the third power (the number of deity) to symbolically describe all the redeemed."[77]

- **William Hendriksen:** "The sealed multitude of Revelation 7 symbolizes the entire Church militant of the old and new dispensations."[78]

- **Jon Paulien:** "So the 144,000 is not some elite group that leaves most of us out. It is a symbol of everyone who has ever been faithful

72. Osborne, *Revelation* (LABC), 85.
73. Bruce Bickel and Stan Jantz, *Revelation: Unlocking the Mysteries of the End Times* (Eugene, OR: Harvest House, 2003), 95.
74. Mounce, *Book of Revelation*, 168, 267, 268.
75. Fiorenza, *Revelation*, 67.
76. Ladd, *Commentary on the Revelation*, 114.
77. LaRondelle, *Chariots of Salvation*, 163, quoting Douglas Ezell. Beasley-Murray dissents: "It is not a timeless picture of the Church [the Church of all ages] which is here given, but a representation of the Church in the climax of history." *Revelation*, 140.
78. Hendriksen, *More Than Conquerors*, 111.

to the God of Israel, no matter when or where (Rev. 7:9)."[79]

- **Hank Hanegraaff**: "144,000 is focused on relationship. It represents true Israel—not by nationality but by spirituality."[80]

- *The New International Dictionary of New Testament Theology*: "The number 144,000 does not denote a numerical limitation of those who are sealed; it symbolizes the final perfection of the people of God."[81]

- **John Randall**: "Again, we are dealing with the symbolism of numbers. . . . To take that literally, as some religionists do . . . is to do violence to the text and meaning here."[82]

- **John Sweet**: "A squared number expresses perfection . . . [Here it] means that the sealed are the totality of God's Israel, brigaded for his service. . . . Judah is put first . . . [and] the true Israel is led by the lion of the tribe of Judah."[83]

- **Jürgen Roloff**: "With the aid of this symbolic number, derived from twelve, John wishes to designate the church as the end-time people of salvation who have taken up Israel's inheritance. He is thinking as little of a reestablishment of Israel as a nation as he is of a special gathering of Christians originating out of Israel. Rather, for him it is clear presupposition of this conception of 'church' that Christians have assumed the rights of Israel in every respect (cf. Rev. 2:9; 3:9)."[84]

---

79. Paulien, *Gospel From Patmos*, 149. Although Neall believes the 144,000/great multitude "symbolize the last phase of the church" (Beatrice Neall, "Sealed Saints and the Tribulation," in Frank B. Holbrook, ed., *Symposium on Revelation – Book 1*, 275), she also writes, "Wherein lies the uniqueness of the 144,000—the final generation of saints? They are not the first ones to be sealed; saints were sealed in Paul's day . . . They are not the first to be persecuted . . . [The 144,000] *share a common heritage with the saints of all ages.*" Ibid., 276. Osborne says, "While this is primarily a description of the church in the final period of tribulation and martyrdom. . ." *Revelation* (BEC), 315.

80. Hanegraaff, *Apocalypse Code*, 125.

81. *The New International Dictionary of New Testament Theology* (Grand Rapids, MI: Zondervan, 1976), 2:695.

82. Randall, *Book of Revelation*, 64.

83. Sweet, *Revelation*, 149.

84. Roloff, *Revelation*, 97.

- *Holman Concise Bible Commentary*: "The sealing of the 144,000 employs starkly Jewish symbols to describe those who know God through Jesus Christ. Clearly John was referring to Christians as the 144,000. For 7:3 refers to the 'servants' of God, a term consistently used throughout Revelation to refer either to Christians in general or the Christian prophet [John], but never to the non-Christian Jew (or Gentile). . . . Those who are in Christ are the beneficiaries of the promises made to Israel (Rom. 4:13-17; Gal. 3:8-9, 15-29)."[85]

- **Phil Moore**: "Satan would be overjoyed if he could use passages like this to distract people. . . . [Jesus] is telling us that he has marked us to dwell in the midst of this age as his agents scattered throughout the earth to worship him, to suffer for him, to preach the Gospel and to win the great multitude from every nation, tribe, people group, and language which is revealed in 7:9. . . . Jesus gave it him for us, to encourage us to press on in the battle for the souls of humankind."[86]

But some will question whether this interpretation in any way prevents God from fulfilling His promises to the Jewish people. Absolutely not! Consider the following:

- *The Expositor's Bible Commentary*: "The identification of the 144,000 with the whole elect people of God, including both Jews and Gentiles, does not negate Paul's teaching to the effect that the majority of the Jews themselves will one day be brought back into a relationship of salvation before God."[87]

- **Earl F. Palmer**: "This text preserves the mystery of God's intention for His original people, founded in Abraham and Abraham's children. The next part of the vision ["great multitude"] envelopes this large number into an even larger fulfillment number, and so Israel is

85. *Holman Concise Bible Commentary*, David S. Dockery, ed. (Nashville: B&H Publishing Group, 2010), 672.
86. Phil Moore, *Straight to the Heart of Revelation* (Oxford, England: Monarch Books, 2010), 95.
87. Gaebelein, ed., *Hebrews Through Revelation*, 481.

itself fulfilled in the universal church of Jesus Christ."[88]

- **Jacques Doukhan**: "The 144,000 depict Israel marching as a whole. It is the 'all Israel' dreamed by the apostle Paul (Rom. 11:26), the 'complete' number of the saved, as alluded to in the fifth seal (Rev. 6:11). . . . Refugees of history. . . . "[89]

To summarize, we have discovered that the majority of Bible scholars agree that the 144,000 are symbolic, and we have seen why they believe that this number represents the church, God's "true Israel." This position is firmly founded on the New Testament and keeps the very dynamics of John's use of numbers in perspective. Needless to say, a proper understanding of the symbolism clearly refutes the notion that Israel has been "replaced."

The great multitude (verse 9)

> *After this I looked and there before me was a great multitude that no one could count, from every nation, tribe, people and language, standing before the throne and in front of the Lamb. They were wearing white robes and were holding palm branches in their hands.*

After John *heard* the number 144,000, he *saw* an innumerable multitude. This is yet another "heard/saw" experience for John. In each case where this happened, what he heard added a spiritual quality to what he saw. And in every case, the two were one and the same. With that in mind, I agree with the majority of Bible scholars who hold that the 144,000 and the great multitude are one and the same, the sum of all of the faithful—God's true Israel. The following commentators speak to this point:

- *Zondervan Handbook to the Bible*: "A symbolic number [144,000]: the total of all God's people (12 x 12 x 1000), identical with the 'great multitude.' . . . We take Israel to mean, not the nation, but God's peo-

88. Palmer, *1, 2, 3 John, Revelation*, 174.
89. Doukhan, *Secrets of Revelation*, 72.

ple—Old Testament believers and New Testament Christians alike."[90]

- **William Hendriksen**: "It is very clear, therefore, that the sealed multitude of Revelation 7 symbolizes the entire Church militant of the old and new dispensations."[91]

- **Herman Hoeksema**: "It is very evident that it is the same throng . . . [one] as standing on the verge of passing through it, and the other pictured as already having experienced it and having overcome. It is, therefore, the same multitude, only in different states, at different periods, and therefore from different points of view . . . [first] upon the earth . . . [and then] already in glory."[92]

- **G. B. Caird**: "The scriptural image had been transformed by the historic fact. . . . [First, the] scriptural image of the army of Israel . . . [and then] the Christian fact of the noble army of martyrs [the great multitude]."[93]

- **Robert Mounce**: "The innumerable *multitude includes far more than the 144,000* of the previous vision. All the faithful of every age are there."[94]

- **Wes Howard-Brook and Anthony Gwyther**: "The countless multitude from every nation, tribe, peoples, and language is the new Israel, the perfectly complete number."[95]

- **George Eldon Ladd**: "They [the two multitudes] represent the same people—the church—seen in two stages of her history in the end times: first, standing on the threshold of the great tribulation, and later having passed through this time of tribulation, martyred but victorious."[96]

---

90. David and Pat Alexander, *Zondervan Handbook to the Bible*, 3rd ed. (Grand Rapids, MI: Zondervan, 2002), 770.

91. Hendriksen, *More Than Conquerors*, 111.

92. Herman Hoeksema, *Behold, He Cometh: An Exposition of the Book of Revelation* (Grand Rapids, MI: Reformed Free Publishing Association, 1969), 267.

93. Caird, *Revelation of Saint John*, 96.

94. Mounce, *Book of Revelation*, 171, italics added.

95. Howard-Brook and Gwyther, *Unveiling Empire*, 210.

96. Ladd, *Commentary on the Revelation*, 116. "[This is] the church on earth *before the last day* . . . [and then] before the throne *after the last day*." Harrington, *Revelation*, 100.

- *Zondervan Illustrated Bible Backgrounds Commentary*: "Here the exclusive tribes of 144,000 Jews are similarly transformed into an inclusive multitude encompassing every race, ethnic group, and nation on earth."[97]
- **Grant Osborne**: "[The] sealed . . . are then part of the multitude . . . so that they constitute all believers of every age."[98]
- And more.[99]

Heaven's victors

The 144,000 "great multitude" is God's army of conquerors, coming out of every nation, tribe, people and language. The vision is the fulfillment of God's promise to Abraham (Gen. 14:5; 32:12).[100] The four-word description denotes universality, and it connects the great multitude with the redeemed of all the ages (5:9; cf. 1:6). Though situated in an end-time context,[101] this scene encapsulates all the ages. From the beginning, Christ has admonished all of His professed followers to overcome (*nike*) (Rev. 3:21). And now, the victors from the seven churches[102] are standing before God's heavenly throne, dressed in white robes[103] (cf. 6:11; 3:5, 18) and holding

---

97. Wilson, *Revelation*, Zondervan Illustrated Bible Backgrounds Commentary, 54.
98. Osborne, *Revelation* (BEC), 303. See also p. 163.
99. "There seems little doubt that the two companies here in view are essentially the same . . . [and] symbolize the entire church of the end-time." Guthrie, *New Bible Commentary*, 1290. "What John *hears*, the traditional OT expectation of military deliverance, is reinterpreted by what he *sees*, the historical fact of a sacrificial death." Sweet, *Revelation*, 125.
100. Osborne, *Revelation* (LABC), 85. See also Rom. 9:6–8; Gal. 3:29.
101. "It ought not to be a matter of theological concern if God should lift a whole generation to a height of holiness rarely achieved before . . . They are perfect in character—they choose only God's will . . . *To exercise this faith under the most extreme pressure is the unique experience of the final generation.*" Neall, "Sealed Saints and the Tribulation," in Holbrook, ed., *Symposium on Revelation – Book 1*, 277–278.
102. "Throughout the book, the emphasis is on one group, the faithful overcomers, and they are linked inextricably with the believers in the seven churches of chapters 2-3, composed of Gentile (probably predominant) and Jewish Christians." Osborne, *Revelation* (BEC), 311.
103. Gaebelein questions how the great multitude can be "the whole redeemed church . . . unless all Christians are to be identified with the martyrs." *Hebrews Through Revelation*, 484. But that is exactly the point. As we have already shown, every victor has undergone spiritual martyrdom under the second seal, and is, therefore, among the righteous under the altar in

palm branches (John 12:13). These were used in celebrations of military victory but are here emblems of spiritual victory.[104] Based on the imagery in the first and fifth seals, the white robes represent the "final justification and victory through sharing the Lamb's sacrificial death."[105]

Palm branches recall the Feast of Tabernacles (also called the Feast of Booths) that served as a reminder of when Israel dwelt in tents in the wilderness.[106] Observed in the fall, this feast was the last annual festival (Lev. 23:39–43), following after the Day of Atonement. It was a celebration for the bountiful harvests, and it reminded the Israelites of God's care and provisions for them during their sojourn in the wilderness on their way to the Promised Land of Canaan.[107]

This heavenly scene is the antitype or fulfillment of the Old Testament type. The celebration is the heavenly feast of Tabernacles: "In our terms we might depict these martyrs as celebrating in heaven, a perpetual Christmas."[108]

After a war, palm branches were waved as a sign of joy and military triumph (cf. John 12:13).[109] But it's not their own victory that the redeemed are celebrating. Rather, "the faithful of all ages [are] celebrating the victory of the Lamb."[110] "Salvation belongs to God and the Lamb," is their cry (7:10)! They know that all of their achievements have come through Christ's sacrificial blood, their testimony of His power, and the spiritual weapons that God provided them—faith, prayer, and the Word (Rev. 12:11, 17; Eph. 6:11–17; Heb. 11–12:2a; 1 John 5:4).

And now, all of heaven joins in with a seven-fold anthem: "Praise and

---

the fifth seal.

104. Doukhan, *Secrets of Revelation*, 72.

105. Sweet, *Revelation*, 151.

106. Keener, *Revelation*, 243.

107. The book of Zechariah concludes with the Feast of Tabernacles (Zech. 14:16–19).

108. Harrington, *Revelation*, 100.

109. Keener, *Revelation*, 244; Guthrie et al, eds., *New Bible Commentary*, 1290; Roloff, *Revelation*, 98.

110. Hamilton, *The Transforming Word*, 1073.

glory and wisdom and thanks and honor and power and strength be to our God for ever and ever. Amen!"

As John ponders the identity of the vast sea of humanity before him (bear in mind that the first-century church was still relatively small), one of the heavenly elders asks him, "These in white robes—who are they, and where did they come from?" As John continues to gaze over the sight, the elder answers his own question, saying that the throng of victors has come out of the "great tribulation" (Greek, *megas thlipsis*, meaning "great pressure").

Trafton finds it "striking" that the great multitude is presently "coming out" (TLB) of the Tribulation. In other words, they "are coming" (Greek, *hoi erchomenoi*) through it presently.[111] Neall explains, "In the book of Revelation the saints are always conquering (marked by the present tense in the Greek); only Christ has conquered (the aorist tense). Even during the seven last plagues the saints are still conquering the beast and its image (15:2, Greek)."[112] In one sense, the victors are already citizens of heaven while still engaged in a spiritual battle on earth. Rather than looking at the Tribulation as only a single last-day event, we ought to view it, as John did, as already occurring in the first century and continuing throughout Christian history.[113] The great Tribulation, then, encompasses *all the trials of the Christian age*.[114] Not only did John use the word *thlipsis* ("tribulation") to

---

111. Trafton, *Reading Revelation*, 85. See also, NASB, "who come out of"; TLB, "the ones coming out."

112. Neall, "Sealed Saints and the Tribulation," in Holbrook, ed., *Symposium on Revelation – Book 1*, 277.

113. Paulien, *Gospel From Patmos*, 157. Guthrie et al note that the text "has in mind one generation of Christians, the last. Yet the latter part of this section seems to refer to the whole church. . . . Those who had gone before, having witnessed a good confession, would doubtless be included in this throng." *New Bible Commentary*, 1290, 1291.

114. Hendriksen notes that this tribulation is "great because it is all inclusive: all the persecutions and trials of God's people, symbolized by the seals, are included in it." *More Than Conquerors*, 114. "Christians were never promised immunity from physical danger." Sweet, *Revelation*, 147.

Although the NIV translation says, "These are they who have come out of

describe his own suffering (1:9), and that of those in Smyrna (2:9–10), but he also uses the words *megas thlipsis* to describe the plight of the unrepentant in Thyatira (2:22). Considering that John uses the word *thlipsis* only here and in the messages to the seven churches (the beginning and the end of Revelation's "opening story"), the word *tribulation* can serve as a link between the victors in the churches and the victorious multitude standing before God's throne in heaven. Thus, Hendriksen can state: "This one tribulation is great because it is all inclusive. . . . [It] gives unity to the entire section, chapters 4-7."[115] (We would go further and say chapters 1–7.)

The elder explains that the victor's robes were made white because they were washed in the blood of the Lamb. This is a reference to placing our trust in the saving blood of Christ's sacrificial victory on the Cross,[116] and our activity in Him (often referred to as sanctification). "The one who has begun his good work in you will go on developing it" (Phil. 1:6, J. B. Phillips). Washing implies purity, and "clean" is one way in which the 144,000 are described ("not defiled," Rev. 14:4). Barclay explains that Christians have a part to play in their salvation, stating that the act of washing is "not passive."[117] This washing "signifies the overcoming of sin in life . . . a retrospect on the whole struggle of life rather than on the moment of conversion."[118] And naturally, the imagery can be likened to the act of baptism.[119]

---

the great tribulation" (verse 14), John actually used a present tense verb. He described the multitude in white as those who *are coming out* of the great tribulation. . . . John's use of the present tense here contradicts the millennialistic notion that God will rapture some believers from the earth to spare them the tribulation. *Judgment day, not a rapture, will deliver the justice* for God's suffering people." Mueller, *Revelation*, 89–90.

115. Hendriksen, *More Than Conquerors*, 114.
116. Ibid.
117. Barclay, *Revelation of John*, 2:38.
118. Guthrie et al, eds., *New Bible Commentary*, 1291.
119. "[The author's statement] refers to the sharing of Christ's death which is begun in baptism." Sweet, *Revelation*, 151. "More than likely it is an allusion to baptismal terminology, for the event of baptism is frequently described in the New Testament as purification by the blood of Jesus." Roloff, *Revelation*, 99. "Often when Christians were baptized, they were dressed in new white robes. These robes were taken to symbolize new life." Barclay, *Revelation of John*, 2:34.

As Osborne points out, "Too many Christians sing 'Victory in Jesus' but then sit idly by, assuming that the work is all God's to do and they will be carried along in the victory."[120]

Christ is not ministering alone in our salvation; the very fact that we are called to believe shows that salvation is relationship based. In His seven messages Christ pleaded with the members of the churches to "overcome," "hold on to what you have," "be faithful," "do my will," "obey and repent," "open the door," and so on.[121] Ultimately, a person must make the decision to invite Christ into their heart. They must be willing to surrender all that they are to Him daily (Luke 9:23). They must choose to "abide" in Him, depending on and trusting in Him (John 15:4). By so doing, they can "walk worthy" in the Spirit and grow up into Christ's character (Eph. 4:1). This is what Paul means when he says, "Just as you have always obeyed . . . *work out your salvation* with fear and trembling; for it is God who is at work in you, both to will and to work for His good pleasure" (Phil. 2:12, 13, NASB).

The symbolism here challenges our logic—we're to believe that Christ's crimson blood can remove our sinful stains and leave us "whiter than snow" (Ps. 51:7). And yet, it is "for this [very] reason" (NASB)—because of the power of Jesus' sacrificial blood—that we can stand before the throne of God as though we are completely innocent. This is why God's "throne," which is the victor's ultimate reward (3:21; cf. 21:6), is given emphasis here at the close of the story (Rev. 7:9, 10, 11, 15, 17).

The ultimate reward for the victor is, of course, not the right to "reign [as a king] forever" (22:5). His greatest joy will be to cast his crown at the Savior's feet (4:10) and serve[122] (*latreuo*) his Creator-Redeemer day and

---

120. Osborne, *Revelation* (LABC), 144.
121. Cf. Matt. 11:29; Mark 11:24; Acts 3:19; Jam. 5:16.
122. I do not subscribe to Phillips's view regarding those who will "serve" God for eternity: "These are not Jews, nor are they members of the church. These are the Gentile victors from the Tribulation" (Phillips, *Exploring Revelation*, 113). As we have already shown, the textual evidence leads us to believe that this group represents all the faithful: "Here is a picture of heaven with the barriers down. Distinctions of race and of status no longer exist; the way into the presence of God is open to every faithful soul" (Barclay, *Revelation of John*, 2:39). "There

night, face to face (22:3)! The Greek word *latreuo* expresses priestly service and carries the notion of rendering religious homage or ministry in worship[123] (cf. Luke 4:8; Rom. 1:25; Heb. 13:10). In the same vein, cultic terms are used to describe the 144,000 in Revelation 14:5 (Greek *amomos*)—"unblemished" or "spotless."[124] All of this is consistent with our understanding of the sacrificial terminology in the second seal. Just as a priest served in the ancient sanctuary, so the victor will serve God in His heavenly temple (cf. Rev. 1:6). Since, in the Revelation the word *naos* ("temple") always refers to the most holy place,[125] it should be understood that the victors "are in the innermost court . . . They are in the holiest place of the sanctuary. . . . They are before the throne of God."[126] You'll recall that Christ promised to make the overcomer a "pillar in the temple" (3:12), implying an intimate fellowship with God, since "the Lord God Almighty and the Lamb are [New Jerusalem's] temple" (21:22).

But the sanctuary imagery doesn't stop here. Now comes a list of promises.

He who sits on the throne will dwell [skenoo] *among them* (cf. 21:3). What a beautiful word picture this is! The word *skenoo* literally means to "tent over," like a shelter. God will "spread his tent over them" (NIV). The imagery evokes memories of when God, after delivering Israel from bondage, instructed them to build a tabernacle in the wilderness so that He could dwell with His people (Ex. 25:8).[127] Barclay adds this wonderful insight:

---

are not two songs sung but one [Rev. 15:3], just as there are not two people of God (Jews and Christians) but one (those faithful to YHWH alone)." Howard-Brook and Gwyther, *Unveiling Empire*, 220.

123. "That 'service' refers to worship and praise (22:3-5)." Osborne, *Revelation* (LABC), 89.

124. "Cultic terminology . . . required in an animal acceptable for sacrifice." Bauckham, *Theology of the Book*, 77.

125. Stefanovic, *Revelation of Jesus Christ*, 336. The ark was located in the most holy place. "Then God's temple in heaven was opened, and within his temple was seen the ark of his covenant" (Rev. 11:19).

126. Phillips, *Exploring Revelation*, 113.

127. Mounce, *Book of Revelation*, 175.

The Greek for *to dwell* is *skenoun*, from *skene*, which means a *tent*. It is the same word as is used when John says that the word became flesh and *dwelt* among us (John 1:14). The Jews always connected this with a certain Hebrew word which was somewhat similar in sound although quite unrelated in meaning. This was the word *shechinah*, the visible presence of the glory of God . . . *Skenoun* always turned the thoughts of the Jews to *shechinah*; and to say that God *dwelt* in any place was to say that his glory was there.[128]

As mentioned already, the palm branches were an allusion to the Feast of Tabernacles, when tents were set up to house the joyous throng. Now we see the redeemed "celebrating a heavenly feast of Tabernacles."[129] Commenting on John 1:14,[130] Goldsworthy says: "In other words, John saw Jesus as resembling the tabernacle in the wilderness."[131] Christ is the everlasting Shekinah, and He will spread His presence over the faithful forever (cf. Ezek. 37:27). "The picture of heavenly blessedness . . . is dominated by the imagery of the feast of Tabernacles. For Jews this was the feast, the crown of the year, when all harvesting was complete."[132]

---

128. Barclay, *Revelation of John*, 2:40. "The Greek verb, coincidentally, has the same consonants as the Hebrew equivalent, škn, from which the word *Shekinah* (the presence of God) is derived." Neall, "Sealed Saints and the Tribulation," in Holbrook, ed., *Symposium on Revelation – Book 1*, 265. "In Greek, *skenoun* (to spread the tent) sounds like the Hebrew word shekinah (from the verb *shakan*, to dwell), which designated the cloud of fire, a symbol of God's 'dwelling' among His people (Ex. 40:34-38)." Doukhan, *Secrets of Revelation*, 72. "The Greek verb skenosei, 'tabernacle,' suggests the Shekinah, the rabbinic term for divine presence or residence." Massyngberde Ford, *Revelation*, 128.
129. Harrington, *Revelation*, 101; Howard-Brook and Gwyther, *Unveiling Empire*, 210.
130. "And the Word (Christ) became flesh (human, incarnate) and tabernacled (fixed His tent of flesh, lived awhile) among us; and we [actually] saw His glory (His honor, His majesty)." John 1:14, *Amplified Bible*. In Jesus the Shekinah became incarnate.
131. Goldsworthy, *Gospel and Kingdom*, 95.
132. Sweet, *Revelation*, 151.

Victory eternal

As the opening story draws to a close, the conquerors are safe with the Lamb in heaven. They will never suffer hunger or thirst again—the true Bread and Water is theirs forever (John 6:35). They will never again feel the pain of heat, for Psalm 23 will be fulfilled—the Lamb, their shepherd, will lead them to springs of living water (cf. Rev. 21:1–2). The Lamb is also the shepherd, another "intriguing exchange of roles" in the revelation.[133] Building on the Old Testament picture of God as the shepherd of Israel,[134] the text, in the form of a chiasm, identifies Jesus with the God of Israel:[135]

A. God (7:15a)

B. he who sits upon the throne (7:15b)

B'. the Lamb in the midst of the throne (7:17a)

A'. God (7:17b)

"The pure river of the water of life" flows forth from the Lamb's throne, nourishing the "the tree of life," from which the victors are free to eat for eternity (Rev. 22:1, 2; cf. John 4:10–14; Gen. 3:22–24). After the saints have endured and conquered through tribulation, God will *wipe away every tear from their eyes* (21:4). Their inheritance—having been obtained through the sacrificial death and atoning "blood of the lamb"—will last forever (21:7; 22:12).

I can only imagine what that glorious sight will be like—a vast sea of conquerors standing before the throne of God. Through faith in Christ, they have triumphed over the Accuser. In the Lamb's power, they have prevailed over the things of the earth. Suddenly, at the cry of the heavenly Commander's voice, a myriad of angels lift their trumpets high and break into a "new song"! This will be heaven's Olympic fanfare, as the conquerors parade into the New Jerusalem and receive their eternal reward (Rev. 21:7).

---

133. Mounce, *Book of Revelation*, 118.
134. Ibid., 175.
135. Trafton, *Reading Revelation*, 83.

But despite the majestic sights and sounds of celebration, no one is able to take his or her eyes off the Lamb, who is standing "at the center of the throne" (NIV).

The Lamb seems to be approaching. His eyes, penetrating deeply, appear to be focused on only one person—*you*. Stopping only a breath away, Jesus holds out a victor's crown with His nail-scarred hands. Inscribed in the gold on the front is *your* new name. As you gaze up into His marvelous face, you can feel the warmth of His countenance—an experience like no other. And then, turning slightly, He stretches out His arm, motioning for you to share a seat with Him on His throne. The Lamb has been waiting for you.

BIBLIOGRAPHY

Alexander, David, and Pat Alexander. *Zondervan Handbook to the Bible*. 3rd ed. Grand Rapids, MI: Zondervan, 2002.

Anderson, Roy Allan. *Unfolding the Revelation*. Mountain View, CA: Pacific Press, 1953.

Aune, David E. *Revelation 6-16*. Word Biblical Commentary 52b. Waco, TX: Thomas Nelson, 1998.

Barclay, William. *The Revelation of John, Vol. 1*. The New Daily Study Bible. Louisville, KY: Westminster John Knox, 1976.

———. *The Revelation of John, Vol. 2*. The New Daily Study Bible. Louisville, KY: Westminster John Knox, 1976.

Barker, Kenneth, ed. *The NIV Study Bible*. Grand Rapids, MI: Zondervan, 1985.

Bauckham, Richard. *The Theology of the Book of Revelation*. Cambridge, UK: Cambridge University Press, 1993.

Bauer, Walter, Frederick W. Danker, and William Arndt. *A Greek-English Lexicon of the New Testament and Other Early Christian Literature*. Chicago: University of Chicago Press, 2000.

Beasley-Murray, George R. *Revelation*. The New Century Bible Commentary. Grand Rapids, MI: Eerdmans, 1981, ©1974.

———. *John*, 2nd ed. Word Biblical Commentary 36. Nashville: Thomas Nelson, 1999.

Bickel, Bruce, and Stan Jantz. *Revelation: Unlocking the Mysteries of the End Times*. Eugene, OR: Harvest House, 2003.

Bickersteth, Edward. *A Practical Guide to the Prophecies*. Philadelphia: Orrin Rogers, 1841.

Blanco, Jack J. *The Clear Word*. Collegedale, TN: Jack J. Blanco, 2000.

Bonhoeffer, Dietrich. *The Cost of Discipleship*. New York: Touchstone, 1995.

Caird, G. B. *The Revelation of Saint John*. Peabody, MA: Hendrickson, 1966.

Carson, D. A., ed. *From Sabbath to the Lord's Day: A Biblical, Historical, and Theological Investigation*. Grand Rapids, MI: Zondervan, 1982.

Charles, R. H. *A Critical and Exegetical Commentary on the Revelation of St. John*. International Critical Commentary Series. 2 vols. Edinburgh: T & T Clark, 1920.

Clarke, Adam. *Commentary on the Bible*. 1831.

Collins, Adela Yarbro. *Crisis and Catharsis: The Power of the Apocalypse*. Philadelphia: Westminster Press, 1984.

Crews, Joe. *The Surrender of Self*. Roseville, CA: Amazing Facts, 2006.

Criswell, W. A., ed. *The Criswell Study Bible*. Nashville: Thomas Nelson, 1979.

Davidson, Richard M. "Sanctuary Typology," in Frank B. Holbrook, ed., *Symposium on Revelation – Book 1*. Silver Spring, MD: Biblical Research Institute, 1992.

Davis, Thomas A. *How to Be a Victorious Christian*. Ukiah, CA: Orion Publishing, 2003.

DeHaan, M. R. *The Tabernacle*. Grand Rapids, MI: Zondervan, 1955.

Doukhan, Jacques B. *Israel and the Church: Two Voices of the Same God*. Peabody, MA: Hendrickson, 2002.

———. *Secrets of Revelation*. Hagerstown, MD: Review and Herald, 2002.

Epp, Theodore H. *Practical Studies in Revelation, Vol. 1*. Lincoln, NE: The Good News Broadcasting Association, 1969.

Expository Dictionary of New Testament Words (Four Volumes in One). W. E. Vine. Grand Rapids, MI: Zondervan, 1952.

Finley, Mark. *Letters From a Lonely Isle*. Nampa, ID: Pacific Press, 2002.

———. *Revelation's Predictions for a New Millennium*. Fallbrook, CA: Hart Books, 2000.

Fiorenza, Elisabeth Schüssler. "The Revelation to John." In *Hebrews, James, 1 and 2 Peter, Jude, Revelation*, ed. Gerhard Krodel. Minneapolis: Fortress Press, 1977.

———. *Revelation: Vision of a Just World*. Minneapolis: Augsburg Fortress, 1991.

———. *The Book of Revelation: Justice and Judgment*, 2nd ed. Minneapolis: Fortress, 1998.

Ford, Desmond. *Crisis: A Commentary on the Book of Revelation*. 3 vols. Newcastle, CA: Desmond Ford Publications, 1982.

Ford, J. Massyngberde. *Revelation: An Introduction, Translation, and Commentary*. The Anchor Yale Bible Commentaries. New York: Doubleday, 1975.

Gaebelein, Frank, ed. *Hebrews Through Revelation*. The Expositor's Bible Commentary, vol. 12. Grand Rapids, MI: Zondervan, 1981.

Gane, Roy. *The NIV Application Commentary: Leviticus, Numbers*. Grand Rapids, MI: Zondervan, 2004.

Gentry, Kenneth L., Sam Hamstra, Robert L. Thomas, and C. Marvin Pate. *Four Views on the Book of Revelation*. Grand Rapids, MI: Zondervan, 1998.

Gill, John. *Exposition of the Old and New Testament*. 1746–1763.

Goldsworthy, Graeme. *Gospel and Kingdom: A Christian's Guide to the Old Testament*. Minneapolis: Winston Press, 1981.

Graham, Billy. *Approaching Hoofbeats: The Four Horsemen of the Apocalypse*. Waco, TX: Word, 1983.

Guinness, H. Grattan. *Romanism and the Reformation From the Standpoint of Prophecy*. London: Hoddar and Stoughton, 1887.

Guthrie, Donald, J. Alec Motyer, Alan M. Stibbs, and Donald J. Wiseman, eds. *The New Bible Commentary: Revised*. Grand Rapids, MI: Eerdmans, 1970.

Habershon, Ada R. *Outline Studies of the Tabernacle*. Grand Rapids, MI: Kregel, 1974.

Hagee, John. *In Defense of Israel*. Lake Mary, FL: FrontLine, 2007.

Hamilton, Mark W., ed. *The Transforming Word: A One-Volume Commentary on the Bible*. Abilene, TX: Abilene Christian University Press, 2009.

Hanegraaf, Hank. *The Apocalypse Code*. Nashville: Thomas Nelson, 2007.

Harrington, Wilfred J. *Revelation*. Sacra Pagina Series 16. Collegeville, MN: The Liturgical Press, 1993.

Hendriksen, William. *More Than Conquerors: An Interpretation of the Book of Revelation*. Grand Rapids, MI: Baker, 1940, 1967.

Henry, Matthew. *Commentary on the Holy Bible*. 3 vols. Nashville: Thomas Nelson, 1979.

Hewitt, C. M. Kempton. *Revelation*. Genesis to Revelation Series. Nashville: Graded Press, 1987.

———. *Revelation: Student*. Genesis to Revelation Series 24. Nashville: Abingdon, 1997.

Hindson, Edward. *The Book of Revelation: Unlocking the Future*. Twenty-first Century Bible Commentary Series. Chattanooga, TN: AMG, 2002.

Holman Concise Bible Commentary, David S. Dockery, ed. Nashville: B&H Publishing Group, 2010.

Hoeksema, Herman. *Behold, He Cometh: An Exposition of the Book of Revelation*. Grand Rapids, MI: Reformed Free Publishing Association, 1969.

Howard-Brook, Wes, and Anthony Gwyther. *Unveiling Empire: Reading Revelation Then and Now*. Maryknoll, NY: Orbis, 1999.

Jamieson, Robert, A. R. Fausset, and David Brown. *A Commentary, Critical, Practical, and Explanatory on the Old and New Testaments*. 1882.

Keener, Craig. *Revelation*. The NIV Application Commentary. Grand Rapids, MI: Zondervan, 2000.

Keil, Carl F., and Franz Delitzsch. *Bible Commentary on the Old Testament*, Vol. 1: *The Pentateuch* (three vols. in one). Grand Rapids, MI: Eerdmans, 1983.

Ladd, George Eldon. *A Commentary on the Revelation of John*. Grand Rapids, MI: Eerdmans, 1972.

LaHaye, Tim. *Revelation Unveiled*. Grand Rapids, MI: Zondervan, 1999.

LaRondelle, Hans K. *Chariots of Salvation: The Biblical Drama of Armageddon*. Hagerstown, MD: Review and Herald, 1987.

———. "Babylon: Anti-Christian Empire," in Frank B. Holbrook, ed., *Symposium on Revelation – Book 2*, 151–176. Silver Spring, MD: Biblical Research Institute, 1992.

Lichtenwalter, Larry. *Revelation's Great Love Story*. Hagerstown, MD: Review and Herald, 2008.

MacArthur, John. *The MacArthur Bible Commentary*. Nashville: Thomas Nelson, 2005.

Maxwell, C. Mervyn. *God Cares*. 2 vols. Nampa, ID: Pacific Press, 1985.

McGee, J. Vernon. *Revelation Chapters 6–13*. Thru the Bible Commentary Series. Nashville: Thomas Nelson, 1975.

Milligan, William. *The Revelation of St. John*. London: Macmillan, 1886.

Moore, Phil. *Straight to the Heart of Revelation*. Oxford, England: Monarch Books, 2010.

Morris, Leon. *The Book of Revelation: An Introduction and Commentary*. Tyndale New Testament Commentaries 20. Grand Rapids, MI: Eerdmans, 1969.

Mounce, Robert H. *The Book of Revelation*. The New International Commentary on the New Testament. Grand Rapids, MI: Eerdmans, 1977.

Mueller, Wayne D. *Revelation*. People's Bible Commentary. Saint Louis, MO: Concordia, 1997.

Naden, Roy C. *The Lamb Among the Beasts: A Christological Commentary on the Revelation of John That Unlocks the Meaning of Its Many Numbers*. Hagerstown, MD: Review and Herald, 1996.

Neall, Beatrice. "Sealed Saints and the Tribulation," in Frank B. Holbrook, ed., *Symposium on Revelation – Book 1*. Silver Spring, MD: Biblical Research Institute, 1992.

Nelson, Loren M. K. *Understanding the Mysteries of Daniel and Revelation*. Self-published manuscript, 2010.

The New International Dictionary of New Testament Theology. Grand Rapids, MI: Zondervan, 1976.

Nicoll, W. Robertson. *The Expositor's Greek New Testament*. Grand Rapids, MI: Eerdmans, 1983.

Osborne, Grant R. *Galatians* (LABC). Life Application Bible Commentary. Wheaton, IL: Tyndale, 1994.

———. *Revelation* (LABC). Life Application Bible Commentary. Wheaton, IL: Tyndale, 2000.

———. *Revelation* (BEC). Baker Exegetical Commentary on the New Testament. Grand Rapids, MI: Baker Academic, 2002.

Palmer, Earl F. *1, 2, 3 John, Revelation*. The Preacher's Commentary 35, ed. Lloyd J. Ogilvie. Nashville: Thomas Nelson, 2002.

Paulien, Jon. *Decoding Revelation's Trumpets: Literary Allusions and Interpretation of Revelation 8:7-12*. Berrien Springs, MI: Andrews University Press, 1988.

———. "Seals and Trumpets: Some Current Discussions," in Frank B. Holbrook, ed.,

Symposium on Revelation – Book 1, 183–198. Silver Spring, MD: Biblical Research Institute, 1992.

———. "The Seven Seals," in Frank B. Holbrook, ed., *Symposium on Revelation – Book 1*, 199–244. Silver Spring, MD: Biblical Research Institute, 1992.

———. *What the Bible Says About the End-Time*. Hagerstown, MD: Review and Herald, 1998.

———. *The Deep Things of God: An Insider's Guide to the Book of Revelation*. Hagerstown, MD: Review and Herald, 2004.

———. *The Gospel From Patmos*. Hagerstown, MD: Review and Herald, 2007.

———. *Armageddon at the Door: An Insider's Guide to the Book of Revelation*. Hagerstown, MD: Autumn House, 2008.

———. *Seven Keys: Unlocking the Secrets of Revelation*. Nampa, ID: Pacific Press, 2009.

Peterson, Eugene. *Reversed Thunder: The Revelation of John and the Praying Imagination*. San Francisco: HarperOne, 1991.

Phillips, John. *Exploring Revelation: An Expository Commentary*. Grand Rapids, MI: Kregel, 2001.

Prescott, W. W. *Victory in Christ*. Hagerstown, MD: Review and Herald, 1987.

Ramsey, William M., *Letters to the Seven Churches*. Grand Rapids, MI: Baker, 1985.

Randall, John. *The Book of Revelation: What Does It Really Say?* Locust Valley, NY: Living Flame Press, 1976.

Revelation. Life Application Bible Studies. Wheaton, IL: Tyndale House, 2009.

Roloff, Jürgen. *Revelation: A Continental Commentary*. Minneapolis: Fortress Press, 1993.

Ryken, Leland, James C. Wilhoit, and Tremper Longman III, eds. *Dictionary of Bible Imagery*. Downers Grove, IL: InterVarsity, 1998.

Ryrie, Charles C. *The Ryrie Study Bible*. Chicago: Moody Press, 1976.

Seiss, Joseph A. *The Apocalypse: Lectures on the Book of Revelation*. Grand Rapids, MI: Zondervan, 1957.

Stefanovic, Ranko. *The Revelation of Jesus Christ*. Berrien Springs, MI: Andrews University Press, 2002.

Strand, Kenneth A. *Interpreting the Book of Revelation*. Worthington, OH: Ann Arbor, 1976.

———. "The Eight Basic Visions," in Frank B. Holbrook, ed., *Symposium on Revelation – Book 1*, 35–50. Silver Spring, MD: Biblical Research Institute, 1992.

———. " 'Victorious-Introduction' Scenes," in Frank B. Holbrook, ed., *Symposium on Revelation – Book 1*, 51–72. Silver Spring, MD: Biblical Research Institute, 1992.

Sutton, Hilton. *The Book of Revelation Revealed: An In-Depth Study on the Book of Revelation.* Tulsa, OK: Harrison House, 2001.

Sweet, John. *Revelation.* TPI New Testament Commentaries. London: SCM Press, 1979.

Swete, Henry Barclay. *The Apocalypse of St. John,* 3rd ed. Grand Rapids, MI: Eerdmans, 1908.

Tenney, Merrill C. *Interpreting Revelation.* Grand Rapids, MI: Eerdmans, 1957.

Theological Dictionary of the New Testament (Abridged in One Volume). Edited by Gerhard Kittel and Gerhard Friedrich, translated by Geoffrey W. Bromiley. Grand Rapids, MI: Eerdmans, 1985.

Trafton, Joseph L. *Reading Revelation: A literary and theological commentary,* rev. ed. Reading the New Testament. Macon, GA: Smyth and Helwys, 2005.

Van Impe, Jack. *Revelation Revealed.* Troy, MI: Jack Van Impe Ministries, 1982.

Walker, Glen. *Prophecy Made Easy: Experience the Future Now!* Fort Wayne, IN: Prophecy Press, 2001.

Walvoord, John F., *The Revelation of Jesus Christ.* Chicago: Moody, 1966.

Walvoord, John F., and Roy B. Zuck. *The Bible Knowledge Commentary: New Testament.* Colorado Springs, CO: David C. Cook, 1983.

Wiersbe, Warren. *Be Victorious.* Wheaton, IL: Victor Books, 1985.

Wilcock, Michael. *The Message of Revelation: I Saw Heaven Opened.* Leicester, England: InterVarsity Press, 1975.

Wilson, Mark W., *Revelation,* Zondervan Illustrated Bible Backgrounds Commentary (Grand Rapids, MI: Zondervan, 2002).

Wohlberg, Steve. *End Time Delusions: The Rapture, the Antichrist, Israel, and the End of the World.* Shippensburg, PA: Destiny Image, 2004.

Made in the USA
Middletown, DE
11 January 2022

57728188R00110